A publication of the

AMERICAN ASSOCIATION FOR HIGHER EDUCATION
National Center for Higher Education
One Dupont Circle, Northwest
Washington, D.C. 20036

G. KERRY SMITH, *Chief Executive Officer*

✿✿✿✿✿✿✿✿✿✿✿✿✿✿✿✿✿✿✿✿✿✿✿✿✿✿✿✿✿✿

The American Association for Higher Education, AAHE,
promotes higher education and provides a national
voice for individual members. AAHE, founded in 1870,
is the only national higher education organization
open to faculty members, administrators, graduate
students, and trustees without regard to rank, discipline,
or type or size of institution. AAHE is dedicated to
the professional development of college and university
educators, to the achievement of their educational
objectives, and to the improvement of conditions
of service.

1870–1970 CENTENNIAL ANNIVERSARY

1945
twenty-five years
1970

G. Kerry Smith

❀❀❀❀❀❀❀❀❀❀❀❀❀❀❀❀❀❀❀❀❀❀❀❀❀❀❀❀❀❀❀❀❀❀

Editor

1945 twenty-five years 1970

Jossey-Bass Inc., Publishers

615 Montgomery Street • San Francisco • 1970

TWENTY-FIVE YEARS: 1945 TO 1970
    G. Kerry Smith, Editor

**Copyright © 1970 by
American Association for Higher Education
Jossey-Bass, Inc., Publishers**

Copyright under Pan American and Universal
Copyright Conventions. All rights reserved.
No part of this book may be reproduced in any
form—except for brief quotation (not to exceed
1,000 words) in a review or scholarly book—
without permission in writing from the publishers.
Address all inquiries to:

*Jossey-Bass, Inc., Publishers
615 Montgomery Street
San Francisco, California 94111*

Library of Congress Catalog Card Number 73-110640

International Standard Book Number ISBN 0-87589-058-X

Manufactured in the United States of America
        *Composed and printed by York Composition Company, Inc.
        Bound by Chas. H. Bohn & Co., Inc., New York*

JACKET DESIGN BY WILLI BAUM, SAN FRANCISCO

FIRST EDITION

Code 7009

THE JOSSEY-BASS SERIES IN HIGHER EDUCATION

General Editors

JOSEPH AXELROD, *San Francisco State College*

MERVIN B. FREEDMAN, *San Francisco State College
and Wright Institute, Berkeley*

Preface

G. Kerry Smith

❁❁❁❁❁❁❁❁❁❁❁❁❁❁❁❁❁❁❁❁❁❁❁❁❁❁

Enrollments in colleges and universities suddenly doubled at the end of World War II as a result of the provisions of the G.I. Bill. Administrators were deeply involved in study and planning to cope with the tremendous job immediately ahead. The task of securing facilities alone—Quonset huts, empty army barracks, and other surplus properties—involved many changes in Federal laws and regulations. In addition, recruiting and preparing additional faculty, reshaping the curriculum, securing funds, and other challenges were faced and dealt with by the total academic community. Since then, the influential events of this quarter century have continued to challenge those responsible for higher education.

In *Twenty-Five Years* thirty of the leading spokesmen of

higher education, representing almost every discipline, chronicle the events of the years from 1945 to 1970 as they influenced the course of higher education. This collection of essays, representing the most definitive selections published in the yearbooks of the American Association of Higher Education, *Current Issues in Higher Education,* reflects the concerns, ambitions, fears, and hopes surrounding the events of those years. The analysis and interpretation of the specific and contemporary responses of the academic community to the problems which arose present many rewarding opportunities for historians. How did higher education react to the launching of Sputnik? To what forces can we attribute the partnership of higher education and the military-industrial complex? How did the civil rights movement influence higher education? Was there any way of knowing that our colleges and universities were nurturing a new breed of student? How long have we been aware of the inadequacy of undergraduate education? These are among the questions answered in *Twenty-Five Years.*

However, in developing this book we had no intention of attempting merely a historical account; we wanted to discover which presentations, if any, make sense for us today and tomorrow. We searched thousands of pages for clues and answers to such ever-recurring and varied questions as these: What should be taught and learned? How can equality of educational opportunity be achieved? Can national demands be harmonized with institutional and individual goals? Our judgment is that the essays in this book are meaningful and that they contribute to the crucial dialogue on the relationship of higher education to American society.

Washington, D.C.   G. KERRY SMITH
February 1970

Contents

Contributors

❀❀❀❀❀❀❀❀❀❀❀❀❀❀❀❀❀❀❀❀❀❀❀❀❀❀❀❀❀❀❀❀❀❀

LLOYD J. AVERILL, *distinguished visiting scholar,* Ottawa University, Kansas

JOSEPH AXELROD, *professor of world literature,* San Francisco State College

KENNETH E. BOULDING, *professor of economics and program director,* Institute of Behavioral Science, University of Colorado

ERNEST L. BOYER, *vice president for university-wide activities,* State University of New York at Albany

OLIVER C. CARMICHAEL, deceased, *formerly president,* The Carnegie Foundation for the Advancement of Teaching

WILLIAM SLOANE COFFIN, JR., *chaplain,* Yale University

W. H. COWLEY, emeritus, *David Jacks Professor of Higher Education,* Stanford University

BRUCE DEARING, *president,* State University of New York at Binghamton

JAMES DOI, *professor of higher education,* The University of Michigan

F. MARTIN ERICKSON, *assistant to the president,* University of Utah

CLARENCE H. FAUST, *formerly president,* The Fund for the Advancement of Education

CHARLES FRANKEL, *professor of philosophy,* Columbia University

MERVIN B. FREEDMAN, *professor of psychology,* San Francisco State College

J. WILLIAM FULBRIGHT, *United States Senator from Arkansas*

JOHN KENNETH GALBRAITH, *Paul M. Warburg Professor of Economics,* Harvard University

PAUL GOODMAN, New York

S. L. HALLECK, *professor of psychology,* University of Wisconsin

STANLEY J. IDZERDA, *president,* College of Saint Benedict, Minnesota

PHILIP E. JACOB, *director,* International Studies in Politics, University of Pennsylvania

RICHARD P. MC KEON, *distinguished professor,* Department of Philosophy and Classical Languages and Literature, The University of Chicago

MARSHALL MC LUHAN, *director,* Center for Culture and
Technology, University of Toronto

LEWIS B. MAYHEW, *professor of higher education,* Stanford
University

TALCOTT PARSONS, *professor of sociology,* Harvard University

NEVITT SANFORD, *director,* Wright Institute, Berkeley

G. KERRY SMITH, *chief executive officer,* American Association for Higher Education

T. V. SMITH, deceased, *formerly Maxwell Professor of Citizenship,* Syracuse University

F. W. STROTHMANN, *executive head,* Modern European
Languages, Stanford University

MARTIN TARCHER, *chief consultant,* Social and Health Sciences, University of California Medical Center

HAROLD TAYLOR, *vice president for education,* Peace Research Institute, New York

DAVID B. TRUMAN, *president,* Mount Holyoke College

PETER VIERECK, *professor of history,* Mount Holyoke College

LOGAN WILSON, *president,* American Council on Education

WHITNEY M. YOUNG, JR., *executive director,* National Urban
League

Prologue

Twenty-Five Years:
1945 to 1970

Joseph Axelrod, Mervin B. Freedman

❀❀❀❀❀❀❀❀❀❀❀❀❀❀❀❀❀❀❀❀❀❀❀❀❀

The twenty-five years from 1945 to 1970 were perilous ones for higher education. That quarter-century ushered in the atomic age with Hiroshima. And shortly thereafter we felt the impact of a new breed of college student—the GI, an older, serious learner who, more often than not, was quite willing to dispense with an education if he could effectively be prepared for a good job. Then came McCarthyism and civil rights, Sputnik and the National Defense Education Act, sit-ins and Berkeley, Vietnam—and finally, most astonishing of all, a new breed of college student who was quite willing to postpone job training until later if only he could find a college or university to give him an education.

The essays that follow reflect those perilous years; and they do more. The sensitive reader will be able to see the past in them and also move through them into the ever-present.

Surely the most dramatic and influential event that the essays reflect is the launching of the first earth satellite in 1957. Hardly a paper in the 1958, 1959, and 1960 volumes of *Current Issues in Higher Education* failed, in some direct or indirect way, to refer to it. By 1959 it was clear to the academic community that America had "overreacted." John Kenneth Galbraith (Chapter Eight) and Stanley Idzerda (Chapter Ten) both gave voice to that concern. At the 1959 National Conference, Idzerda expressed the fear that the shrill cries for academic rigor might bring on rigor mortis; and Galbraith commented, "It was less the blow than the fragility of what it struck that caused the attention and created the alarm."

Galbraith analyzed why the reaction to Sputnik, on the whole, did American education—and the nation in general—more harm than good. For one thing, he stated, it brought on an era of tough, practical, hard-headed men in positions of leadership. This was the wrong kind of leader. We needed men who could cope with our problems; and our problems demanded study, thought, and perception rather than immediate action based on simplistic analyses. But the deepest harm that was done, according to Galbraith's analysis, was to increase the nation's "continuing failure to see . . . the relation of education . . . to the economic and social order."

Thus the pressures of an uneasy peace following World War II had provoked an oddly motivated relationship between the society and the university—a relationship of convenience, basically different in its nature from the entirely emergency character of the one that existed during the war years. Then, in 1958, Sputnik provoked a shotgun wedding between the two giants—the governmental-industrial complex and the higher education establishment. However, it turns out that the two did not trust one another, and thus love was out of the question. William Sloane Coffin, Jr., writing in 1964 (Chapter Nineteen), expressed regret at this turn of events; for one could not have a lovers' quarrel if the partners were not lovers, and lovers they surely were not. This, Coffin declared, was the source of the trouble: "The relationship I would like to see between university and society is that of a lovers' quarrel, with the accent equally on lover and quarrel." For there are two things, he went on to say, that neither society nor the university can risk: alienation or identification. But for most of us in higher education today—six years after Coffin's address was delivered—alienation from or identification with the powers that be are the only alternatives that are open.[1]

Galbraith put his finger on the crucial point in the society-university relationship when he told his audience in 1959 (Chapter Eight) that a private, capitalist economy, which works so well when the investment is in material capital, presents serious faults in the way it is compelled to handle its investments in human beings. Still, the system works fairly well when there is economic stability, but it falls apart when there is inflation—"the implacable enemy of the public sector of the economy," Galbraith labeled it.

A half decade later, James Doi (Chapter Twenty-One) picked up Galbraith's theme. Doi posed this question: We can measure the productivity of a commercial enterprise in fairly easy ways, but how do we measure productivity in those organizations that are nonprofit in nature and committed to service? Since university budgets are allocated—or, in any case, reviewed and justified—by reference to educational productivity, the discovery of more valid measures than those currently used by the bookkeeper mentality of finance departments in state capitols becomes crucial. The survival of higher education—and consequently the survival of our society—is at stake.

Can one say, with the certainty with which we have just said it, that if the American college and university do not survive, then American society will not survive? Nevitt Sanford thinks so: "If colleges did not exist," he stated at the 1962 National Conference (Chapter Thirteen), "they would have to be invented." And Kenneth Boulding thinks likewise. In his address before the 1966 Na-

---

[1] Many aspects of this point are explored in the sections that open the 1968 and 1969 AAHE *Current Issues* volumes. The 1968 volume is *Stress and Campus Response* (San Francisco: Jossey-Bass), and the 1969 volume is *Agony and Promise* (San Francisco: Jossey-Bass).

tional Conference (Chapter Twenty-Six) he stated that the present society is "fundamentally suicidal," and our international system "fundamentally unstable and unviable." But he was, as he called himself, a "long-run optimist," and he saw our society moving toward a new era, one he described as characterized by "the integrative system." During the years of transition to that system, which he predicted would be a difficult period, the university will play the central role: "If any organization is responsible for this transition—and it is a frightening one—it is the university."

Boulding was not speaking here of the university as an arm of the government (as at Los Alamos or at the Metallurgical Laboratory that mysteriously replaced football on Stagg Field at Chicago) or the university as a service department to industry or neighborhood community, but of the university as a major force in the shaping of a new society. This development—the formation of a powerful academic "system" intimately interrelated with all of our social institutions—is, according to Talcott Parsons (Chapter Twenty-Four), the "most important sociocultural change which has occurred in the structure of society . . . in this century." In 1945 this system had not yet emerged; in 1966, an eminent sociologist told an audience at the National Conference on Higher Education that it was already in existence.

That change inevitably brought with it another: national visibility. The image of the egghead researcher and the absentminded, good-natured, rather foolish old professor was gone for good. It seemed, just after the mid-sixties, suddenly to have happened. Of course, the Free Speech Movement had already attained high national visibility. But Berkeley remained something special; few viewers associated the Free Speech Movement with American higher education in general. It felt somehow different when we marched in the inaugural ceremony for John Summerskill at San Francisco State College in Spring 1967 (he had taken office the preceding autumn) and faced peaceful demonstrators carrying placards condemning Summerskill for cooperating with the Chancellor of the State College System and with General Hershey in releasing grades to draft boards: we were astonished to see the ABC camera crew busily photographing the protestors. This was our first experi-

ence with a national television news program; and, as members of
the college community, we felt important.

We did not then realize the price that would be exacted.
But six years earlier, Charles Frankel had spelled it out in his address to the 1961 National Conference (Chapter Twelve). "Just to
report the news," he stated, "is to make news"; and that process,
in turn, "plays back on the event, expanding its area and transmuting it into something other than it would have been if it were
allowed to play out its career in private." How well we were all to
learn that lesson in the years ahead. We had not known it then; we
cannot say we had not been warned, for Frankel noted in his 1961
talk that for the first time in history, "a very large and broad public
is looking upon all of us with considerable curiosity and interest."
He ended that address on a prophetic note: "If we do badly, we
will hear about it."

No one could have dreamed, in the first decade following
World War II, what the new breed of students in the sixties would
be like—and how it was that conflicts were no longer to be a private
matter between a recalcitrant, ill-tempered student, barely more
than a child, and an all-knowing and all-powerful parent-surrogate
dean or faculty member. Suddenly students acquired *rights*—like
any other citizen protected by the laws of the land—and became
grown-ups all at the same time. In an earlier day, the professor had
known a great deal more than his student, not only in his special
field but about almost everything else too. One reads, with nostalgia
perhaps, Philip E. Jacob's profile of the typical college student of
the fifties (Chapter Seven), written in 1957: He was "gloriously
contented" and "unabashedly self-centered"; he held moral values
high (*our* moral values, that is, the moral values of the adult
world); and his campus environment was characterized by social
harmony, with an easy tolerance of the student who was different.
By 1964, on the fateful October day when participants in the American Council on Education meeting in San Francisco—the first that
was ever held west of the Mississippi—read that stunning headline
in the San Francisco *Chronicle,* "STUDENTS RIOT IN BERKELEY," it
was obvious that things had changed.

Curiously enough, the 1964 National Conference on Higher

Education, which took place a half year earlier, was full of fore-boding; a whole section of the conference was devoted to "tur-bulence among students." Among the speakers, F. Martin Erickson reviewed the situation (Chapter Seventeen) presenting some of Kenneth Keniston's findings, and suggesting that the basic solution might be a different attitude toward students: "It is necessary to develop a different relationship than we have traditionally sought with students. This relationship [is] one of trust." By 1966 the cat was out of the bag, and academia was buzzing with explanations. Talcott Parsons offered one of the more interesting ones (Chapter Twenty-Four): The father (the professor) had deserted his children (the undergraduates) and was spending his days working outside of the family ken (that is, doing research); and the children could hardly be expected to react other than by howling. At the 1968 Na-tional Conference, Seymour Halleck did the profession a vast service by analyzing all of the main explanations and interpretations of student disturbances that had been offered, classifying them into twelve hypotheses on student unrest (Chapter Twenty-Nine).

As a new breed of student developed in the sixties, so did a new breed of faculty. Who would have thought, a decade earlier, that a single faculty member could defy a whole board of trustees, that an academic senate could create and depose presidents like corporations, and that some faculty members would consent to be-come—of all things—unionized?

It seems hardly conceivable that the two politician-professors represented in our collection—T. V. Smith and J. W. Fulbright—should be warning professors in the early and middle fifties to take it easy and not rock the boat. To think of businessmen as the enemies of higher education, T. V. Smith stated in 1952 (Chapter One), "that is a suicidal thought in a capitalistic society"; to think of legislators as working against the interests of higher education—"that too," Smith said, "is a completely suicidal thought to have of the men without whom we can do nothing in public education." Fulbright emphasized (Chapter Five), as did Smith, that academic freedom is primarily a means rather than an end; and he took a jibe at the colleges and universities that are "at a loss how to define the ends they mean to preserve through academic freedom."

We must remember that these men were writing during the

unhappy days of McCarthyism. When, in the first stage of selecting essays for this collection, we were reading volumes of *Current Issues in Higher Education,* especially those of the early fifties, we were amazed at the degree to which the Communist scare had penetrated almost all discussions on higher education. Even Fulbright himself, far-seeing as he was, digressed at one point in his 1955 address to assure his audience that in his evaluation of American colleges and universities, "their key weakness is *not* that they breed Communists"; and he added: "It is arrant nonsense to say that they do."

However, the Communist scare that was reflected in T. V. Smith's and J. W. Fulbright's addresses before the National Conferences on Higher Education in 1952 and 1955 continued on far into the sixties, influencing those responsible for planning and administering American education. In 1960, Harold Taylor (Chapter Eleven) protested the trend in America to make crucial decisions in education on negative grounds, that is, in order, as he put it, "to maintain American prosperity and military security." Taylor suggested instead a positive goal, such as the establishment of "a just and peaceful world order," and argued that the real issues are not ideological but practical: poverty, the armaments race, unemployment, and so forth. The only possible means are cooperative efforts, he asserted, and nothing less will do.

Can a group of human beings work together to attain cooperation, or must interaction follow the "conflict model," whereby enforced cooperation is sought by some balance of power? This question lies behind a number of essays in this collection. In the first chapter, T. V. Smith expressed a down-to-earth point of view: human beings are built, he said, "on an animal chassis." He went on to explain: "The will to power no less than the will to perfection is of the very essence of our lives." Kenneth Boulding (Chapter Twenty-Six) presented a different view: While conflict can at certain times be creative, the conflict model is not the answer; human society will reach the point where it is organized to follow what he called "the integrative model," or it will by then have wiped itself out.

What of higher education itself?—its over 2,000 campuses, complex social organizations each of which consists of trustees, administrative officers, faculty, staff, alumni, students, and, in some cases, important groups of nonstudents? What is the right model of social organization—of governance—for them? W. H. Cowley's address before the National Conference in 1963 (Chapter Fourteen) presented an analysis of each of the major decisions that have shaped American higher education. Cowley showed that for the most part these were cooperative decisions, involving participation of all interested groups, not only those inside the institution but certain outside groups as well. Cowley's thesis was that no single group should monopolize the decisions of social institutions; "The most successful system," he stated, "involves all interest groups—the general public, the faculty, the administrators, the alumni, the students."

By the late sixties, the universities of the nation were carrying out with great efficiency the tasks demanded of them by American industry, by the government bureaus, and by the war machine. It is ironic that during the very years those tasks were being performed so well, American higher education should have been so heavily criticized for its "irrelevance." Thus began a series of conflicts of interest that marked the period of disenchantment.

Interestingly enough, the theme of relevance is a major theme in eight of the chapters in this book (according to our analysis), and it is a minor theme in perhaps fifteen more. Richard P. McKeon's essay is the first actually to use the word *relevant* as a central term in its argument (Chapter Sixteen). McKeon presented a new definition of the liberal arts, after first asserting that the liberal arts as most colleges define them are characterized by irrelevance. For him, the liberal arts must liberate man by equipping him to be active in four ways: with respect to other men (communication), the world around him (knowledge), the achievements of men (appreciation), and his own potentialities and actions (individuality). Nevitt Sanford, in an earlier address (Chapter Thirteen), moved toward a similar conception of relevance, using a totally different approach and a different set of terms.

Although they followed diverse routes and used different terms to arrive at their conceptions, the authors of the first five essays of the collection also speak directly to the subject of relevance. For T. V. Smith, the "middle-sized values" are the relevant ones: "the discipline of doubt" which science teaches; "the virtue of sensitivity" which the arts teach; and "the virtue of tolerance" (which

includes magnanimity and a willingness to compromise) which the
social sciences, and especially politics, teach. For Oliver Carmichael
(Chapter Two), the "greatest single weakness in the American college" is the inadequacy of liberal education. Clarence Faust (Chapter Three) showed, among other examples, how the opposition often
posed between book learning and direct experience is a false opposition; for it is obvious that a certain balance between these two educational means must be sought in order to make a college education
both effective and relevant.

Peter Viereck presented an address to the 1954 National
Conference (Chapter Four) that can only be described as con-
sciousness-expanding in character. He decried the exploration of
outer space without simultaneous exploration of the "fabulous new
continent within the skull." For Viereck, the path toward relevance
is the path away from "the outer mechanized world of massmen and
robots." He asserted that the college professor must become a model
not for the well-adjusted man but for the new hero to emerge in
America: the Unadjusted Man. (He was of course not speaking of
psychological maladjustment nor, as he explained, of "the drugstore
nonconformist.") "Our great universities," Viereck went on to say,
"are killing intellectuality . . . by turning an entire generation of
graduate students into trained seals." Our hope, according to him,
lay with our "most daring and individualistic young students."

In his essay, J. W. Fulbright quoted another professor-politi-
cian, Woodrow Wilson, on the ideal of the "community of scholars."
Such a community, Wilson had said, will provide the means
whereby "the classroom itself might some day come to seem a part
of life." Two later essays deal with this subject explicitly. David
Truman's (Chapter Twenty-Five) deals in its entirety with curricular
relevance. "We should not wonder if students raise the question of
relevance," he told his audience; "their intelligence should compel
them to." And Martin Tarcher (Chapter Twenty-Eight) gives a
concrete plan for bringing life into the classroom without killing the
one or contaminating the other.

No discussion of relevance can be complete without a consideration of the relationship between the civil rights movement and
higher education. Various of the National Conferences on Higher
Education during the fifties and sixties dealt with this question. The

address of Whitney Young (Chapter Twenty) begins with one of the basic tenets explored at those conferences: "Education has failed to teach what democracy is all about." The case cannot be more simply or more cogently stated.

If goals and functions are misconceived, there is virtual certainty that structures will grow lopsided. Several of the chapters in the book stress structural and organizational problems, from Carmichael's essay in 1953 to Boyer's in 1967. A thesis that pervades the collection is that the majority of American colleges and universities are wrong to set as their model a handful of prestigious universities that emphasize graduate education and research. Logan Wilson declared at the 1965 National Conference (Chapter Twenty-Three) that the primary obligation of American higher education is to students, and therefore the top priority must go to the teaching function. The research function is second in priority, Wilson asserted, and third in priority is public service. He stated that the nation cannot, and need not, support more than forty or fifty research-oriented institutions. Bruce Dearing's address at the same conference (Chapter Twenty-Two) analyzed why undergraduate teaching was so bad and what might be done about it.

Among the many criss-crossing themes to be found in the essays here, perhaps the one that emerges most strongly is the inadequacy of undergraduate education on American campuses. This is the major thesis of Carmichael's essay; and the emphasis continues with Faust, Viereck, Jacob, Frankel, Sanford, Averill, and McKeon. At the 1965 National Conference, the first after the impact of the Berkeley turbulence was felt, this theme was pervasive. Four years earlier, Frankel, speaking on the same subject (Chapter Twelve), stated that the acute problems in undergraduate education would not "be solved by great, sweeping programs." They will be solved, Frankel said, "by getting educated, liberal teachers."

Where are such teachers to come from? The preparation of college teachers has been a fundamental problem with which the profession has not been able to come to grips. There were noble but sporadic efforts in the fifties—F. W. Strothmann's address to the 1957 Conference (Chapter Six) is especially interesting in the light of his work as a member of the Committee of Fifteen. During the sixties there was less talk but, fortunately, some action: two institutions, Carnegie-Mellon University and the University of Washington, established a doctor of arts degree, specially designed for college teachers.[2]

No discussion of teaching at the college and university level can afford to overlook the revolution in electronics that occurred precisely during the twenty-five-year period under discussion. The major essay in the current collection on this subject is by Marshall McLuhan (Chapter Nine), delivered at the 1959 Conference. It is possible that some of his listeners then thought his position was either extreme or a passing fad, but they must surely know better by now. McLuhan's main argument can be simply stated: In the world of tomorrow new educational media and traditional educational procedures must coexist, and this coexistence must be "based on awareness of the inherent powers and messages of each of these unique configurations." McLuhan argued that this development will enable us to educate "more of each person"; and he demonstrated that we are no longer in need of teachers who are merely "the sources of data." McLuhan pointed out that old-fashioned teaching devices, such as a single teacher in front of a classroom, are akin to the old-fashioned medium of print; whereas "two or more teachers in dialogue with each other and with class or audience" create the same sense as the television screen does. But most important of all, in the new type of college classroom, the student is producer as well as consumer: "He is coauthor and coproducer, so that the new teaching must increasingly cast the student in coteacher roles." The essay by Martin Tarcher (Chapter Twenty-Eight) most aptly illustrates McLuhan's thesis.

The title of this book might well have read *Twenty-Five*

[2] William C. DeVane was a leading spokesman for a special doctor's degree ("not less rigorous, but different," as he described it) directed toward preparing men and women to teach effectively in college. His position is spelled out in two reports that appeared in the fifties: F. W. Strothmann (on behalf of the Committee of Fifteen), *The Graduate School Today and Tomorrow* (New York: Fund for the Advancement of Education, 1955) and Joseph Axelrod (Ed.), *Graduate Study for Future College Teachers* (Washington, D.C.: American Council on Education, 1959). A 1969 Carnegie Commission report again proposed a new doctor of arts degree for college teachers —E. Alden Dunham, *Colleges of the Forgotten Americans: A Profile of State Colleges and Regional Universities* (New York: McGraw-Hill, 1969).

Good Years; but we rather think *Twenty-Five Bad Years* would be
more accurate. It was a quarter-century that started out full of
promise—both for society and for higher education. A war had
ended in which a great foe of democracy had been vanquished;
a world organization of nations had come into being, and it seemed
possible that an era of international cooperation was in the offing.
Instead, Russia and the United States invested their resources and
energies in competition. Their education systems suffered, because
the national needs that guided educational development were conceived basically in terms of that competition. In a society at war,
every aspect of life is distorted as priorities go topsy-turvy. Educators
were optimistic during the earlier years of the quarter-century from
1945 to 1970; but as the essays here reveal, the optimism ebbed
away as the nation moved toward 1970.

The spirit of optimism is strongly reflected in the earlier
essays in this collection—the essays that were written in the fifties—
even though one suspects that in some cases (for example, in Faust's
essay), the optimism may have been included for rhetorical purposes.
By the sixties, that optimistic spirit had all but disappeared. Nevitt
Sanford quipped (Chapter Thirteen): "The situation is serious but
not hopeless." And the year before, Frankel (Chapter Twelve)
cheerily called it a "happy" crisis; but, in truth, he did not *sound*
very happy.[3] The typical attitude of the balance of the essays in the
book—that is, after 1960—is suggested by a phrase of Boulding's; in
his essay (Chapter Twenty-Six), he speaks of himself as "a long-
run optimist." This, we submit, is a nicely *positive* way of expressing
how difficult the years ahead are likely to be.

Within the next few years it seems unlikely that disruption
and disorder within our colleges and universities will decline appre-
ciably. Extrapolating from the current social scene in our cities and
our nation and assuming that colleges and universities, particularly
urban and public colleges and universities, reflect the wider social

---

[3] Frankel's essay in the 1968 *Current Issues* volume, not reprinted in
this collection, is far more pessimistic—indeed grim in comparison with his
1961 essay. Charles Frankel, "The Educational Impact of American Foreign
Policy," in Smith (Ed.), *Stress and Campus Response* (San Francisco:
Jossey-Bass, 1968).

system of which they are a part, confusion and disruption seem almost inevitable.

This prediction, however, has to be tempered. We were talking a short while ago to a somewhat older colleague who said, "Well, you're too young to be optimistic." He was making the point that things have really been worse in the United States—for example, in the twenties, in the days of the Palmer raids, or for that matter, during the Senator Joseph McCarthy period. He was making the point that during such periods colleges and universities were very vulnerable; that is, various Congressional and state un-American activities committees essentially invaded the campuses and hauled people off to testify before committees at their will. Faculty members who took the Fifth Amendment to protect themselves from having to testify against themselves were in many cases summarily fired from colleges and universities. He was saying that perhaps things are not that bad now. There may be something in what he said. But when we look about us, at the war in Vietnam or at social conflict in our cities, it is really difficult to be optimistic. However, let us look to longer-range predictions, that is, predictions beyond the next few years of possible immediate disruption or chaos. Presuming that we get by such a period, what is likely to face us in thirty years? One possibility is that things will remain much as they are. This opinion is held by a number of our colleagues. Their feeling is essentially that most faculty members and students like the system we now have, that the rebels among them are relatively few in number and rather atypical, and that nothing very much will change. We doubt this very much, but it is a possibility.

Another possibility, assuming that chaos and disruption persist for some time, is that we would evolve in our colleges and universities something of a dehumanized system, a kind of knowledge factory. The reaction of many faculty members to turmoil on the campus is essentially to turn their backs on it as quickly and effectively as possible. These faculty members would like to teach their courses and have their office hours and get out—to go to the library or home, where things are quiet and safe. A distinct possibility, and a very pessimistic one, is increasing dehumanization and impersonality on our campuses.

There are also optimistic possibilities. By this we mean education for freedom in Erich Fromm's sense, that is, the full realization of individual potentialities, together with the ability to live actively and spontaneously. Such an education will permit and aid an individual to develop his personality (in the sense that Sanford develops this idea in his essay) to the fullest extent possible. We would regard such education as the only kind appropriate to a democracy. Some years ago we were quite sanguine that this hope for higher education would be realized. The big question now is whether we have sufficient time, given some of the crises that face us immediately in our society and on our campuses.

In thinking about educational procedures that would enhance desirable qualities in young people, the question arises: Whence will the leadership come? We doubt very much that leadership of this kind is likely to emerge from faculty and administrators on our campuses. Since the end of World War II we have witnessed considerable erosion of morality on the part of faculty members and administrators. To some extent this has resulted from involvement in various kinds of programs and activities—for example, research for agencies of the federal government—that have little relationship, in some cases no relationship, to the kinds of things an institution of higher education should stand for. When a role shifts in a bureaucracy and people take on roles that were not intended within the legality of the original system, concern for the protection of this role by the exercise of power frequently ensues. We are not criticizing faculty members and administrators for being despots in the worst sense. For the most part their exercise of power has been benevolent. Nevertheless, we think we have witnessed increasing concern with the protection of their roles by means of exercise of power and abdication of the moral sense that should devolve upon teachers when they are involved actively with students in the process of liberal education.

In considering other reasons for abdication of leadership among faculty and administrators, we must recognize that faculty and administrators are fallible human beings, and this means that in time of stress they are likely to react with what may be described as primitive morality. Recently we have had occasion to attend various meetings of faculty members and administrators at which discussion of rebellious and disruptive students took place, and we must say that on these occasions we could sense little difference between the outlook of many faculty members and administrators and the general ethos of Orange County, California. The predominant attitude of these faculty members and administrators toward student protestors is essentially punitive. They display a primitive kind of conscience—a punitive response to transgression without concern for understanding of the motives of the transgressors. Increasingly apparent on campuses is the absence of true teachers among the high officials. By true teachers we mean people who explicate complex issues, who go to the heart of the matter. On occasions when faculty members or administrators respond to student protest with primitive punitiveness, the president or another prominent administrator should say to the faculty, "You are extremely annoyed that the kinds of things you think are important have been disrupted. Nevertheless, I think it is very important that you recognize that you cannot allow yourself the luxury of this immediate need for punishment. It is essential that you rise above this level of immediate response and act with greater wisdom, greater magnanimity. In the long run your treatment of students must serve *educational* ends." We see few college presidents or important administrators exercising educational leadership in this fashion, and the situation is likely to get worse instead of better. Apparently the quality of people who are becoming educators and administrators seems to be going down rather than up.

Now if we were designing the optimal kind of college or university system for the future, our chief concern would be the development of faculty members rather than students. Faculty members need such help, for they are being ground down at the present time by a dehumanizing system. If we had an educational system that promoted the optimal development of faculty members, we should not have to worry about students. The development of students would take place very well quite automatically. A system designed to promote the optimal development of faculty members would be essentially noncompetitive. People would publish when they had something to say rather than to advance their tenure. This would be a great boon to all engaged in scholarly activities. That is, we would not have to face the plethora of fragmented publications that induce vertigo, if not nausea. We would have a system that countered the professionalism of graduate education.

We are troubled by the bypassing of language or denigration of language as a medium of communication. Language is a fine moral sieve. What we can put into words and communicate to others, we can control. We are fully aware that language is not the only way in which we communicate; and we should hardly like to see our life or our society based on communication by language alone. Nevertheless, for certain kinds of social functions, for example politics, language is still the best form of communication for promoting mutual understanding. In her book, *Philosophy in a New Key,* Susanne Langer describes how it is the fascination with a new idea can lead to overworking it. And Samuel Taylor Coleridge had a very apt description of this process: "Every reform, however necessary, will by weak minds be carried to an excess, which will itself need reforming."

William Blake wrote:

> *When the rich and learned Pharisee*
> *Came to consult him secretly,*
> *Upon his heart with iron pen*
> *He wrote, "Ye must be born again."*

We need an educational system that will enable faculty members and administrators to be born again. If we had such, we would not have to worry about student development, because what is best in the sense of development of the fullest humanity and potentiality of one group of constituents within a total system is best for all. But this rebirth is not likely to happen from within. Within a bureaucracy the power structure rarely does anything serious about reforming itself. If we contemplate innovation and reform in higher education, we have to think that the basic initiative will come from students.

PART One

1945 to 1957

❀❀❀❀❀❀❀❀❀❀❀❀❀❀❀❀❀❀❀❀❀❀❀❀❀❀❀❀❀❀

We require freedom. Let there be no misunderstanding about that; but it is a freedom of means. It is a freedom so we may do other things in the field of value; and if we let it become an end in itself, the only thing it does for us is to make us think that the business community is against us—a community which has established the system, after all, from which and on which we live, privately and publicly. It makes us think that businessmen are our enemies—and that is a suicidal thought in a capitalistic society. It makes us think that the politicians, the legislators, are somehow out conspiring every night, and that they are after us, us teachers. That too is a completely suicidal thought to have of the men without whom we can do nothing in public education and not much in the long run in private education.

from the address of T. V. Smith
before the 1952 National Conference on Higher Education

I

1952
Middle-sized
Values

T. V. Smith

❀❀❀❀❀❀❀❀❀❀❀❀❀❀❀❀❀❀❀❀❀❀❀❀❀❀❀❀❀❀❀

"It is a gloomy moment in history. Not for many years, not in fact in the lifetime of most men who are here, has there been so much grave and deep apprehension; never has the future seemed so incalculable as at this time. In France, the political cauldron seethes and bubbles with uncertainty; Russia hangs, as usual, a cloud, dark and silent, upon the horizon of Europe; while all the energies, resources and the influences of the British Empire are sorely tried and are yet to be tried more sorely. It is a solemn moment, and no man can feel indifference, which happily, no man pretends to feel in the issue of events. Of our own troubles, no man can see the end." The foregoing quotation is from *Harper's Weekly,* October 10, 1857.

There is a story which Plutarch tells in his *Parallel Lives of Greek and Roman Statesmen* of a certain Pyrrhus, the Pyrrhus of Pyrrhic victory fame in the annals of military life, who one day called to him his wise man, that is, the fool of the court, and told him to get ready, that tomorrow morning at dawn the armies would march on a little conquering expedition.

This was an early Mussolini from Greece. The fool said, "Yes, sire, I shall be ready, of course, as you command; but do you mind my asking where are we going?"

"Well," he said, "we are going over and conquer the Italians."

"Sire, this is something of an undertaking—to conquer the whole of Italy. They are divided among themselves, and we will have to conquer them in segments. No doubt you can do so if you have made up your mind; but have you thought carefully about it?"

"Yes, I have thought it out. Have your pajamas and tooth-brush ready in the morning. We march at dawn."

"Yes, sire, I shall be ready. But after we have conquered Italy, where then do we go?"

"Then," he said, "we shall cross over the Straits at Messina, and conquer Sicily."

"Yes, sire, but the Sicilians are much better fighters than the Italians and this will be something of an expensive undertaking. Have you considered carefully the cost?"

"Yes, I have considered the cost. Be ready at dawn to march."

"Indeed, sire, I shall be ready, but after we have conquered Sicily, then where do we go?"

The monarch had not thought much further than this, and a little impatiently he replied, "Then, we will cross the Mediterranean and conquer Carthage."

"Yes, but sire, this Carthaginian conquest is going to be very expensive in treasure and most expensive in lives. These are the best fighters in the world. Where do we go from there?"

And the monarch very impatiently said, "We will go to the Valley of the Nile, and we will conquer that rich empire."

"Yes, sire, no doubt you can do all things that you determine upon, but may I ask one more question before I go. Where do we go from Egypt?"

And the monarch, as Plutarch says, very impatient and somewhat irritated at his court fool and wise man, concluded the colloquy thus: "Then we shall sit down and take our ease."

"But, sire, if that is the only end for which we go through these heroic endeavors, why do we not sit down *here* and take our rest *now?*"

In the backwash of a troubled world in which we have been through not only two great world wars but are still in the aftermath of these wars, when we are fed up with the will to power and have lost confidence in the serviceability of men of power to achieve anything of the ends of perfection for which we ourselves struggle, we are likely to think that in that argument between the monarch and his fool, that the fool had the better end of the argument; and perhaps so he did. But he did not have the whole of the argument. We human beings are built on an animal chassis, whatever may be the Fisher body of our minds and of our towering spirits.

Just as certain as the sun rises and sets, given a time of peace in which we have settled ourselves down to take our ease here and now, extended a little beyond the hedonic level to the level of the cultivation of the arts and sciences and all of the adornments of the human spirit, we shall be just as ready to march again, if not in military formation, then under some other phalanx of the protest of the human spirit, as we were to devote ourselves to the ends of perfection. For the will to power no less than the will to perfection is of the very essence of our lives; and for us to keep this in mind, that we do not set our values so high that they appeal only to the dried up, so high that men of action, men who want to do things in the world rather than to think things or feel things more intensely, shall not be interested in them is, it seems to me, of the very essence of wisdom in approaching such a problem as values for higher education.

I take it that academic values are primarily concerned with the problem of means. That is the reason why we put a very great deal of emphasis upon academic freedom, as we call our white elephant, our sacred cow. Not that liberty is not an end in itself; it is, of course, the most precious of human ends; but we, ourselves, are primarily concerned not with that when we talk about academic freedom. We are concerned with the conditions, rather, under which we can foster and perhaps implement other ends than our own freedom.

To get too preoccupied with academic freedom as the end of higher education is indeed one of the most suicidal things that can happen to us. I think we sometimes fall into that. We make it an end. It is an end, but the less we think about it as an end, the better off we are. When we get to thinking about academic freedom as an end, we entirely overestimate our own significance in society; and having estimated it beyond the level where objectively it is estimated, we find people not observing our estimates of ourselves. This frightens us and puts us on the defensive, and then we become more avid to maintain academic freedom until finally we treat our friends as our enemies, and we look for a member of the board who is a plutocrat or some unscrupulous politician under the bed every night before we go to bed, and forget who our friends are in the world.

We do ourselves the greatest wrongs. It was a very fine day in my life, for example, when I woke up to the fact that grievances are usually self-inflicted. I do not want to be unjust to anybody, but it seems to me true that the people who cry the most about academic freedom are often those with whose freedom our profession does not altogether stand or fall.

I think I might claim credit, a thing that is rather hazardous to do in the political world, for having made a difference one day in the Senate of Illinois. It is the only time I can think of when things were really different because I was there. It was the day when the teachers' loyalty oath bill was introduced in the lower house and got 151 of 153 votes. Then it came to the Senate. It would have passed if we had not stalled and worked the day and night shift against it for weeks—and finally it came to a vote, and got only nine votes. And those nine apologized for it. I fought against it tooth and nail.

It never occurred to me, however, nor would it ever occur to me in terms of academic freedom or anything else, that if the bill had passed, I would not have been the first to sign it, and glad to sign it. I think myself we ordinarily do more harm than we do good by making the kind of issues we do make of this peculiar academic predicament. We require freedom. Let there be no misunderstanding about that; but it is a freedom of means. It is a freedom so we may do other things in the field of value; and if we let it become an end in itself, the only thing it does for us is to make us think that the business community is against us—a community which has established the system, after all, from which and on which we live, privately and publicly. It makes us think that businessmen are our enemies—and that is a suicidal thought in a capitalistic society. It makes us think that the politicians, the legislators, are somehow out conspiring every night, and that they are after us, us teachers. That, too, is a completely suicidal thought to have of the men without whom we can do nothing in public education and not much in the long run in private education.

I shall pay for these bold words, no doubt; but I shall not repent them. I think it is most useful to us to consider academic values primarily as things concerned with the means of life, the effective condition under which we can implement some other values that could better be considered as our ends.

The freedom that is an end in academic freedom is the freedom that we get apart from being school teachers. It is a freedom that belongs to us as citizens and can be discussed elsewhere. Let me now jump the moral values for the moment, and say a word that to me at least is helpful on the problem of spiritual values.

I am going from Omega to Alpha at one jump. The term "spiritual value" describes the vaguest of all values, and in some very large sense is the most precious formulation which we give to the life of our values. I myself have the impression that just as values conceived as means are too small for the daily preoccupations of intelligent men, so the values conceived as spiritual values are too large for the daily preoccupations of men engaged in higher education. In between we have to find those middle-sized values to which we can devote ourselves. I make that distinction about middle-sized values, largely because I know all the line of patter about the nobility of the teaching profession, and on proper occasions, I indulge in it—and nearly always I believe nearly all I say. We are, indeed, the custodians of all the high values in the world. Wisdom is with us, and will almost die with us. We are the parents of all the children of all the people, and with us civilization grows. Through us, it will flourish, and with our demise, civilization would die. This we all understand well enough.

On the blue Saturdays, however, I sometimes indulge the general thought that only those who sleep on the floor never fall out of bed—and I like to inquire where the floor is, not where the ceiling is. I like to put to myself, as a teacher, this question: "What would be the least function that I could perform, that I would be willing to settle for, without a sense of guilt, in taking my salary from whatever school I happen to be serving? What is the least of the functions that I could settle for, and still keep my self-respect?" When I put it to myself, the illustration comes to me from the Senate of Illinois, of my political enemy, but my personal friend, Jim Monroe of Collinsville. I still read his editorials. We had a bill up recognizing the high virtues of the public-school teachers in Illinois—we were going to increase their earnings. Teachers were entitled to it, and I was fighting, as any representative of the teachers would, to get this bill passed. This man, an extremely intelligent man, was against it. I went to him one day and I said:

"Jim, this is a very anomalous situation. You are one of the most intelligent men I have ever known; and here you are against this bill. I am really afraid you do not know what education is all about."

He said: "That is really going too far, that I do not know what education is about. I know all it is about."

I said: "What, for instance?"

Confronted with the specific question, he said: "Education is—it is to keep the kids out of their parents' hair a sufficient number of hours every day so that the parents can lead their own lives." Then he said: "I think it is worth all it costs. Maybe after all I will vote for the bill," which I think he finally did.

I often come back to that. I would be willing to settle for that—only a baby-sitter, of adolescence—so that we would not have this business of each generation's living for the sake of the next generation, which will live for the sake of the next generation. It means the whole show will some day be over, and nobody will have lived for life itself. Parents have their rights; and education conceived as entertainment of kids, as baby-sitting—this is not too bad a conception. I would call that a middle-sized evaluation of education.

I have found as a teacher that just as I approach the problem described in these terms, as an *intellectual* entertainer, I do a really better job of not getting too wrapped up in the implementation of ideas that are too high ever to be implemented. I would myself define, without meaning to be unctuous, spiritual values as concerned with ends in themselves, as over against academic values, which are primarily concerned with means. Ends—in themselves—are the highest level of human experience. They are that formulation or discovery or projection of the life of the human spirit that changes only with changes of the cosmic seasons. We all have these types of values unquestionably. You just take truth, which the scientists can talk about, and put a capital "T" on it, and you have made a spiritual value out of truth—but by doing so, you have promoted it out of the reach of any complete implementation by human beings. You can take beauty and spell it with a capital "B" and you have made beauty a spiritual value; and by that, you have promoted it to a level where it balks full implementation. To insist upon these biggest values in the fullest way is but to invite peptic ulcers.

The teaching profession is a peculiar victim of this. We indulge nervous breakdowns, if we can afford them; if not, ulcers; or at least galloping hiccoughs. Statistically, one out of every twenty-two people in any group will spend some time in a mental institution before his day is done. I suppose that among teachers the proportion is higher, because we do such homage to these very high values. That is, in the life of value, there comes a time in which whatever ideal we may be talking about demands more of us than we can ever give. You talk about truth easily; but suppose you spell it with a capital "T" and go out in the world determined twenty-four hours in the day to tell the truth, the whole truth, and nothing but the truth, so help you God. So help you the Devil, too, as, before it is done, you will need more help than there is. So it is with Beauty. So with Justice. So with Holiness.

The only end of the devotion of the human spirit to these ideals that are too high for implementation by ordinary men in ordinary life—the only eventuation of this is tragedy; it is the presence of such ideals, these spiritual ideals, that constitutes the tragic note in all human life. We do not have to deny that fact; but we have to make acknowledgment of the fact. If we make as the goal of education these highest values, we have made as our end something for which there are no means, and which in turn will depreciate the effectiveness of the means which we do have.

This was the reason why our fathers set up from the very first day of this republic what came to be called the doctrine of the separation between church and state. It was to keep men who served the spiritual values, these highest of all values, from inflicting their view of these absolute values upon other people who had values, but who had other views as to what the values were. Those who go around criticizing our great systems, from the public schools to the state universities, and who despair of this generation, and who say we have become completely secular—in my opinion, they do not know what they are talking about. Secularization is not anything to be feared. If you did not have it, the saints would be cutting each other's throats because they would not agree as to what the spiritual values meant. When you get into that situation, you have to declare a truce. The state has to become neutral, and therefore, secularization is not the enemy of religion. Sectarianism is the enemy. These values are too precious for us to make them common. Men differ too much about them. They are too private. They are completely private; and the only way we can serve them is by leaving all men free to serve spiritual values in whatever way they themselves may think best.

This is a tragic problem, not only in our day in which this doctrine is under the most strident attack since the day of the founding fathers—this doctrine of the state as a secular arbiter between religious groups—but this was a tragic problem before this republic was founded. Take, for instance, the controversy between John Cotton and Roger Williams—we have the literary documents of it. Roger Williams wrote a pamphlet, addressed to the Parliament in England, after he had been driven out of Massachusetts, in which he said that these Puritans came over here to get freedom for their conscience, and now they had driven him out because he followed his own conscience. John Cotton replied to that with "The Tenet of Bloody Prosecution Washed and Made White in the Blood of the

Lamb." Roger Williams responded to this reply—these arguments cannot be settled, they have gone on for all these years, and will continue—in a pamphlet "The Tenet of Bloody Prosecution Made More Bloody Still by Being Washed and Made White in the Blood of the Lamb."

The moral of the story is the tragic element in all human life; that is, the higher we make our values, the more certainly they will divide us. John Cotton said that they did not drive Roger Williams out of Massachusetts because he followed his conscience, but because he refused to follow his conscience in doing what he well knew to be right.

Every value has its absolute aspect. It has a surplus of significance that cannot be implemented by human beings.

In our experience during World War II as military governors —the first time we had ever trained men to follow the army and take over from army officers the civilian administration so the army men could go on fighting the war—our first effort was on a little island in the Mediterranean, which we took while on the way to Sicily. We had our first experience there as military governors. The official historian of that occupation wrote: "We thought our principles only had to be heard, in order to be accepted." These are high spiritual values—these principles that men had died for. "We found other people had a different set of principles which they regarded as equally self-evident, and to which they were equally devoted. In spite of the tiny size of the newspaper published there, it taught us this great philosophical lesson. The sergeant sat down and wrote an editorial in which he urged the citizens to observe the four freedoms, and to cease defecating on the public highway. A delegation came to the sergeant and said this: 'What good are these four freedoms which you are ramming down our throats, and which we never heard of before, if you deny us a freedom we have always known, and our fathers before us?' The sergeant scratched his head and said: 'All right, then, never mind about the other freedoms for awhile. You go away, and don't commit nuisances in the piazza.' Within an hour, the citizens assembled, and with one accord struck a blow for freedom."

That brings me to the third formulation of the topic, the

moral values. I am not trying to impose definitions. I am suggesting
a distinction which seems to me to make sense in a sea of semantic
ambiguity.

Moral values are what I call medium-sized values. They are
neither mere means nor mere ends. They are what the progressive
educators have been taught to call "ends-in-view." They direct human activity. I would rather put it in this way: Moral values are
such elements of spiritual values as can be agreed upon without
coercion. These are the values that we, as higher educators, are primarily concerned with. It is not that we overlook or depreciate
spiritual values. The fact is that we know that the highest and the
best is private. It is not public. The effort to make it public always
leads to coercion. The final test of spirituality is self-containment of
ideal impetuosities.

There is a wide field in human values over which we do have
agreement, and an agreement more solid than that achieved intellectually. To the extent that we can keep ourselves disentangled from
such things as academic freedom as an end in itself and can count
the values of our academic life as precious means which must be
maintained so that we may be more effective in dealing with ends,
just to that extent can we achieve that wise tolerance of the founding fathers seen in their doctrine of separation between church and
state and in their divorcing of spiritual values and religion (religion
is only one type of spiritual value); just to that extent will we free
our minds for doing what can be done, and what I think we are
doing magnificently as a matter of fact in our American education
system. We can free ourselves through preoccupation with the values
on which there is sufficient agreement to make our means effective
for these intermediate ends.

I would like to risk an aside about our secondary education.
I hear university professors, and have all my life, who are criticizing
the high schools, commenting on the ill-prepared students we get in
the freshman year in the universities and colleges. I have never
understood what they are talking about. I have never been able to
document it. It seems to me every year that the freshmen I get come
ever better prepared for all the things that seem to me finally to
count, and that they themselves are better educated—and I would

measure my words—they are better educated now in science and
art and social studies than I was when I graduated from the university some 30 years ago. To me, it is simply magnificent, the
changes in the thinking, the ingenuity, and the habits of work, as
compared with what I knew in my youth.

I have the impression also that at the higher educational level
we are doing a magnificent job of touching the only values that we
can really serve collectively—these middle-sized values. Training in
science, as I said, is effective at the secondary level; and I think it is
more than highly effective in American colleges and universities.
Training in science is a concrete implementation up to a very far-
reaching extent of one of the chief moral values—the value called
"truth" spelled with a little "t," not with a big "T." The latter spell-
ing makes it a spiritual value. Science, after all, is the one great,
organized, established way that the human race has found of developing scrupulosity in human beings, when we start life without
any of it whatsoever. We start life with a lot of other things, and
some are very beautiful—but we do not start with scrupulosity. We
are not an unbelieving world. We are a believing world. I suppose
it is a sort of law that any child would believe anything that is told
him by anybody, until he discovers some reason for not believing it.
Scrupulosity of belief is not surrendering to beliefs because they are
old or because they make people more comfortable or more popular.
It is not a capacity which is a natural inherent thing for human
beings. It is an achieved capacity, for most of us would not know
truth if we met it in the road. Yet we need people who know how
to get it when we do need it; and that is the role of science. I was
reading the other night the letter which Galileo wrote to Kepler in
which he referred to his calling on the professor of philosophy—
which is to say, of theology—at Padua University. Galileo said he
asked the professor to look through the long glass, the newly invented telescope. The professor said he could not do it. Galileo said:
"You had better take an evening off. Come down and look at it."
(I communicate only the meaning, not the words.) "There is a new
planet there never before seen by mortal eyes."

"No," the professor said, "there is not such a planet."

"Well," replied Galileo, "come down and look."

"No," he said, "it is not there. I have read Aristotle carefully and I know the Bible backwards and forwards. It is not mentioned anywhere. I know it is not there."

"But I say come down and look at it, and see for yourself."

No, he was not going to do it because he was afraid if he looked, he would see it and he knew it was not there. The professor went on to say that if he saw it, it would be a temptation extemporized by the Devil to win him away from his faith. Now think of the putridity of a mind like that—a man afraid of opening his eyes and looking out on the vast universe of God and finding out what is what and what is not what. Even the humblest freshman in high school is long over the fear that has dogged the human race, the fear to use one's own mind.

But I have no right to say this. I am not a scientist. I am only an admirer of the gadgets and technology of science, and an admirer of this magnificent moral virtue of scrupulosity which science, above all things else in the world, developed. Let me quote a man who had the right to say what I have just said, Pasteur. Accepting 500,-000 francs by the grace of school children's contributions, two million from the French government, millions more from other governments and scientific societies, he said, accepting his scientific home:

Gentlemen of Science, what I am asking of you here today, you in turn must ask of your students who gather in the laboratories throughout the world, and it is the most difficult thing which can be asked of human beings: namely, after believing that you have discovered a great truth, after being filled with an eager desire to make that truth known, not to make it known but to impose silence upon yourself for days, for weeks, sometimes for years, while striving to destroy your own conclusions; and permitting yourself to announce it as the truth in the name of science only after all adverse hypotheses have been exhausted.

"After all adverse hypotheses have been exhausted," I repeat. It is easy to convince our wives if our marriage is one in which "you and I are one," but "I" is *the* one. We may convince our children. We can always get a group of like-minded sectarians around us and convince them. But the test of truth is convincing those who are not going to have that belief, by getting enough evidence together so when they look at it, they either go to the insane asylum or they accept it, and not making up your own minds until you have exhausted all hypotheses. This to me, this austerity of spirit, is the nearest approach to spiritual values that is ever achieved by organized men.

Now the development of the virtue of scrupulosity through science is our first and perhaps greatest contribution to the field of values in higher education. But just as the sciences cultivate that, so all of the arts, beginning with the fine arts and coming down to the humble arts, cultivate another great moral virtue, the virtue of sensitivity—not the scientific discipline of doubt, but this discipline of opening all the senses to all the sights and sounds and colors and cadences that move in our world, until finally, looking where other people look, we see what they do not see; or listening where they attend, we hear what they do not hear. This is the fruitage of art and literature.

We are cultivating, I think, at a high level, the great values clustering around beauty. Upon this we can agree, that it is a magnificent thing for human society. Once we get over the invidious comparison between the fine arts and just "arts," and then between arts and crafts, we shall be much further on our way to developing in all the ranges of education this fine sensitivity that I described as the middle-sized virtue that the arts themselves suggest.

There happened to me in New Orleans, once when I was visiting at Tulane University, a beautiful thing. I was having trouble with my car and was getting terribly fed up on all automotive mechanics. I was just ready to conclude pessimistically that there were not any who knew their jobs and had some pride in their skills. I drove finally into a garage and said, "I will try it once more."

A middle-aged mechanic was there. "Will you look at my engine and see what is the matter with it?"

"No, let's listen to the motor. Start it up."

I did so.

"All right, lift the hood." I lifted the hood, and he made some adjustment. The engine purred very beautifully as it had not done for weeks. In this case, I will say, the cure proved lasting, too.

Filled with admiration, I said, "That is marvelous. By listening to that engine you can tell what is wrong with it."

He said, "How else but?"

I said, "Don't tell me that in that tone of voice. I have spent forty dollars in the last few weeks with three mechanics. 'How else but?' "

Then he said (maybe it is a famous quotation, but not knowing, I gave him credit for it): "He who works with his hands is a laborer; he who works with his hands and his mind is a craftsman; he who works with his hands, his mind, and his heart is an artist."

Now this business of investing our whole emotional nature in the enterprise destroys the invidiousness of the levels at which we work, and transforms labor into skill.

My final illustration is of politics. I happen to think that in the schools we are doing as good a job as we are doing anywhere else in the world, sensitizing people to the great moral virtue which arises almost exclusively out of our two-party politics. This is the virtue of tolerance, the virtue of magnanimity. This is the cultivation of the middle-sized virtue of which politics is the great exemplification, let us say, the virtue of magnanimity. The politicians, by and large, are the only people who achieve this because it is so hard to achieve—you do not achieve it unless you have to, and they are the only ones that have got to—namely, the discovery that the great difficulty about the life of virtue, of value, is that it is not bad men, it is not a bad system of politics; the trouble is with good men, with men who insist on being good in such cussedly queer ways, namely, their own way. The more intelligent men are, the more they will differ upon the high values. That is the reason, I repeat, why we cannot make the spiritual values our objective. They are so high that different men mean different things when they use the same word. We have to leave them in their magnificent isolation, and make our approach in solitude.

The politician has to discover that the more intelligent men are, the more they differ one from another; and the more honest they are, the more steadily they hold to those differences; and, therefore, because men are good and are intelligent, the highest level of agreement which can be achieved in the great strident issues of life is the level of compromise, which you think to be remarkably low and which I admit to be low. But this is the highest level that can be achieved as we approach the higher values.

It would be a great moral advance if we could wake our students up to the moral majesty of a two-party system of politics in turning out people who can differ one with the other, as Senator Taft and I have done, on the radio and everywhere else, with mutual respect. I would swear to high Heaven that Senator Taft is one of the most intelligent men I have ever known; that he is one of the most patriotic men I have ever known; that he is the hardest-working man I have ever known; and that above all odds, he is a paragon of courage in American political life. And I believe he would say of me that I am an honest and intelligent man. But I did not like originally to admit this. I had to learn how to admit it. Politics is the only game in which men have to learn that the other man's error is his way of seeking the truth, and have to come to terms on whatever level you can as a compromise measure. To insist upon higher values than scrupulosity, sensitivity, and sportsmanship is to lower these without achieving higher values.

As masters of means, we are the connecting link between the higher values of solitude and the middle-sized values of society.

1953

Weaknesses in the College

Oliver C. Carmichael

❀❀❀❀❀❀❀❀❀❀❀❀❀❀❀❀❀❀❀❀❀❀❀❀❀❀❀❀❀❀

Any appraisal of higher education requires a look at its background, at the history of the changes which have taken place since the fixed curriculum was abandoned in the last half of the nineteenth century. Three revolutionary movements in that period are chiefly responsible for the fantastic growth in numbers of students attending colleges and universities, for the proliferation of courses, and for the present character of American higher education. They are the Land-Grant

College Act of 1862, the introduction of the elective system, and the development of the conception of the modern university. At the risk of being tedious, I should like to examine each of these in some detail.

The Morrill Act, providing for agricultural and technical training, was a basic departure from the tradition of higher education as it had developed in Europe and America. It boldly declared that its purpose was to provide educational opportunities for those who worked with their hands, to break with the historical conception that college was for the elite alone, and to establish a new and more democratic system of higher education than had hitherto been known. Courses in agriculture had been developed experimentally as early as 1850 but had no standing educationally. When the federal government with its prestige and economic resources declared that they should be admitted to the fold as a part of the curriculum of higher education, their status was completely changed. While some states set up separate institutions to carry out the provisions of the Act, twenty-six state universities incorporated the new courses in their programs, thus increasing the respectability of "agriculture and the mechanic arts" as subjects of study. Gradually research and experimentation were added to the training courses in agriculture, and engineering programs were encouraged.

The effect of this innovation was manyfold. First of all, it unlocked the door of opportunity to a vast segment of the population that had up to that time no thought of education beyond that provided by the local school. This was of great significance socially and politically, as well as educationally. It had a profound effect upon the development of the democratic conception of life characteristic of America and stimulated enormously the aspirations of the average citizen. This in turn meant great numbers clamoring for admission to college and an increasing interest in vocational and technical courses. Broadening the base of the college population meant a lowering of the average of ability, while an emphasis on *training* rather than *education* lowered the intellectual tone of the campus.

But all these changes would not have affected the purity of liberal education if the college curriculum had remained fixed. These courses might have developed as discrete segments of post-high school education, much as they have done in Europe, except for a concurrent change which was taking place in the colleges. Eliot was elected president of Harvard in 1869, seven years after the passage of the Morrill Act. He began early to insist upon the admission of new courses to the college curriculum, such as history and economics, and the privilege of selection on the part of the student from among the college offerings. Thus, the adoption of the elective system was proceeding simultaneously with the gradual acceptance of vocational and technical training as legitimate elements of higher education. It was, therefore, natural that the practical courses should find their way into college programs.

The third important development in higher education was signalized by the founding of Johns Hopkins University (1876). It heralded the advent of the modern university. Before that time many professors were active in research, some institutions granted Ph.D. degrees, a few had professional schools, but research and professional training were not generally regarded as essential functions of universities. Johns Hopkins, with its great emphasis upon research and graduate work and upon medical education from the beginning, set a new pattern that was quickly followed by two new institutions—Chicago and Clark Universities. Gradually the older institutions moved in the direction of the new program until today in most universities the college is only one small segment of the total offerings. The graduate and professional schools enroll the majority of the students, while research gets the lion's share of the budget. Harvard, for example, in addition to the college, has ten professional schools, while its graduate and research programs dominate the educational picture.

The effect of the development of the modern university has been felt throughout the educational system. The relatively minor role of the college, hence of liberal education, in the overall university picture has resulted in its loss of prestige and influence. The importance of the professional schools and their preprofessional demands upon the college have still further weakened its position. The graduate schools, with their emphasis upon highly technical research as a basis for the Ph.D. and the requirement of that degree for teaching in the college, have been responsible for the tone and quality of college instruction, if not for the curriculum itself. Thus, the university development has exercised a preponderant influence over the college throughout the period of change which it has been experiencing.

With these facts in mind as a background, perhaps we are ready to consider the strengths and weaknesses of higher education as we know it today. What we consider to be its assets and liabilities will depend, however, on what we conceive the role of higher education to be in modern society. It is necessary, therefore, to indicate the assumptions underlying the discussion which follows.

It is assumed that the classical curriculum of fifty years ago will not meet the needs today; that post-high school education for 20 to 25 per cent of the population is inevitable, and that it is to the best interests of the country that this should be so, provided the program is adapted to the abilities of the student and the needs of society; that technical and vocational interests of students are legitimate concerns of post-high school education, though not of liberal arts colleges; that general studies should be emphasized in all curricula on the ground that whatever the vocation or profession, the individual should be educated for effective citizenship; and that the role of colleges and universities in American society is to provide (1) education, interpreted in the broadest terms, to youth and adults, (2) scientific, technical, and professional training, and (3) the advancement of knowledge through scientific and technological research.

In the light of these assumptions let us look at higher education as a social enterprise in an effort to suggest its major elements of strength.

The first feature of the American system which strikes the visitor from other lands is the variety of offerings of colleges and universities and the proportion of youth who enroll in them. Despite the criticisms of the quality of those offerings and of the level of intelligence of the college population, the assets of the system from the standpoint of social and economic progress seem to outweigh the liabilities. A few facts will illustrate the uniqueness of the American system and indicate the reasons for this conclusion.

For example, Great Britain has a population of approximately 50,000,000, some 80,000 of whom are enrolled in their colleges and universities. On the basis of that ratio, the college population in the United States should be 240,000 (approximately the number recorded for 1900) instead of 2,200,000. It is, of course, true that the two systems are in some ways not comparable, for many institutions in this country unworthy of being called colleges are listed as such, while a number of the British schools provide relatively advanced courses though they are not called colleges. Moreover, the British do not count part-time students. Even when these differences are taken into account, it is still true that the ratio of college students to the total population is five to eight times greater in this country than in the United Kingdom. The same holds true for the countries of Europe. The importance of this fact to the social and economic welfare of the United States is not fully appreciated. Our preeminent economic and industrial power as compared with the rest of the world is not unrelated to it. It is difficult to imagine what the status of the United States would be today if higher education had been confined to the few.

This widespread interest in higher education is a relatively late development. Its origins date back only three quarters of a century. Harvard was two hundred years old before Horace Mann began his crusade for public education. In 1850, our total college population numbered less than 12,000. Today, we have only a little more than six times as many citizens, but some two hundred times as many youth in college. This vast increase in the numbers given educational opportunities has had a profound effect on the outlook of the American people. The democratic spirit as we know it today would not have been possible if the colleges and universities had been opened only to the few.

Thus, our system of higher education, which provides opportunities for so large a proportion of youth, has made two great contributions to American life. It has raised standards of living through technological advances and thereby has been largely responsible for our current economic and industrial supremacy. On the other hand, by opening the door of opportunity to the masses, it has been a chief factor in developing the characteristic American outlook and attitude, the democratic spirit of the people.

A third significant contribution has been made by the universities through their development of the most adequate program of research and professional education that the world has ever seen. They have not only raised professional standards and leadership but have created an unprecedented respect for research and scholarship which is shared by many who have little understanding of its meaning. Many examples might be cited to illustrate the point, but one will suffice. The discovery of nuclear fission by university professors working in their own laboratories gave the public a new faith in scientific investigation and a new respect for the investigator. The evidence is clear from the overwhelming demands made upon institutions by government, business, and industry since World War II for research assistance in the solution of their problems. The ivory tower conception of the university has been largely displaced by a belief in the almost magical powers of the scholar-scientist.

Despite all these achievements, the most encouraging fact in the college and university world today is the unprecedented ferment and concern for the improvement of their programs, which is discernible in every section of the country and in every type of institution. In practically every college, in most of the graduate schools, and in many professional schools, discontent with the program is the characteristic of these postwar years. A still more noteworthy fact is that the chief concern is not to improve the technical aspects of their training but rather to provide a broader base, a more thorough general education, a more vital social outlook, and a better understanding of our highly complex society.

In the college the stirrings of the faculties have been described as a "silent revolution." The meaning and purposes of liberal education are subject to more widespread scrutiny and discussion than at any previous period in our history. Interdepartmental courses of all varieties and at all levels are being developed on an experimental basis in scores of institutions. Princeton University has been engaged for five years in a study of the total impact of the college experience on undergraduates. The administration, the faculty, the students, and the alumni have participated. Columbia, Yale, Harvard, and Chicago have maintained for several years internships in general education for younger faculty members gathered from all sections of the country. Brown University has recently announced a five-year effort at curriculum revision in the college that may result in a new pattern for undergraduate courses. The Great Books Program at St. John's College, modifications of which are beginning to appear in different places, is another example of curriculum reform.

This concern for more basic education is not confined to the colleges. Several of the stronger engineering schools are now engaged in quite ambitious programs designed to provide more effective offerings in the humanities and social sciences for future engineers. Several medical schools within the past few years have added sociologists to their faculties on the theory that more than technical competence is required of the physician and surgeon. Leaders in the field of legal education are much concerned over the inadequacy of law schools in providing fundamental courses in the ethics and philosophy of the profession. In graduate schools which prepare for teaching, a growing discontent is appearing over the emphasis on specialized research and the lack of breadth in their programs.

This picture of widespread interest and efforts on the part of educators in the professional fields is both a tribute to the importance of liberal education and an implied criticism of the colleges from which their students are recruited. Whichever aspect you may choose to emphasize, the clear inference is that the chief problem in American higher education is to be found in the area of liberal education.

Beardsley Ruml, in discussing the liberal arts college, recently declared that the administration had lost control of the faculty, that the faculty had lost control of the curriculum, and that as a consequence, it had become a desperately inefficient institution. The grain of truth in this extreme statement is sufficient to warrant serious consideration. But for the purpose of this discussion let us examine only the facts with regard to the relation of the faculty to the curriculum.

In the changes which have occurred since 1900 it must be admitted that the faculty has generally fought a rearguard action. Under the elective system the student demand has been largely the determining factor. Requirements for this degree or that set up by the faculty have held the line at various points for a time, but have been gradually modified over the years with the result that the current version of the liberal arts curriculum bears little resemblance to that of fifty years ago.

First of all, the division of the humanities fifty years ago provided the bulk of the instruction; today only a skeleton program remains in the average college. Philosophy—logic, ethics, metaphysics—figured heavily in the earlier programs; now it is in many institutions merely a museum piece attracting only a handful of students. Science, which formerly went under the name of natural philosophy, occupies a major place as physics, chemistry, biology, and geology with a plethora of courses listed under each. Moral philosophy has now become anthropology, sociology, economics, and political science, under the title of the social sciences.

A middle states university (accredited) with 765 full-time and 200 part-time students listed 361 separate courses; a New England college with 1,000 students listed 320 courses; a southern institution with 406 students listed 169 courses. In such a vast array of courses the question arises as to which are central to a liberal education and which are peripheral. More important still, one wonders whether the educational vitamins may not be so widely dispersed throughout the menu that it is impossible for the student to get a balanced diet without overstuffing his mind. That does indeed seem to be one of the current difficulties which the interdepartmental courses are seeking to overcome. By concentrating the essentials in a few courses, the consumer may get not only a balanced diet but also adequate nourishment for his mental growth and development, neither of which is possible in such cases as those cited.

The shift from philosophy to science suggests a series of issues in the liberal arts program that warrant examination. Philosophy represents a search for truth, whereas science is a search for knowledge. A curriculum built around the former focuses attention on meaning, while one dominated by the latter is likely to overemphasize the importance of facts. Perhaps all would agree that current undergraduate instruction exhibits just this weakness. For example, in history, which traces the course of events, too frequently the *where,* the *when,* and the *how* are stressed, while the *why* is passed over lightly, since that is in the realm of speculation. Or, again, in economics, sociology, and political science, facts are gathered and classified, observations are recorded and analyzed, value systems are described and explained, but the question as to what constitutes the *good society* is scarcely raised. While facts must be mastered as a part of the educational process, when they become the *end* as well as the beginning, higher learning, defined as the pursuit of truth, has lost its meaning.

Again, while science has made possible man's understanding and control of nature and the technological advances characteristic of our age, it has through its very success in this area left on man's outlook and attitude a profound impression which has exercised a subtle influence over all education. In his emphasis on more and more specialized research, the scientist has accumulated many fragments of knowledge useful in solving specific problems, but of little value in interpreting life's deeper purposes. Indeed, because the meaning of life and the reason for striving are not subject to scientific treatment, the weight of modern scholarship tends to discourage their consideration. The result is that in the entire field of higher education little attention is focused on goals or purposes or a sustaining philosophy of life, which is surely the greatest need of our time. The tensions of our day demand a dedicated search for the absolutes of faith that are the source of moral direction. It is the dim consciousness of this fact which underlies much of the discontent with the present program of liberal education.

To put the matter in another way, the emphasis on scientific analysis which characterizes undergraduate instruction in practically all fields and the failure to devote adequate attention to synthesis, to putting the pieces together to form a meaningful design, frequently leaves the student adrift and without motivation. No more harmful fallacy has plagued education than the notion, implicit in the unit and credit-hour system, that discrete fragments of knowledge, however well mastered, will automatically mold to produce the liberally educated graduate. Failure to make a conscious attempt to help the student construct a logical philosophy of life frequently leaves him bewildered, without chart or compass.

Perhaps the greatest single weakness in the American college is the lack of adequate provision for considering questions of basic educational policy such as those just raised. The presidents and deans are too absorbed in organization, administration, and promotion to devote sufficient time to it, as I can testify with some feeling after serving in those capacities for twenty-five years. The professors, concerned chiefly with scholarly pursuits or departmental development, give little thought to the overall objectives of the college as a social enterprise. In the state, regional, and national educational associations the personnel participating are mainly the presidents and deans whose energies and efforts are largely devoted to administrative problems, to housing, equipping, staffing, and financing the enterprise. When the professors meet in their associations, it is usually as historians, psychologists, chemists, economists, and so on, whose interests are in their specialties rather than in institutional policy. Thus it is that the matter of the direction of educational change has fallen between two stools with the result that it has been determined largely by pressure rather than by planning, by outside influences rather than by statesmanship. The great need is for educators to become masters in their household with a view to reversing the process. The ferment now going on at all levels and in all types of institutions may indeed be the prelude to a significant move in that direction.

III

1954
Specialization and Liberal Arts

Clarence H. Faust

❀❀❀❀❀❀❀❀❀❀❀❀❀❀❀❀❀❀❀❀❀❀❀❀❀❀❀❀❀❀❀❀❀

Higher education in America has two tasks, for all members of a modern democratic society are faced with two kinds of problems. First, there are the specialized, technical, professional problems we face individually as a consequence of our special role in society as doctors, lawyers, businessmen, housewives, or educators. The solution to these problems requires special knowledge, special training, and special experience. Second, we are confronted with certain common problems, not as specialists, but as men and as citizens. The selection of the chief executive for this country and of the members of our legislatures is not a matter for specialists, but a common responsibility. Nor do our common problems lie wholly in the political realm, rising from our membership in a democratic society governed by majority rule. There are problems which all men face in their relationships with each other, in their relationships with the natural world, and in those decisions which involve determinations concerning the ends we seek and the means we employ in seeking them which will reflect for better or worse our views of what is good and evil, our convictions about the meaning of life; in short, our general outlook or philosophy.

Education is pressed to perform these two tasks by the needs of society on the one hand and the interests of individuals on the other. It is not surprising that there should be differences of emphasis among educators and in educational institutions with respect to these tasks. These differences go, however, beyond mere differences of emphasis. They reflect differences in educational philosophy which have their roots in differences concerning the processes of learning, the nature of the individual and of society, and, indeed, the nature of the world and of man's relationship to it.

What troubles me about the controversy thus engendered is that, though its roots lie deep in the most fundamental problems of the modern world and run far back historically in the development not only of American education but of American life and thought, the debate between the proponents of specialization and the proponents of the liberal arts is, for the most part, carried on at a superficial level of clichés and slogans.

I am troubled by the simple oppositions which are set up in the debate. Distinctions made between academic education and preparation for life, between verbal and practical education, between education in abstractions as against learning from experience, between traditional and progressive education; or, again, between adjustment to life and society (seen as mere conformity) and education for independent thinking.

Each of these oppositions, when one examines it closely, appears at best an oversimplification and, at worst, an actual confusion of thought about education. Take, for instance, the opposition of the verbal and the practical. What seems to be assumed is that language is artificial, unrelated to reality, or at least a feeble instrument for coming practically to grips with reality. Yet a little observation and reflection seem to make clear that the social life of human beings and all sustained cooperation among human beings depend upon communication. It would appear, too, that all knowledge effective for more than one individual—that is, all shared knowledge—requires verbalization. It seems clear also that any chance of practical effectiveness in wide areas of human life must take into account the fact that what we must learn practically to deal with are signs and symbols. When as a people we choose each four years a chief executive for the nation, we cannot do so by some firsthand experience of the individuals from among whom one is to be selected. We are bombarded by words presenting the case for one candidate or another; and, insofar as we are able to check their verbal assurances and those of their supporters by reference to the facts, we learn of these through channels of communication. In short, it is impractical to separate the verbal from the practical.

This is not to say that the use of language is either easy or without its dangers. It is to say that, though gaps may exist between facts and our ideas or interpretations of facts and again between our ideas and the words we use to express them, these gaps present a profoundly important human problem, the solution of which cannot lie in attempting to eliminate the verbal aspect of life or of learning, but must lie in the acquisition of wisdom concerning the ways in which language can be made adequate to ideas as well as ideas made adequate to the state of the world and the nature of things.

Similar oversimplifications or confusions seem to me to lie in the distinction between education in abstractions or general principles as against education from experience. A case might be made, I think, that experience is the worst of all teachers; that indeed, in the absence of understanding through general principles, experience is a great buzzing confusion. One would not suppose that a student would master chemistry by being turned loose in a chemical laboratory to have as wide a range of unguided experiences as possible. Experience can be directed and rendered intelligible only through generalizations about it. Raw experience is a chaotic succession of impressions. One thing after another happens to us, strikes upon our consciousness, leaves one mark more in the vast and confused collection of marks on our memories. If we read a lesson into the succession of things that happen to us, it is because we interpret experience, that is, we discover ideas into which experience is fitted and in the light of which it is understood, contributes to knowledge, and provides the basis for learning. Now it is, of course, also true that, in view of the relationship between generalization and experience or between abstraction and experience, the process of abstraction presents certain dangers. One danger is that fixed attention upon an erroneous generalization may blind one to the truth by preventing the observation of relevant data for correcting it. But here, as in the case of verbalism, the problem is to establish the right relationship between generalizations and particular experience, and that problem cannot be solved by attempting to avoid abstraction.

In much of our discussion of the problem of specialization and liberal education, there is, it seems to me, a parallel superficiality. Mere information about particulars is a heterogeneous and confused collocation of unrelated elements. On the other hand, the possession of generalizations without a knowledge of their roots in particulars or without capacity for application to particulars can hardly be called knowledge or be a worthy object of an educational process. Put more concretely, the acquisition of the particular techniques of a vocation or the firm fixation of appropriate habits for performing a vocational task degrades vocational activity to a purely mechanical or slave operation. A vocation, or any other specialized activity, becomes properly human only when the reasons for operations are understood and the relation of specialized activity to society and to the individual is in some sense comprehended. Doctors, lawyers, businessmen, teachers, tradesmen, and craftsmen of all sorts are human beings and citizens as well as specialists. Mere technicians —that is, specialists who do not understand the relations of what they do to society, have no sense of social responsibility, and do not conceive of what they are engaged in in relation to their own development as human beings—are pitiful as human beings, dangerous as citizens, and, I am convinced, ultimately not good specialists.

My purpose here is not to set forth a series of answers to the questions raised by our contemporary controversies in education, but to suggest that we need much fuller and more penetrating analyses of these problems than the superficial debates of conflicting schools of educational philosophy at present provide. In the absence of these answers, our conflicts become battles of slogans and clichés, and our discussions tend to be mere debates in which each party looks for an effective collection of rhetorical topics to sustain its position, instead of seeking penetration into the profound problems underlying our educational tasks.

In this situation, it is easy for opposed schools to strengthen their positions, or at least to comfort themselves, by burlesquing the practices of their opponents. If one takes the weakest extremes in practice of, let us say, vocational training and education in the liberal arts, both positions can be made to appear ridiculous. If an institution in a dynamic American community sets up a curriculum by surveying the occupations currently practiced in its surroundings and offers specific courses in these vocations, it invites a considerable amount of not unjustified ridicule. The community, at least the typical American community, is likely to be engaged in a quite different set of occupations ten years hence. Furthermore, the students in the typical American community are unlikely to settle down to spend their lives in it, even if it remained unchanged. Above all, the practices of current vocations and occupations change so rapidly that, even if the community were frozen and students forced to remain in it, the operations they had learned to perform would be shortly out of date. If, with some such considerations as these in mind, one turns to the curriculum of some liberal arts colleges, disappointment with current practices may be equally sharp. It may be observed that the structure of the curriculum all too often reflects the history of the departmental disciplines in American education and the organization of graduate schools as of several generations ago. It seems to be assumed that the world of things to be known falls neatly into the compartments historically developed in the relatively recent history of the American graduate school. The organization of the curriculum, the structure of individual courses, and the kinds of problems dealt with in these courses have been determined not by the urgent realities of the world and the urgent demands for the solution of critical questions, but rather by the internal evolution of academic disciplines. A great gap, consequently, develops between the needs which a course might serve and the purposes it achieves.

In the present shrinkage of the world, in the increased communication between nations of various language habits, in view of the tremendous problems raised by the propaganda machines of our day, the need for understanding the problems raised for mankind by the fact that we do not all speak the same language and that, when we do, the devices of language can be employed not for the communication of truth but for the propagation of prejudice and error, presents a tremendous challenge to the teachers of foreign languages. And yet, in all too many instances language courses deal with the questions that have emerged in the development of philology as an academic discipline and serve merely to communicate the results of academic endeavors to solve them.

As a consequence of the kinds of debates of which the controversy concerning specialization and the liberal arts is an instance, we are threatened with the development in American education of two almost separate traditions—what might be roughly termed the tradition of the liberal arts and the educationalist tradition. Anyone who moves about in American education at its various levels must be impressed by the lack of communication between these groups. They begin with separate assumptions and reach opposed conclusions. They speak in languages so different that communication is almost impossible. Consequently, we make much less progress than we need to in penetrating beneath the surface of controversies to come to grip with the urgent educational questions of our time.

What is required and indeed urgently demanded, it seems to me, is an attempt to uncover these basic questions, to make a more penetrating and thoroughgoing analysis of them, and to reformulate our problems at a more fundamental level than we presently achieve. There is much, for example, which we need to think through and perhaps to acquire information about with respect to the relationship of specialized training and education in the liberal arts. One aspect of the question certainly is the extent to which the processes of education can be generalized and the extent to which they must deal with the particular situations with which students later on need to deal. Problems of the psychology of learning are here involved, such matters as the transfer of training. Profoundly difficult social questions emerge, such as the extent to which individuals of our dynamic modern society need early to be committed to particular roles in a highly specialized civilization. What, moreover, is to be done about the rapid shifting of the content of specialties? Behind these problems lie profound philosophical and even metaphysical questions concerning the meaning and significance of man's career in the universe.

I am far from pleading for uniformity in educational theory. We profit so much in America from free enterprise in ideas, and I am so little confident that any final and ultimate solution for our problems can be once and for all worked out, that uniformity strikes me as far from desirable and, indeed, as positively dangerous. What I am pleading for is greater penetration and more adequate communciation between our conflicting schools of thought in education.

To serve these purposes, the confrontation of opposed schools and the discussion of the differences between proponents of the various positions must go beyond being a mere exhibition of the toleration of differences. It must not be content with mere compromise in which valuable insights on both sides may be sacrificed. It cannot aim toward the mere addition of all the practices which anyone happens to favor. It will not have achieved its purpose if agreement in practice takes place without full understanding of reasons for practice.

The hope of American education lies in systematic discussion of the issues with which we are all concerned. I suppose that fruitful discussion calls for at least two things. Those who hold one position must assume that those who hold another have at least some grain of reason for holding it and that it might be well to try to discover what that reason or those reasons, however limited they may later appear to be, actually are. The second requirement is that the proponent of a particular position, especially if it is a position which has been fairly elaborately developed and fairly fully articulated, be willing to review his own assumptions and principles and be prepared to give serious thought to the difficulties and objections which may be raised with respect to his views.

I have not undertaken to answer the problems I have uncovered, though I suspect that I have revealed certain presuppositions about them. What I am concerned with is the development of the means at our disposal in American education for the full and fruitful exploitation of our habit of conference and discussion. I was much struck recently by the observation of a visitor from abroad who remarked that he had at first been greatly confused about American education and unable to formulate with any clarity or conviction an answer to the question he knew would be asked of him when he returned to his native land, namely, what is the American educational system? He had at first been obliged to conclude that there was no system and that thousands of independent school districts and hundreds of independent institutions of higher education each pursued what seemed best to it. This conclusion he said had, however, been changed as he came to see more of American education. Our education, he said, has a definite character and a surprising coherence, despite its seeming confusions and contradictions, by virtue of two things. First, unlike those in most older countries, American educators are committed to change and confident of making progress. Secondly, the vast number of organizations of teachers, administrators, and institutions constantly holding conferences and exchanging views produces not uniformity of belief but a rough agreement with respect to what the major problems of education are and provides a ready and vibrating mechanism for the rapid diffusion of ideas.

IV

1954
Frontier Behind the Forehead

Peter Viereck

❀❀❀❀❀❀❀❀❀❀❀❀❀❀❀❀❀❀❀❀❀❀❀❀❀❀❀❀❀❀❀❀❀❀

The number of cells in the brain and the number of the stars in the universe are said to be exactly equal in number. So-and-so-many trillion stars apiece. From this unprovable fancy emerges a metaphor: the gigantic scale of reality, which forever weighs dream versus matter, is balanced exactly evenly at the fulcrum of the forehead. Soul versus cosmos: imagine them balancing with a one-to-one correspondence between the units without and within the skull, between the stars and the no less radiant brain-cells.

This true metaphor is defied—this scale is upset—by any philosophy which deems *either* side of the equal scale as "more real." In the case of America, there is no danger of overweighing the inner side, the aesthetic and spiritual side. America's danger is over-emphasis of the outward side—the star matter, not the gray matter.

Obviously our society needs and should be grateful for the measurable facts of positivism and the measurable statistics of pragmatic science. These will indeed take us far—just as far as any material measurements can take us.

But the total human being moves beyond this boundary; he hungers not only for measurable facts but for unmeasurable truths. He needs the intangible—the spiritual and aesthetic—beyond the gadget world of tangible things. In this exploration of that "beyond," the complete man turns for guidance to the classics and humanities, in their way, and to religion in its kindred way. These may be flickering and fitful lamps, yet they are the only lamps we have once we cross the boundary beyond measurable material facts, the boundary where the top-of-the-brain man prudently stops. Prudently he stops, but meanly, unimaginatively, with every hunger satiated except that ultimate hunger which separates us from the beasts, which makes us often lower than the beasts and occasionally higher, but never the same.

Therefore, let us stop being defensive, stop being apologetic about affirming the dignity and importance of the humanistic and the spiritual studies. Today they receive more lip service than a decade ago, but are more squeezed in practice in the campus curricula. These curricula reflect an atomic age which puts a new premium on the technician and on practical outer applications of inner theory. Yet, without the understanding of man's inner nature which art and literature give us, and without the inner ethical restraint which religion gives us, our outer mechanical progress is paving our road to hell with good inventions. That is why the teacher of humanities need not lose morale in this technical age. Rarely have the dignity and importance of his oft-neglected field been affirmed more effectively than in the following brief quotation from the 1948 report of "The Commission on Liberal Education of the Association of American Colleges" (emphasis mine):

> *Our society is preoccupied with activities that obscure and in*

effect deny the importance of knowing and understanding letters. This unhappy situation arises partly from technology's promise of great physical comfort, partly from the material rewards most esteemed in a materialistic society, and partly from the dangers of our time that seem to demand immediate and material solution. Young people, therefore, take inordinate interest in what they think is practical *study, failing to realize that self-knowledge, which is indispensable to the most practical judgments, is the highest practicality. . . .*

Literature arrests the rapid flow of experience, holds it up for contemplation and understanding. . . . It thereby leads to self-discovery and self-realization.

In a period of technological prodigies and of economic complexity, the crucial problem of education is to sustain and develop the individual. If social and economic welfare *are realized, we are told, the individual can take care of himself. It is at least equally true that if an adequate number of* individuals *are unusually elevated, society can take care of itself.*

An occupational disease of all of us college teachers is the filling of scholarship-recommendation blanks about students aspiring to higher groves of academe. Here is a new development in blanks, increasingly frequent, that gives me the "1984" shudders: more and more scholarship blanks are asking, "Is your student well adjusted? Popular? A good mixer?"—in effect, a Regular Feller? I can only answer, "I hope not," and wonder how many credit points for adjustment to mediocrity would be won by, say, a young Kafka of the future.

Against this menace of the all too well-adjusted man—what David Riesman calls the outer-directed man, what Ortega y Gasset calls the mass-man—*a new hero emerges in America today: the Unadjusted Man.* Unlike the days of the Renaissance, today the scholar, the educator, the teacher of the humanities can no longer be the prophet and seer, the unriddler of the outward universe; modern science has deprived him of that function. Instead, he can assume a less dramatic but actually nobler role. His twofold role now is: first, to be more than ever the explorer of the inner universe, the universe behind the forehead; second and simultanously, thereby to be the

Unadjusted Man, stubbornly and deliberately maladjusted to the outer mechanized world of mass-men and robots.

Outer civil liberties are not enough. We can also lose inner freedom, even if we do save all our outer liberties from the left or right totalitarians. You can talk civil liberties and prosperity and democracy "with the tongues of men and angels," but it is merely a case of "free from what?" and not "free for what?" if you only use this freedom in order to commit television or to go lusting after comic books.

Hence, America needs downright desperately—as its inner-directed man, its antimass man—whoever is so gloriously impractical as to love and to teach the arts and the humanities in our colleges and high schools.

When I say the new hero of American education is the Unadjusted Man, I am, of course, not speaking psychiatrically. I merely mean: be unadjusted toward current ephemeral fads. But do adjust —for God's sake, do adjust—to the great permanent ethical and cultural and religious traditions. For the sake of inner freedom, it is better to adjust to what your conscience says is eternally right than to your neighbor's expediency. It is better to adjust to the ages than to the age. If accused of being "maladjusted" to the century of the common man, because you do not yearn for a television set, for example, then remember that "one man and God make a majority."

Let us distinguish between two entirely different kinds of nonadjustment. The lower kind is merely the cheap and easy Babbitt-baiting and conformism-baiting of adolescent radicalism, of Greenwich Village, of Bohemia, which refuses to adjust even to valid norms. The higher kind does adjust gladly to higher norms but rightly rejects—out of thoughtful maturity, not out of adolescent affectation—the shoddy norms of keeping up with the Joneses. An exciting example of this higher kind are the dying words of Thomas More on the scaffold: "I die the king's good servant, but God's first."

There speaks Western man! (as Herbert Agar once pointed out). There speaks the voice of liberty for our own age also. For our own age, you must in that quotation substitute "Servant of the state" or "Servant of secularism" for "king's good servant"; and for

"God" some may wish to substitute "universal moral standards, the need to use good means and nothing but good means, no matter what your political or secular goal." I am using the word "secular" not in any denominational clerical sense but in order to mean *vanitas, vanitatum*—the selling of one's soul for a mere utilitarian mess of pottage (or, for that matter, pot of message).

Note this additional point: even though More is being executed by his king for putting God first, yet More does not say: "I die the king's bad servant," or "I die refusing to serve the king in anything, even in those duties which must be rendered not unto God but unto Caesar." This attitude contrasts with the radical, who revolts indiscriminately against authority; More's revolt against secularism and statism is essentially conservative because he is revolting only when forced to some ultimate moral extreme; short of such an extreme, he remains voluntarily and gladly the king's servant.

Not only does this attitude distinguish More from the Western radical. It also distinguishes him from the other-worldly oriental attitude found, for example, in Buddhism. Here, therefore, in still another sense speaks Western man. Unlike the passive other-worldly Buddhist, Western man—even when rejecting secular reality —knows he must (in this life) live within it; he cannot evade its moral choices by fleeing from reality to some inactive Nirvana. Western man does not let religion relieve him of the duty to face and master the material problems of this earth. He must, for example, favor for religious reasons—rather than reject for religious reasons— those thoroughly material social reforms which make a free society more equitable, more just. Without such material reforms, freedom becomes an empty phrase, in which all men are equal but some (as Orwell put it) more equal than others and in which equality means only (as Anatole France put it) imprisoning the rich as well as the poor man for stealing bread. In short, even while rejecting the vanity of this world, Western man remains not only its servant but its *"good* servant." But he remains so only up to the point where being its servant does not encroach on God, on conscience, on those ethical norms within which all social reform must operate if it is to avoid 1984 or November, 1917.

Unlike the evader who flees from reality even when it is not necessary to do so, Western man, with his not-to-be-despised material and organizational achievements, rejects being "the king's servant" only as the last resort, never as the first resort. That last resort did occur when the "king" was Hitler or Mussolini or Stalin or Malenkov. Let us make sure (despite our Huey Longs and McCarthys) that it will never occur in America. But, if it does occur in whatever country you happen to inhabit, in that ultimate moral choice (that dark night of the soul that occurs also in every man's private life when he must choose between the secular reality of self-interest and God), *then* the nonmaterialist, the Christian, the man with inner liberty, walks to his scaffold smiling and unhesitant, like St. Thomas More, because he is "God's servant first" and not the servant of a chummy well-adjustedness.

Unfortunately the Thomas Mores, the examples of the higher kind of nonconformism, are rare in any age. The examples of the lower kind are frequent; let us try to analyze why they are today both more frequent than ever before and more difficult to detect. Why difficult to detect? Because chameleon-like, because, at mid-century, mass-man shoddiness has become so slick, so sophisticated that it masquerades as its opposite.

In the literary and scholarly world today, nonconformism has become one more conformist pose. Avant-garde is one more rear-guard movement, consisting of the arthritic somersaults of those aging *enfants terribles* who had once seemed "new" in the days when Joyce and jazz were considered shocking and when *The Waste Land* and rumble seats were considered expressions of Rebel Youth. This change you will already have noted in the mechanically "cultural" uplifters of the lecture platforms and in the professionally arty quarterlies; highbrow nonconformism has succumbed to its own kind of popularizers and hack educators, almost as completely as have *Screen Romances* and *True Detective Stories* (on their infinitely *lower* level). The latter are only more openly robotized; they frankly try to kill a spiritual and humanistic education by open attack on it, while the high-brow hack kills by hugging it to death.

For reasons which I recently tried to analyze in my books, *Shame and Glory of the Intellectuals* and *Conservatism Revisited*, and which need not be repeated here, philistine-baiting has become only a more high-brow mask for the same old philistia. Hence, we must inspect very closely the credentials of those artists, scholars, poets, educators who most loudly proclaim their nonconformism, their anti-Babbittry, their sensitivity. We must distinguish between genuine sensitivity—that is, amateur sensitivity—and the professional sensitive plant, the professional wincer, the drugstore nonconformist.

Picture to yourself a whole army of regimented robots, consisting of "noble"-browed educators, sonorously "eloquent" guardians of culture, and hearty, tweedy, pipe-smoking teachers of "creative-writing" courses, which—with "lovable" whimsy—they call "workshops." Picture this robot army on the march toward soulfulness and Advanced Ideas, each robot intoning dutifully: "I'm a real human being, an independent, nonconforming, embattled individualist, just like everybody else!"

In other words, as educators we now have a third important alternative in addition to the two confronting us in the past. Let us call them Alternative One, Alternative Two, Alternative Three, and try to define them. Of the three, only Alternative One is worthy of our calling. Alternative One for American education is the Unadjusted Man, cultivating his inner riches of liberty and reverie. Alternative Two is the wholesome adjusted Rotarian, with his robot values in a world of cellophane, plastics, and hygiene-worship. Between these two original alternatives, we as educators have naturally been choosing and teaching the former, usually without success, occasionally with a success so inspiring and breath-taking that it redeems our profession. The new, the third alternative, I have not seen sufficiently discussed and would like to put up for discussion. Like the first, it seems to affirm the humanities and spiritual values—but in an entirely mechanical uninspired way, so that it only masks more subtly the crass utilitarianism of Alternative Two.

In the 1930's, the phrase "parlor socialism" was used to describe those who became socialists not out of inner conviction but because it was then fashionable in the intellectual salons to be leftist, materialist, and obsessed with economics. In the 1950's, Alternative One has taught us, and taught us rightly, to turn instead to the traditional cultural, humanistic, and religious values of the spirit. Alternative Three is parloring God just as snobbishly today as the professional or conformist "nonconformist" of the 1930's was parloring socialism. Fully weighing my words, I assert that this manicuring of our sacred humanistic and spiritual values into mere fashionable fads may kill these values more surely, even though more subtly, than if open barbarians, torch in hand, were burning down our churches, our libraries, our universities.

It is no-go holding annual meetings only for purposes of self-congratulation. It is no-go listing proudly the current growth of college courses in Great Books or Great Issues or Great Classics, the growth in courses in how to become a creative writer or a creative reader in ten lessons, when all these Great Books or Great Issues— for which our ancestors toiled in loneliness and faced the rack if necessary—when all these Great Classics are studied as gregarious, comfortable, painless parlor games. Yes, American youth is indeed turning back to religion and to more creative interests than in the shallow, Marxist 1930's. Yet before we herald that salutary development with premature trumpets, remember this caution: when religion is handled by the yard and wrapped in cellophane, when artistic creativity is sold like dry goods, with spontaneous inspiration left out, then all we have is commercialism triumphing all over again, this time in the name of anticommercialism.

Our great universities, steeped in the sin of intellectual pride, are killing intellectuality and killing the humanities not by the now-old-fashioned vulgarity of the Nineteenth-Century Gilded Age but by turning an entire generation of graduate students into trained seals. For such docile circus animals, literature no longer means the shudder of awe before the beautiful; nor does it mean the mass-man's at-least-honest and open shudder of contempt. The trained seal's love of literature means leaping sleekly through the endlessly receding hoops of the criticism of the criticism of criticism, and, after each successive hoop of the newest New Criticism, gratefully swallowing some fishy "explication" in mid-air.

The most corrupting, most insidious development is the substitution of technique for art; the substitution of the mass-produced "just as good" for the real thing. What once resulted from the inspired and audacious craftsmanship of a heartbreakingly lonely individual is now mass-produced in painless, safe, and uninspired capsules. Is this not often true today of every category of education and of literature? For example, the "stream of consciousness" for which James Joyce wrestled in loneliness with language, the ironic perspective toward society which Proust attained not as entertainment but as tragedy, all the quick, sensitive insights over which a Virginia Woolf or a Katherine Mansfield bled her heart out—all these intimate, individual achievements are today mass-produced as the standard props of a hundred hack imitators, mechanically vending what is called "the *New-Yorker*-type short story." Do not underestimate that type of story; though an imitation job, it is imitated with magnificent technical skill. And think of the advantages: no pain any more, no risk any more, no more nonsense of inspiration. Most modern readers are not even bothered by the difference between such an excellent but bloodless machine job and the living product of individual heart's anguish.

Synthetic food pills we already have. Why not synthetic culture pills and finally synthetic mass-produced souls? If the humanities survive the external materialist assault, then will they survive it only in order to succumb from within to the slick substitutes of synthetic humanities, synthetic religion? Is it accidental or is it typical of our civilization that precisely our most commercialized industry, the cinema, includes a firm whose motto (with a straight face) is *ars gratia artis?*

What, then, is the test for telling the real inspiration from the almost-real, the just-as-good?

The test is pain. Not mere physical pain but the joyous pain of selfless sacrifice. The test is that sacrament of pain, that brotherhood of sacrifice, that aristocracy of creative suffering of which Baudelaire wrote: *Je sais que la douleur est l'unique noblesse.* The great creative masterpieces and great educational institutions of the past were privately sweated for and bled for, not publicly lip-serviced.

My criticism of contemporary self-congratulation about culture has been sufficiently nasty to avoid any danger of being accused of a booster spirit for America. Therefore, when I nevertheless end on a note of optimism, it is because the optimism is rooted not in boosterism but in the objective historical situation. The objective historical situation can still help us save the day from Alternative Three by prodding mid-century America toward an exciting new frontier. This frontier is not the material one of old; it is what, at the very beginning of this essay, I called the universe behind the forehead.

America's old or outward frontier had two forms, geographic and ticker-tape. The geographic form was Horace Greeley's "Go West, young man." It ended when it bumped up against the Pacific Ocean. The ticker-tape form was the big-boom, big-business spree of George Babbitt's Zenith City and of the stock-market illusions of the 1920's. It likewise bumped up against a couple of things that made it untenable: namely, Sinclair Lewis plus 1929.

Bouncing against outward barriers, America—judging by historical parallels with past cultures—will now turn rapidly and increasingly inward. Not in its mass, but in its most daring and individualistic young students, if only we educators do not "adjust" them. Let me end, as I began, by again emphasizing that the time has come to discover in the brain-cells all the beauty and all the potential explosions that America has been discovering in its outer atoms. Our new Columbuses will sail the seas of education, literature, and the holy spirit of man. And what they discover may be some fabulous new continent within the skull.

V

1955
Maintenance of
Freedom

J. William Fulbright

❀❀❀❀❀❀❀❀❀❀❀❀❀❀❀❀❀❀❀❀❀❀❀❀❀❀❀❀❀❀

Some time ago, a warden at the Joliet penitentiary played host to a conference of criminologists, called to consider ways and means of reducing the crime rate. One speaker seemed to carry the day with his thesis that the way to do this was by requiring all young people to study mathematics intensively. For the discipline gained in this way, so the speaker claimed, would lead the young to think logically, and so make them virtuous when they came of age.

There was great applause when he reached the end and sat down. The warden alone seemed unimpressed. He asked an aide to fetch a certain prisoner, introduced him to the meeting, and then at once sent the prisoner back to his cell. "That man you just saw," the warden explained to the criminologists, "is the most brilliant mathematician in the whole prison. So brilliant, in fact, that it took bank examiners ten years before they found that he was embezzling funds by juggling bank ledgers. Obviously, he was not deficient in mathematics. What he lacked was a sense of grammar and rhetoric. He simply didn't know the difference between the words 'mine' and 'yours.' "

The criminologist who saw in the science of mathematics the means to create a nation of moral men and good citizens is not alone in his approach. He is joined by a chorus of voices, each with a special educational emphasis leading to the magic formula. To one person, it is training in physics, or medicine, or plant life. To another, it is training in business, or home making, or athletics. Let this or that be the cornerstone for higher education—so they say—and the arrangement of its own force will meet every danger, solve every problem, remove every evil, and gain every good.

As for myself, I am inclined to favor the "warden theory" of education, if I may call it that. I am inclined to favor it, subject to three qualifications.

First, no system of higher education, however arranged, can bear the whole load of cultivating what lies in the human spirit. For that spirit, as the ancients taught us long ago, is a mixed thing. It is formed and ruled not alone by reason. It is also formed, and it is all too often ruled, by the will and by the passions. And if there are those who may deny this ancient fact, the rule of Adolf Hitler in Germany, and Mussolini in Italy, and the careers of a variety of imitators in the United States, each in the land preeminent of its literacy and enlightenment, are case studies of how reason can be set on its head by willful men who know how to play on passions, and so make the worse cause appear to be the better one.

The second qualification follows from the first. It is that if the education of the individual is viewed in its entirety, then disciplined hearts must dwell in the same body as disciplined minds. And in this light, not the schools alone can carry the burden of the work that needs to be done. Nor can they be charged, as they now often are, with full responsibility for any defective products. Our homes, our churches, our political institutions, our economic enterprises, all our media of communication, are, and must be, considered a part of what educates the individual. None can absolve itself from the end result. All are jointly responsible for what it is like.

The third qualification is addressed to those who would have the schools and colleges emphasize this or that specialized science and art. Let me say here that I have the utmost respect for the specialist. It is plain, for example, that we urgently need scientists and technicians who can lend their expertness to the defense of America and the free world. So, too, as a further example, do we need men, skilled in the art of economic management, who can perfect the way we organize production and distribution. This work is of supreme importance; for though it is true enough that man does not live by bread alone, at least he lives by bread. And we need places specifically set aside for the purpose of cultivating the science and art of making bread, and defending it.

Yet divorced from all else, this specialization in art and science is not an education for a democracy. There is nothing to distinguish it from an educational system in a totalitarian state. Men like Hitler, Mussolini, and Stalin may have boasted of a Nazi, or a Fascist, or a Communist science and technology. Yet these bits of knowledge are not political or moral by nature. The same textbooks dealing with them can be used by students in both democracies and tyrannies. For the subjects themselves are equally useful to free men and slaves alike; and indeed, in ancient times, they were cultivated chiefly by slaves.

This specialization does not form an education for a democracy. It does not create an atmosphere in which the mind can be opened to every intimate impulse and voice, in free contact with other minds of a like sort. Specialization, by definition, focuses on only a small part of the human battle line. It orients no one toward a view and a place in the battle line as a whole. It orients no one toward the whole intellectual life and tradition of a country. It orients no one toward an understanding of man as he appears in a particular moment of current history, and in the history of the ages.

And it is precisely at this point, as I shall try to make plain later on, that the comment of the warden at Joliet seems to apply on all fours. Here, let me digress to say that from what I have seen of our colleges and universities, their key weakness is not that they breed Communists. It is arrant nonsense to say that they do. Yet there is a weakness in our colleges and universities. In my view, at least, it lies in our failure to teach grammar and rhetoric—to teach the difference between "mine" and "yours." In the largest sense for which this difference in words is but a symbol, it lies in our failure to keep intact as a unifying reference point for the undergraduate body, a common intellectual tradition, or a sense of an intellectual community leading to a sense of the continuity of human experience.

One used to find all this in the old prescribed courses of the humanities before a rampant, free-for-all, excessively individualist elective system ripped everything apart. But now we live in a setting where doctors only know how to make their meaning plain to other doctors; or engineers to other engineers; or lawyers to other lawyers; or businessmen to other businessmen; and so on. Each of these talks, and talks well within the range of a profession. But they do not talk up and down and across their professions. They do not talk up and down and across the whole range of human experience, stimulating and stimulated by that experience, to perfect the spirit of their age in the light of the spirit of all ages. They do not and they cannot do this, because they do not have in common a vocabulary they all understand—a vocabulary that was once drawn from the common fund of knowledge embraced by the humanities.

All of this lends an air of paradox to our commitment to democracy. On the one hand, we assert our devotion to a system of government that is based on free and intelligible communication between citizen and citizen, and between the leaders and the led. On the other hand, we weaken the effectiveness of that system by a prevailing educational process that tends to narrow down communication by limiting it to an "Information Please" program and a *Reader's Digest,* or by rendering meaning altogether meaningless. This paradox is made to order for exploitation by the demagogues. When our higher institutions of learning came under attack from that quarter, all too many of them were bewildered by what they were called on to defend. They seemed at times to flounder in an inner darkness of their own making, equal in density to the darkness the demagogues meant to impose on them from without. The best that many of them could do was to raise the rallying cry of academic freedom. Yet academic freedom, while of supreme importance in the educational process, is not the end-aim of the process. It is but a means to an end. And under conditions where so many of our institutions of higher learning lacked any coherent, general, and organized body of knowledge they meant to impart to their students, they were at a loss how to define the end they meant to preserve through academic freedom.

I am not implying that our colleges and universities ought now to sit down in a solemn convention and agree on a body of doctrine which they will then impose as a new orthodoxy on their student bodies. I see in any such proposal the death of all education; of an education, at least, whose aim ought to be the infusion of the spirit of learning among students, and whose method ought to be not indoctrination, but the constant exercise of the mind in meaningful arguments. Also, I see in any such proposal for orthodoxy, something of the ludicrous outlook of a university trustee who strongly objected to the text of a university president's commencement address. And when the president said to the trustee, "Well, don't you want your students to hear the truth?" the trustee answered, "Of course! But can't you print the truth on the back of the convocation program, and hand it to the graduates as they file out of the chapel?"

The tradition of the humanities, for whose restoration I am pleading as the heart of any educational system that can best serve democracy, is not a tradition of orthodoxy. It is a tradition of continuous disagreement between parties in a great dialogue extending back over the ages. All that these parties agreed upon were the topics they felt were worth talking about. And beyond this, the sense of unity that is present in what they said back and forth was hinged to the fact that when they disagreed, they knew what they were disagreeing about. Today, by contrast, we are inclined to rush ahead pell-mell with our solutions, without first asking what the question is we want to solve. Today, also, it happens all too often that people differ violently without recognizing that they are talking about different things in the first place.

In the long retrospect, I think it is fair to say that the strength of our political institutions is a strength drawn originally from men who shared the common heritage of education in the humanities. Indeed, in this respect, there probably was no institution of higher learning in history equal to the community of men who formed the Constitutional Convention. All were preeminent in practical affairs. Yet they were also men who knew how to speculate, who brought a broad range of human experience to bear first on their thoughts and then on their practical work. This is not to say they re-echoed each other. They disagreed sharply. But when they did, they shared a common vocabulary which made the eventual agreement possible. So, also, in later years, a Thomas Jefferson and an Alexander Hamilton, whose thoughts form the basic fabric of our national life, disagreed sharply. Yet they were children of the same tradition. And because they were, each in the act of stating his views brilliantly served the nation so that we can now turn to Jefferson for guidance under one set of circumstances, and to Hamilton under a different set. And in this way, we profit from both.

I am saying here that tradition does not mean uniformity. It means diversity within an embracing unity. And it is to this end, I feel, that we must reconceive and reorganize the life that is lived in our schools of higher learning. We must make them, as Woodrow Wilson pleaded in 1909, "a community of scholars and pupils—a free community but a very real one, in which democracy may make its reasonable triumphs of accommodation, its vital process of unity. I am not suggesting," Wilson continued, "that young men be dragooned into becoming scholars or tempted to become pedants, or have any artificial compulsion whatever put upon them, but only that they be introduced into the high society of university ideals, be exposed to the hazards of stimulating friendships, be introduced into the easy comradeship of the republic of letters. By this means the classroom itself might some day come to seem a part of life."

A final remark. I have no illusion that even if all this is done, all will be well with us in a present and future hour. For we face the fact that what we are educating is, after all, the son of Old Adam. And like his ancestor who rebelled against a teaching from the highest possible quarter, so can the son of Old Adam rebel against what he is taught, and reach for forbidden fruit. Yet this much, at least, can be hoped for: that a familiarity with what the many generations of man have talked about and experienced in their career on earth, can, by pointing up the consequences, reduce the danger of such a rebellion, though it may not eliminate it altogether. Indeed, without this heroic hope that education can inch humanity forward toward the vision of human perfectibility, life itself would have no purpose.

In all that touches existence, free men everywhere look to America for leadership. When we wobble, they feel unsteady. When we creak, they groan. When we slip, they fall. But when we act with the clarity of a great purpose, they feel braced and uplifted. Our schools of higher learning must view themselves as the cradle for that which can enable America to give free men the leadership they want. Yet America cannot exercise that leadership if, within the borders of our own land, we are in danger of losing the ability to talk to one another. It is to the restoration of that lost art, in all its admitted difficulties, that I hope our schools of higher learning will bend their chief energies.

VI

1957
Preparation of
College Teachers

F. W. Strothmann

❀❀❀❀❀❀❀❀❀❀❀❀❀❀❀❀❀❀❀❀❀❀❀❀❀❀❀❀

When we speak about the "advancement of learning," we may be
using a timeworn phrase with a somewhat archaic, rationalistic
flavor. Yet we know exactly what we mean by it. We mean that
every one of our various academic disciplines has a "frontier," that
is, a line which is gradually being pushed forward by research into
hitherto unknown or unconquered territory.

My ideas concerning the training of future undergraduate

teachers are based on the conviction that the relation of this ever-advancing frontier to the classroom task varies from discipline to discipline and from level to level.

It varies, first, from discipline to discipline. In physics, in archeology, or in any other endeavor whose task is the intellectual conquest of the unknown, the frontier is the only thing that counts; for all excitement, all life goes on at that frontier; and success or failure is measured exclusively, one might say, in terms of square inches, that is, in terms of facts or relationships uncovered for the first time.

That is the reason a seminar on Galileo is not offered by a modern physics department. To delve into Galileo may be the legitimate task of a historian working on *his frontier;* it is no longer the legitimate task of the natural scientist. The knowledge which Galileo gained has become part of the standard equipment with which the modern scientist is sent to the front line. How this equipment was first forged has nothing to do with its efficiency. To forget, or not to forget, Galileo's agony is therefore a question of piety, not of scientific competence.

The humanities, too, have their advancing lines: for instance, the description of the semantic function of intonation patterns in linguistics, or the impressive structure of Shakespeare scholarship. As far as this advancing line itself is concerned, human individuals and their lives are again unimportant.

On the other hand, a seminar in ethics does not supersede Plato or Kant in the same sense in which Newton superseded Kepler. To be sure, the leader of such a seminar knows today something about the subconscious and about several other behavior-controlling factors of which neither Plato nor Kant was aware. Nevertheless, after all the factors which influence human behavior have been analyzed, when the old problem of good and evil has been once more formulated in new terms, failure or success of the seminar is not judged by what the students *write* at the end of the semester. The question whether the seminar did or did not "take" is answered only by their lives.

Similarly, the value of Shakespeare scholarship is not measured by the mass of codifiable knowledge about Shakespeare, but by the effect which this knowledge has on our capacity to relive, without distortion, a Shakespearian tragedy. If, in the opinion of our progeny, the reliving of such a tragedy should ever become an unworthy experience, then the scholarship that makes it possible would become a waste of time.

In short, within the humanities, the gaining of knowledge at the frontier has only a preliminary, an auxiliary, function. The sciences—astronomy, physics, archeology, psychology—have a value in themselves. In the humanities, however, the goal is not *scientia,* but *prudentia;* the goal is conduct—the perfection not of intellect, but of will and emotion. Any attempt to define the value of humanistic disciplines without reference to emotive and affective life is to me like the attempt to find in a pitch-dark room a black cat that is not there.

There was a time when the prestige of both scientific and humanistic research made it almost impossible to gain recognition on the American campus for any activity which, by rehashing or reliving an old problem, aimed at formation rather than information. That time has passed. The necessity for affective teaching is recognized, and the new situation will soon have an effect on all programs aiming at the training of college teachers. What has not passed is the danger created by the very importance of the frontier and by the legitimate enthusiasm of the workers who man it. This brings me to my second point, that is, to the assertion that the relation of frontier work to the educational task varies not only from discipline to discipline, but also from level to level.

The statement "not to work at the frontier is not to be a scholar" holds true for all disciplines, but we tend to forget, I believe, that there is a passive as well as an active participation in the advancement of learning. We also tend to forget that the frontier itself will collapse unless there are observers in the front lines who, without fighting themselves, tell the people back home what it takes to maintain a frontier, and who, on the basis of what they have observed, shape the training of the new recruits.

Let me illustrate what I mean by passive participation in research. Let us assume that the two best textbooks introducing our college freshmen or sophomores into world history or into the natural sciences have been written by active and successful researchers, that is, by men whose work on the Harding administration or on white dwarf stars has gained them worldwide recognition. Nevertheless it is true that only a very small fraction of the total number of pages making up these textbooks deals with that section of the frontier at which they have made their lasting contribution to the advancement of learning. For every page which gives an account of their own research, there are at least 50 pages dealing with work at those sections of the advancing line where the two authors have never been personally employed.

And that is not all. Even that portion of each book which deals with their own special field—that is, with the Harding administration or with the density of white dwarfs—is not presented by these gentlemen to the freshmen in the same way in which they first presented it to their colleagues. It is presented in a form and in a language appropriate to undergraduate students. At least for the time that it took these researchers to write a textbook, they stopped being researchers and became educators. And their books are good, good enough to fill several generations of freshmen with the desire to man the frontier, not because their authors possessed that kind of creative intelligence which is prerequisite for a Nobel prize, but because they have that other kind of creativeness which enabled them to encompass with critical circumspection their whole discipline. As a result, the chapters dealing with Egypt, written by our Harding specialist, read as if he himself had supervised the building of the pyramids from his cubicle in the library.

Within the walls of a liberal arts college which is not connected with a graduate school, active frontier experience on dwarf stars or on Harding is almost impossible. Not only are research facilities limited, but the demands on the college teacher's time generated by the very scope of his teaching are appalling. To keep his work up to date, he must spend almost all of his free time reading the periodical literature, not just of a small specialized field, but of a whole discipline. No wonder the number of Nobel prize winners in our liberal arts colleges is as small as it is—namely, zero.

Exclusive—and I say "exclusive," not "excessive"—exclusive admiration of the advancing frontier sometimes blinds us, so it seems to me, to the sober realities of educational facts. Good undergraduate teaching is not dissociated from research. It absorbs research constantly. The problem confronting the college is not "teaching versus research," but "creative absorption versus creative production." The one is as necessary as the other. It is good high school and college teaching which keeps the supply of men flowing into our research institutions; and judging by statistics, some of our small liberal arts colleges are sending, percentage-wise, more men to the front lines than the undergraduate divisions of some of our great universities, which have apparently been blind to the facts.

If, then, the American four-year college has a legitimate function—and I, for one, believe it has—then undergraduate teaching is a legitimate profession with a dignity of its own; and we may well ask whether the future college teacher deserves a training significantly different from that of the future researcher.

As long as the graduate courses offered by a specific department cover the major areas of that discipline, as long as a good look at what is going on in related disciplines is demanded of all graduate students, so long the future college teacher might have the same courses and the same seminars as the future researchers; though I do believe that a great deal of the course work we demand might just as well be accomplished by independent study.

However, there are three educational experiences desirable, or perhaps even necessary, for the future undergraduate teacher which he should have over and beyond his course and seminar work, experiences which are at present not always demanded of him.

First of all, he should participate for a short period in some research project not set up by himself. What I mean by participation is not some dull coolie labor like checking bibliographies or mark-sensing IBM cards. I have in mind some share in a genuinely creative activity. At least once in his life, the future college teacher should taste the thrill and the fascination inherent in research—in actual research, not in some project dressed up for training purposes to look like research.

Second, the future college teacher ought to write a special kind of Ph.D. dissertation. In general, we demand that every dissertation, in order to be acceptable, be a contribution to knowledge, that it be a step in the slow process called the advancement of learning. By definition, then, a descriptive dissertation on "The Present State of Genetics" or on "Changes in Plato Interpretation During the Last Ten Years" is not a contribution to knowledge. Yet such a dissertation would represent exactly the kind of work which the college teacher has to perform if he is to stand above his textbook. The ability to passively participate in research and to pass the digested and reformulated results of research on to an undergraduate class ought therefore to be demonstrated, and demonstrated by a written piece of work.

The suggestion that he participate in some exciting creative work for a short time, but not write a research dissertation, involves no contradiction. I am interested in saving some time. I am thinking not of the few graduate students who find, formulate, and solve by themselves an exciting problem. I am thinking of the many who waste a whole year or two in the attempt to write a dissertation that almost looks like a contribution to knowledge, who often lose all taste for research while doing it, and who are then recommended to a college without having demonstrated their ability to keep abreast of their whole discipline.

Third, the future college teacher should learn—in the undergraduate divisions of our universities—how to conduct a sophomore or senior class, and finally demonstrate, in the presence of his examining committee, that he can present a body of up-to-date material by clear exposition and that—in the case of the humanities —he can conduct a discussion which aims at formation rather than information.

This brings me to my last point. I wish we could devise some method of judging, with a certain degree of objectivity and fairness, the quality of college teaching. The development of suitable tests and procedures for rating college teaching, it seems to me, is one of the most urgent tasks confronting us. This task, it should be clear, cannot be performed without the full cooperation of the schools of education.

Before such an undertaking can possibly be fruitful, before the long and tedious research work necessary can even be organized, something else is necessary. The graduate departments must realize that college teaching, in the four-year liberal arts colleges as well as in the undergraduate divisions of our large universities, is a legitimate profession, that it is a man's job, that it is not dissociated from research, and that, unless college teaching is rewarded as it should be, we will no longer have competent college teachers.

VII

1957
Student Values

Philip E. Jacob

❀❀❀❀❀❀❀❀❀❀❀❀❀❀❀❀❀❀❀❀❀❀❀❀❀❀❀❀

The colleges and universities must take stock of a hard fact about their present accomplishment before they can plan realistically for their future role. For the most part, they seem to lack the capacity to *influence* students. Or maybe it is that today's students are *incapable* of being influenced by higher education. In any case, a study of what happens to the values held by American students as they pursue a college degree shows that hardly anything fundamental does happen to them. The college experience barely touches a student's standards of behavior, quality of judgment, sense of social responsibility, perspicacity of understanding of himself and others, or his guiding beliefs and attitudes.

75

This means that if institutions of higher learning are expected to fulfill the historic humanistic mission of what we have called liberal education, they will have to learn how to do it, because they are *not* doing it now with most of their students.

This conclusion stems from an analysis of three main types of data: studies of student attitudes over the last fifteen years; recent evaluations of the impact of general education and other courses, and of various methods of teaching; and a number of comprehensive self-studies by particular institutions. The data are incomplete in many respects. For instance, some types of institutions are not covered; and "depth" data about individual students are scarce, but enough is now known, and the consistency of the material is sufficiently great to warrant tentative generalizations along these lines.

Fortunately, not all of the evidence is negative. There are some institutions where students' values seem to develop. There are some teachers whose influence penetrates and stays. There are some educational techniques which help open the sensibilities as well as the intellectual perceptions of some students. To identify more clearly the factors which make a difference in the value students derive from college, to find how these can be multiplied and transferred across the board of American higher education, are critical questions which need to be answered before *liberal* education at any rate is ready to claim a pivotal role in the lives of the next college generations.

First, in identifying the pattern of values of American college students today, the most striking characteristic about these values is their homogeneity. American students seem generally to think alike, believe alike, almost feel alike, regardless of economic, social, ethnic, racial, religious, or geographic background, or the nature of the colleges at which they are studying. The profile which follows is a composite of attitudes which appear to be held by at least 75 to 80 per cent of recent college generations.

They are *gloriously contented* both in regard to their present day-to-day activity and their outlook for the future. Few of them are worried—about their health, their prospective careers, their family relations, the state of national or international society, or the likelihood of their enjoying secure and happy lives. They are supremely confident that their destinies lie within their own control rather than in the grip of external circumstance.

The great majority of students appear unabashedly *self-centered*. They aspire for material gratifications for themselves and their families. They intend to look out for themselves first and expect others to do likewise.

Social harmony with an *easy tolerance of the dissident* and the different pervades the student environment. Conformists themselves, the American students see little need to insist that everyone conform to the socially accepted standard. They are for the most part (with some allowance for sectional differences) ready to live in a mobile society, without racial, ethnic, or income barriers. But they do not intend to crusade for nondiscrimination, merely to accept it as it comes, a necessary convention in a homogenized culture.

The traditional *moral virtues are valued* by almost all students. Although they respect sincerity, honesty, loyalty, as proper standards of conduct for decent people, they are not inclined to censor those who choose to depart from these canons. They do not feel personally bound to unbending consistency in observing the code, especially when a lapse is socially sanctioned. For instance, standards are generally low in regard to academic honesty, systematic cheating being the custom, rather than the exception at many major institutions.

Students normally express a *need for religion* as a part of their lives and make time on most week ends for an hour in church. However, their religion does not carry over to guide and govern important decisions in the secular world. Students expect these to be socially determined. God has little to do with the behavior of men in society, if widespread student judgment be accepted. His place is in church and perhaps in the home, not in business or club or community. He is worshiped, dutifully and with propriety, but the campus is not permeated by a live sense of His presence.

American students are likewise *dutifully responsive toward government*. They expect to obey its laws, pay its taxes, serve in its armed forces—without complaint but without enthusiasm. They will discharge the obligations demanded of them though they will not voluntarily contribute to the public welfare. Nor do they particularly desire an influential voice in public policy. Except for the ritual of voting, they are content to abdicate the citizen's role in the political process and to leave to others the effective power of governmental decision. They are politically irresponsible, and often politically illiterate as well.

This disposition is reflected in *strangely contradictory attitudes toward international affairs*. Students predict another major war within a dozen years, yet international problems are the least of the concerns to which they expect to give much personal attention during their immediate future. The optimism with which they view their prospects for a good long life belies the seriousness of their gloomy prophecy. They readily propose some form of supranational government as a means of preventing war, but a very large number display only a limited knowledge of and confidence in the United Nations as an instrument of cooperative international action.

Turning to their immediate preoccupation, the pursuit of an education, students by and large *set great stock by college* in general and their own college in particular. The intensity of their devotion varies quite a bit with the institution and sometimes with the nature of the students' educational goals, and the real point of the devotion is not the same for all. Only a minority seem to value their college education primarily in terms of its intellectual contribution, or its nurturing of personal character and the capacity for responsible human relationships. Vocational preparation, skill, and experience in social adjustment head the rewards which students crave from their higher education.

These values are not the unanimous choice of American college students, it should be emphasized. Many individuals forcefully refute some or all of the generalizations. Furthermore, on some issues students have no common mind—for instance, on how much discipline children should have, how much government the country needs, how far power should be relied on in international affairs, and to what extent political dissidence should be repressed for the sake of national security. For the most part, a campus norm of values prevails coast to coast, at state university or denominational college, for the Ivy Leaguer or the city college commuter.

Against the background of earlier generations, the values of today's students look different. The undergirding of the Puritan heritage on which the major value assumptions of American society have traditionally rested is inconspicuous, if it is present at all. Perhaps these students are the forerunners of a major cultural and ethical revolution, the unconscious ushers of an essentially secular (though nominally religious), self-oriented (though group-conforming) society.

Coming now to the impact of college on students' values, the inescapable conclusion seems to be that on most fundamentals, students come out pretty much as they go in. There is, to be sure, somewhat more homogeneity and greater consistency of values among students at the end of their four years than when they begin. Fewer seniors than freshmen espouse beliefs which deviate from the going campus standards. The student has ironed out serious conflicts of values or at least achieved a workable compromise. Changes which occur are rarely drastic or sudden, and they tend to emerge on the periphery of the student's character, affecting his application of values, rather than the core of values themselves.

To call this process a *liberalization* of student values is a misnomer. The impact of the college experience is rather to *socialize* the individual, to refine, polish, or shape up his values so that he can fit comfortably into the ranks of college-bred men and women in the American community.

The values of the college graduate do tend to set him off in some respects from the rest of the society though the tendency is not very marked. He is more concerned with status, achievement, and prestige. Proportionately more college graduates distrust welfare economics and strong government than do citizens in the country at large. Paradoxically, they tend to be somewhat more tolerant and less repressive of radical ideas and unconventional people, also less prejudiced toward minority groups and alien cultures. They share few of the cold war suspicions of the subversiveness of college faculties, nor do they support the popular stereotype of the colleges' godlessness. Religiously, they may be less superstitious or otherworldly than their fellow countrymen. The college man or woman thus tends to be more self-important, more conservative, more tolerant, and less fearful of evil forces in this world and outside than those who have not been "higher educated."

Generally, values and outlook of students do not vary greatly whether they have pursued a conventional liberal arts program, an integrated general education curriculum, or one of the strictly professional-vocational options. The more liberally educated student may take a somewhat more active interest in community responsibilities, and keep better informed about public affairs. But the distinction is not striking and by no means does it occur consistently among students at all colleges. It does *not* justify the conclusion that a student acquires a greater maturity of judgment on issues of social policy or a more sensitive regard for the humane values because he has had a larger dose of liberal or general education.

This negative conclusion applies specifically to the effect of social science courses. The values expressed by those who are most interested in social sciences are little different from those of other students. This is true not only of personal moral and religious values, but also of attitudes toward social and political issues regarding which the social science students are presumably more concerned and better informed. Neither the students' interest nor their instruction in social science seems to exert a broad influence on their belief or their judgments of conduct and policy.

Equally disturbing is evidence that the quality of teaching has relatively little effect upon the value outcomes of general education—in the social sciences or in other fields—so far as the great mass of students is concerned.

Yet by and large the impact of the good teacher is indistinguishable from that of the poor one, at least in terms of his influence upon the values held and cherished by his students. Students like the good teacher better, and enjoy his classes more, but their fundamental response is little different than to any one else teaching the course. With important individual exceptions, instructors seem equally *in*effective in tingling the nerve centers of students' values.

In the process of mass education, many students appear to take the instructor for granted, as he comes, good or bad, a necessary appliance in Operation College. His personal influence washes out in such an atmosphere, especially in regard to the deeper issues of life direction, and the recognition and resolution of basic value conflicts. A teacher can be recognized as a *good* teacher by his students, but with increasing rarity is he an *effective* teacher in the communication and maturing of values. Something in the contemporary social or educational climate curtains him off from the inner recesses of his students' character and freezes their motivational responses.

Student testimony and perceptive observation by educators and counselors indicate, however, that some teachers do exert a profound influence on some students, even to the point of causing particular individuals to reorient their philosophy of life and adopt new and usually more socially responsible vocational goals. What it is that ignites such influence can hardly be defined, so personal, varied, and unconscious are the factors at work. It is perhaps significant, however, that faculty identified as having this power with students are likely to be persons whose own value commitments are firm and openly expressed, and who are outgoing and warm in their personal relations with students. Furthermore, faculty influence appears more pronounced at institutions where association between faculty and students is normal and frequent, and students find teachers receptive to unhurried and relaxed conversation out of class.

The method of instruction seems to have only a minor influence on students' value judgments. Student-centered techniques of teaching and a stress on discussion in contrast to lecture or recitation have been strongly advocated as effective means of engaging the student's personal participation in the learning process, and encouraging him to reach valid judgments of his own on important issues. Studies of the comparative effectiveness of such methods tend *not* to support such a conviction.

Under certain circumstances, notably a favorable institutional environment, student-centered teaching has apparently resulted in a somewhat more satisfactory emotional and social adjustment by the students, and a more congenial learning situation. But there is little indication of a significantly greater alteration in the beliefs or behavioral standards of students taught by one method or another.

The response of a student to a given type of instruction often reflects his personality or disposition previous to entering upon the course. Some students react very negatively to a more permissive teaching technique. They feel frustrated and uneasy without more direction and authority exercised by the teacher. Consequently, they may actually learn less, and be less profoundly affected by a course taught in this manner than by a more formal, definitely structured approach. In any case, the evidence is not conclusive that the potency of general education in influencing student values may be consistently strengthened by using a particular method of teaching.

Similar as the patterns of student values appear on a mass view, the intellectual, cultural, and moral climate of some institutions stands out from the crowd. The response of students to education within the atmosphere of these institutions is strikingly different from the national pattern.

The very individuality of these places makes comparisons unreal, but they do seem to have in common a high level of expectancy of their students. What is expected is not the same. It may be outstanding intellectual initiative and drive, profound respect for the dignity and worth of work, world-mindedness or just open-mindedness, a sense of community responsibility or of social justice, a dedication to humanitarian service, or religious faithfulness. Everyone, however, is conscious of the mission to which the institution stands dedicated, though this is not necessarily loudly trumpeted at every convocation, nor elaborated in fulsome paragraphs of aims and purposes in the college bulletin.

Where there is such unity and vigor of expectation, students seem drawn to live up to the college standard, even if it means quite a wrench from their previous ways of thought, or a break with the prevailing values of students elsewhere. The college serves as a cocoon in which a new value orientation can mature and solidify until it is strong enough to survive as a maverick in the conventional world.

A climate favorable to a redirection of values appears more frequently at private colleges of modest enrollment. In a few instances, something of the sort has also emerged within a particular school or division of a larger public institution.

With a distinctive quality of this kind, an institution acquires a personality in the eyes of its students, alumni, and staff. The deep loyalty which it earns reflects something more than pride, sentiment, or prestige. A community of values has been created. Not that every student sees the whole world alike, but most have come to a similar concern for the values held important in their college. The hold of these institutional values evidently persists long after graduation and often influences the choice of college by the next generation.

Recent research has identified certain personality characteristics of students which filter their educational experiences. Some students have a set of mind so rigid, an outlook on human relations so
stereotyped, and a reliance on authority so compulsive that they are
intellectually and emotionally incapable of understanding new ideas,
and seeing, much less accepting, educational implications which run
counter to their preconceptions. This particularly limits their re-
sponsiveness in the social sciences and the humanities whenever controversial issues arise. Such students quail in the presence of conflict
and uncertainty. They crave right answers. They distrust speculative
thought, their own or that of their fellow students. They recoil from
creative discussion.

Under most conditions of general education, where content
and teaching method have been more or less standardized to suit
what faculties consider the needs of the average student, the personalities just described become deadwood. They appear impervious
to a real educational experience, even though the brainier ones may
survive academically by parroting texts and instructors on examinations. Many educators have concluded that such students do not belong in college; others insist that at least some liberalizing influence
may rub off on them if they are obliged to run a lengthy gauntlet of
general courses in social science and humanities, distasteful as the
students may find them. A few institutions, however, are exploring
special approaches to general education for this type of student, with
promising results.

Not enough is yet known to insure the general success of such
teaching, and a few of these students will achieve the autonomy of
those whose personality was freer to start with. But they have shown
striking gains in critical thinking and developed more responsible
and sensitive social values when their general education in social science has been so tailored to their particular needs. Because the
number of students with such personality characteristics is large and
growing, this type of experimentation seems unusually important.

The implication of all this is that no specific curricular pattern of general education, no model syllabus for a basic social science
course, no pedigree of instructor, and no wizardry of instructional
method can be patented for its impact on the values of students. Student values do change to some extent in college. With some students,

the change is substantial, but the impetus to change does not come primarily from the formal educational process. Potency to affect student values is found in the distinctive climate of a few institutions, the individual and personal magnetism of a sensitive teacher with strong value commitments of his own, or value-laden personal experiences of students imaginatively integrated with their intellectual development.

PART *wo*

1958 to 1964

❋❋❋❋❋❋❋❋❋❋❋❋❋❋❋❋❋❋❋❋❋❋❋❋❋❋❋❋❋❋

The relationship I would like to see between university and society is that of a lovers' quarrel, with the accent equally on lover and quarrel. For there are two things neither society nor the university can risk: alienation or identification.

from the address of William Sloane Coffin, Jr.
before the 1964 National Conference on Higher Education

VIII

1959
Social Balance

John Kenneth Galbraith

❀❀❀❀❀❀❀❀❀❀❀❀❀❀❀❀❀❀❀❀❀❀❀❀❀❀❀❀❀❀

The past year or two will no doubt have a minor place in our history as the time when we chose to have a serious discussion of education. This discussion had, perhaps, a certain inevitability—like the approach of the Second War or the Great Depression. Deeply disruptive forces had been at work and at some point they were bound to come strongly to our attention. Much importance has been attributed to the first Sputnik—indeed, the word has come to suggest less the Russian searching of space than the American searching of the soul. But, in fact, the Sputnik had much the same precipitating effect as the stock market crash in 1929 or the Japanese attack

87

in 1941. It was less the blow than the fragility of what was struck
that caused the attention and created the alarm.

It is to be hoped that this discussion of education since the
first Sputnik has done some good. Perhaps it has. But we are entitled
to wonder. Three things have kept the results from being as salutary
as they might have been.

First of all, we have been living through another era of the
tough, practical, hard-headed man. The idealization of this man—
the instinctive man-of-action—is a recurrent phenomenon in our society. In recent years we have had an especially severe attack, although, hopefully, one that is now subsiding.

The problems of our time, as indeed those of all time, yield to
study, thought, and perception. Particular experience rarely provides
general qualification. It can be a profound disqualification if it is
supposed to qualify the man for unstudied action or snap decision.
And this is often the nature of the so-called practical judgment. It is
based not on thought, but either on unexamined dogma or surface
phenomenon. The first has a very good chance of being wrong. The
second almost invariably sacrifices the long run to the short.

The point is well illustrated by the reaction of those who are
called hard-headed and practical men in the present administration
to the period since Sputnik. They have expressed dutiful concern
about education. That, unfortunately, has been about all. And the
reason is that they have a deeper commitment. That is to the paramount importance of lower taxes, lower expenditures and a balanced
budget. (We may falter and fall, but we will do it in a financially
impeccable way.) There has been no great concern, other than of a
purely oral sort, for the oncoming crowd of children which is now
taxing our schools and will presently engulf our universities. These
are more distant (marginally more distant) phenomena, and anything however slightly removed from the present is in the province
of the planner or the theorist.

As I have mentioned, we are coming to the end of the era of
the tough-minded, hard-headed man. Perhaps the reason lies partly
in the imagery. People may well have begun to wonder if brains
should be praised for their resemblance to leather and the head for
its value as a blunt instrument. But the more important reason is
probably in the nature of the world. Keynes once reminded us that

in the long run we are all dead. It is no longer true. In the long run people are still alive and suffering from the errors of omission of those who declined to look ahead. So it has come about that the practical genius of the springtime is the Charlie Wilson of the fall.

Yet we should not underestimate the residual power of these attitudes. In the last two or three years, they have yielded very little to the proponents of federal aid to education. This was by far our best chance for getting dramatic improvement, especially in the states and localities of greatest need. And, needless to say, the states and localities have their hard-headed men too. They have been busy defeating the school bond issues and opposing the increases in state and local taxes. Some of this is to be attributed to old-fashioned selfishness. However, I find this an understandable and amiable trait as compared with the proud and self-righteous rejection of foresight which has lately been in fashion.

The genuine and valuable concern over education which developed after the Sputnik took flight was also the victim of another of the disturbing tendencies of our time. That is for speech to become almost completely divorced from consequence. President Eisenhower, it has often been said, clearly feels that a long and heartfelt statement of his concern for a problem is a substitute for doing anything about it. In defense of the President, I think it must be said that he faithfully reflects a tendency in the country at large. Once men said what they were going to do. Now, they consider it sufficient to say what should be done. Speech was once a portent of action. It has become a substitute.

As speech has become an end in itself, we have come increasingly to concentrate our energies on the magnificence, or anyhow the grandiloquence of expression. We live in the era of the memorable speech. If a man cannot be practical, he at least can be memorable. I could perhaps enlarge on the components of the memorable speech. Its principal ingredients are fanciful exaggeration, foolish prophecy, and silly heroics in about that order of importance, although in recent years there has been increasing resort to extreme piety. But I do not need to go further. Our concern for education after the Sputnik was partly buried by a crushing avalanche of memorable speeches.

However, there has been a deeper factor in this loss of mo-

mentum. I would also stress—this is far from a modest assertion—
our continuing failure to see with clarity the relation of education,
at different levels, to the economic and social order. Until this is
clearly perceived, the case for education will rest on a defective
foundation. The passing fear and envy excited by a Soviet technical
achievement will be a poor substitute for a secure and permanent
base. I should like, in the remainder of this article and with no
ambition to be memorable, to deal with the relation of education to
economic and social change.

The problem begins with the curious and complex duality of
the role of man. Man is a goal—an end himself. We need look no
further for justification for his intellectual development or his intellectual adventure. It is for these, or such as these, that he lives. A
great many intellectuals, including many educators, have declined to
look further for a rationale. If the ultimate purpose of education is
agreed on, why search for a lesser one?

Yet there is a more vulgar view of man, and it is idle to deny
its hold. This regards him as an instrument of production—as a con-
verter of energy, or as a servomechanism, or in a more dignified role
as a directing force in productive activity. If the society sets great
store by production, as ours so obviously does, then it will set great
store by man as an agent of production. And this our society does.
We are not at all tolerant of the individual or group whose pursuit
of happiness brings him or them into conflict with production. We
have no praise for the idle or easygoing workman and certainly none
for the featherbedding union.

Yet our view of man as a producer is also an archaic one.
Given its endowment of natural resources, the productive power of a
country depends on its stock of capital and its supply of labor and on
the skill with which these are combined. Both capital and labor have
two dimensions—the dimension of quantity and that of quality. Of
a steel mill, one needs to know *both* its rated capacity and the efficiency of its blast furnaces, open hearths, and rolling mills. And as
one wants to know both the quality and the capacity of a mill, so
one wants to know not only the size but the quality of a labor force.
Along with numbers are the questions of literacy, skill, discipline,
technical guidance, and leadership.

In the early years of the Industrial Revolution, it was at least arguable that the decisive factor for an economy was simply the supply of capital. The demands of the early machines on human talent were simple. The supply of clerical, supervisory, and administrative talent seemed to be forthcoming more or less automatically. Invention and technological change appeared to be the product of haphazard inspiration and genius. They were not easily related to any specific training or preparation. The evidence for this point of view is not absolute. Adam Smith began the *Wealth of Nations* by attributing the productivity of a nation to the proportion of gainful workers to total population and to "the skill, dexterity and judgment with which [the nation's] labor is generally applied." But it is not in doubt that from the beginning of modern economic society, the supply of capital had a central fascination for the economist and through him, for the public at large. The total valuation of the nation's capital became the measure of its national wealth. The annual volume of its saving and capital investment became the measure of its growth. It is the annual investment in capital—tangible capital in the form of machinery, plant, generating plant, transmission lines —which remains the measure of our progress.

There can be very little question that this measure is technologically obsolete. We can probably lay it down as a law that in an advancing economic society, human beings gain in importance in relation to the capital with which they are associated. Machine production, paradoxically, diminishes the machine in relation to the man. This is partly because the improvement of capital—what we call technological change—comes increasingly to be one of the recognized paths toward increasing productivity. Technological change is the result not of amassing capital. It is the work of human beings. And increasingly, of course, it is the result of a deliberate and purposeful investment in human beings. According to the National Bureau of Economic Research, for roughly 75 years until the decade 1944–1953, national output in the United States had been increasing at the rate of 3.5 per cent a year. Slightly less than half of this can be attributed to crude increases in the stock of capital and to increases in the number of workers. The rest must be imputed to technological advance and to improvements in the abilities and skills of the people who operated the better equipment. The part of the improvement attributable to technological change has been increasing.

Some technological change is unrelated to education. And some of the advance in industrial skills and aptitudes represents a general accommodation by people who are on the job. But we are entitled to attribute much, if not most, of this advance to our investment in people. We almost certainly owe more of our economic gains in the last seven decades to investment in people than to saving and the amassment of capital. And the margin in favor of people is increasing.

To say that investment in people has yet to establish itself in comparison with investment in material capital would be a remarkable understatement. For ages, the road company philosophers have been making the point that people are just as important in their own way as things—and just as worthy as objects of expenditure. And the poets in their audience have been nodding their agreement. The operative consequences have been remarkably slight. On weekdays wealth is still measured by physical capital and progress by the additions thereto. Part of this can be attributed to the force of tradition. Part must again be credited to our old friend the practical man. That which is inconsistent with established belief is not only untrue but vaguely foolish. And you can see capital and you cannot see learning. Only the impractical theorist reacts to what he cannot see.

Investment in human capital as opposed to material capital has also been damaged, I think, by the fact that the material calculation is not the only and not the primary justification. Man, to repeat, is an end in himself. We eat for the purposes of improving our productive efficiency. But with even more enthusiasm, we eat to avoid hunger and enjoy the food. Education increases our productivity. It is also a nourishing alternative to ignorance which, like food, has its own enjoyments and rewards. Like food, it is not only an aid to production, but a prime object of consumption. But the very attitudes which caused us to set such store by capital cause us also to accord an inferior role to consumption. It is by saving—refraining from consumption—that the capital stock is increased. Anything that interferes with saving is inferior. Expenditures on education, because they are consumption, get in the way of the higher claims of saving and capital investment.

And let no one suppose for a moment that this is a theoretical argument without operative content. Outlays for education are regularly opposed on the grounds that the community cannot afford them. Even more explicitly, it is said that the high taxes interfere with saving and investment and thus with enterprise and economic health. Education is agreeable and even worthy, but it is not a utilitarian or productive employment of resources. The taxes for the new high school, a consumption good, may cost the community a new brewery which is a capital good. This is a horrendous prospect, so the community must proceed warily. Those who speak for education have rightly and, I think, wisely insisted that education is both a means and an end. But this has handicapped them in arguing what is ordinarily a superior case on purely economic criteria.

I come now to the final problem in asserting the economic claims of education. It is the most serious. And were I writing a memorable paper, I might even claim that it is the one that will eventually ruin us.

This concerns the profound structural difference in our type of economy between the machinery which provides for material investment and that which provides for investment in human beings. In a private capitalist or market economy, the provision for investment in material capital is integral to the system. When there is a prospect for gain from a particular capital outlay—when the marginal return from an investment exceeds the going return on savings —the investment proceeds more or less automatically. No public decision is ordinarily required. It is not necessary to arrange a specific transfer of funds from some other employment. A very large part of modern investment occurs within the business firm. The latter has a ready-made supply of investment funds from its own earnings.

In contrast, investment in human beings is very largely undertaken by the state. And quite a bit of the remainder is in the domain of private conscience and charity. The return to the investment accrues partly to the individual and partly to the community. It is not as in the case of a public utility something on which the in-

vestor can levy a claim. Hence support for this investment is dependent on a decision to transfer funds from other uses. If there is
an increased need for investment in people or an increased opportunity, there is no automatic process by which it will be recognized
or exploited. The need or opportunity must be seen and then a decision must be taken to raise and apply public revenues to the purpose.

We should expect serious faults in machinery so designed.
Since the estimate of return from investment in people, unlike the
estimate of return in investment in capital, is almost completely subjective, we should expect, or anyhow fear, serious underestimation.
The diversion of revenues from other purposes raises the question of
who is to supply them. It is also entangled with the question of using
taxes to promote greater equality. This would lead us to expect that
underestimation would be coupled with underappropriation. And
let me remind you that the criterion here is a strictly economic one.
The test is whether we are keeping a parity of investment as between
people and material capital.

This is a problem that Socialist-Communist countries do not
have. In the nature of their organization, resources are in the public
sector. They have, I would imagine, grave problems of education,
but they do not have this problem of subtraction and transfer.

In the spring of 1958 when I was in Poland—a very poor
country—I was questioned closely by the students of one of the universities on the rate of pay of students at American colleges and universities. They were surprised when I told them we had no regular
student stipends. They wished to know how our students lived. The
rector of the university told me afterward that he thought I had dis-
appointed my audience. They had hoped my answers might be useful for purposes of collective bargaining. The fact that rich America
did not pay people who studied was a serious blow.

My purpose in these comments was analysis and exposition.
I would be running a risk were I to go further. It is the mark of the
memorable writer that he courageously outlines a course of action
for other people. But perhaps I may be permitted to suggest one or
two consequences—which in any case are sufficiently obvious.

We must recognize that our society has a critical and as yet un-
solved problem of investing in people. We can neglect no hopeful and

realistic solution. I have urged, not to a rousing chorus of applause, that we should not, as one example, bar any tax which promises to ease the problem. By the same token, all who are interested in education must align themselves strongly on the practical measures for economic stabilization. (I do not have in mind the combination of prayer, incantation, and higher interest rates on which the present administration relies.) Inflation is the implacable enemy of the public sector of the economy. It means that we must have constantly increasing allocations to the public sector in order to remain even. Especially in the case of states and localities, where revenues are inelastic, this is a source of formidable difficulty. But most of all I would plead for the utmost self-confidence on the part of those who argue for, and work for, increased investment in education as well as other outlays for productive human capital.

Neither timidity nor an academic inferiority complex should constrain the case for an increasing allocation of resources to these purposes. Those who say it cannot be afforded are not only wrong, but must be protected from the consequences of their own error. This latter is of no small importance. While it is well established that the Lord looks after fools and drunk men, he is said not to intervene on behalf of the chronically shortsighted.

IX

1959
Electronic
Revolution

Marshall McLuhan

❀❀❀❀❀❀❀❀❀❀❀❀❀❀❀❀❀❀❀❀❀❀❀❀❀❀❀❀❀❀❀❀❀

Today in the post-mechanical age we are in the same position as horse-minded people when confronted with the automobile. To horse-minded people the most striking fact about the car is that it is a horseless carriage. In the same way radio appeared as wireless to those who had become accustomed to the miracle of the telegraph. Automation to machine-minded people strikes fear as being an extreme form of mechanization; but as Peter Drucker says in his

Landmarks of Tomorrow, automation "is merely a particularly ugly word to describe a new view of the process of physical production as a configuration and true entity."

So rapidly have we begun to feel the effects of the electronic revolution in presenting us with new configurations that all of us today are displaced persons living in a world that has little to do with the one in which we grew up. Most of us can recall the days when children pushed hoops along sidewalks and roads. There are more hoops than ever now. But no child will push one. For children today live in a space whose configurations are not those of thirty years ago. Instead of being attracted by an outer space designed in lineal fashion, children now nucleate their own space, ballet style. Living, for example, with electronic imagery in which the image is formed by light *through* rather than light *on* (one major difference between TV and film), children respond with new sensory configurations and new attitudes to their world.

Educators naturally feel that their job is to maintain the educational establishment and to preserve and advance the values so long associated with its procedures.

Right now this means, for example, that we are going to insist that Johnny acquire the art of reading, if only because print is the matrix of Western industrial method in production, and print teaches consumer habits and outlook as well. Print teaches the habit of sequential analysis and of fragmentation of all motion into static units. Print teaches habits of privacy and self-reliance and initiative. It provides a massive visual panorama of the resources of our mother tongue which preliterate peoples know only by ear. In fact, print is not only access to our culture and technology, it is our culture and technology. That is why in the electronic age we are threatened by new fast-moving and flexible media—while we sit in a Maginot Line convinced of the importance of our position.

Of course Johnny must read. He must follow the lines of print. He must roll that hoop down the walk. He must roll his eyes in lineal, sequential fashion. We have only to proceed to engraft the old right-handedness on his new left-handedness in order to win our point. But in the meantime we shall have lost his attention, and he may be subdued, but he will be utterly confused.

Taken in the long run, the medium is the message. So that

when, by group action, a society evolves a new medium like print or telegraph or photo or radio, it has earned the right to express a new message. And when we tell the young that this new message *is* a threat to the old message or medium, we are telling them that all we are striving to do in our united social and technical lives is destructive of all that they hold dear. The young can only conclude that we are not serious. And this is the meaning of their decline of attention.

I have said that the medium is the message in the long run. It would be easy to explain and confirm this point historically. Print simply wiped out the main modes of oral education that had been devised in the Greco-Roman world and transmitted with the phonetic alphabet and the manuscript throughout the medieval period. And it ended that 2500-year pattern in a few decades. Today the monarchy of print has ended, and an oligarchy of new media has usurped most of the power of that 500-year-old monarchy. Each member of that oligarchy possesses as much power and message as print itself. I think that if we are to have a constitutional order and balance among these new oligarchs, we shall have to study their configurations, their psychodynamics and their long-term messages. To treat them as humble servants (audiovisual aids) of our established conventions would be as fatal as to use an x-ray unit as a space-heater. The Western world has made this kind of mistake before. But now with the collapse of the "East," that is, with its recognition that no viable society can be built anywhere except on Western modes, it would be a very bad time to allow our own new media to liquidate the older media. The message and form of electronic information pattern is the simultaneous. What is indicated for our time, then, is not succession of media and educational procedures, like a series of boxing champions, but coexistence based on awareness of the inherent powers and messages of each of these unique configurations.

In his book on *Film as Art*, Rudolph Arnheim, the psychologist, wrote: "The history of human ingenuity shows that almost every innovation goes through a preliminary phase in which the solution is obtained by the old method, modified or amplified by some new feature."

In the past thirty years all of our traditional disciplines in the arts and sciences have moved from the pattern of lineal cause to configuration. Nowhere is this more true than in biology. Yet the methods used to reach configuration are still the old Cartesian methods of classical mechanics applied to the study of living organism. And configuration concepts such as *stress* or *metabolism ecology* and *syndrome* are essentially aesthetic terms.

As we move into the world of the simultaneous out of the era of mechanism and of the lineal succession types of analysis, we not only move into the world of the artist but we see the disappearance of the old oppositions between art and nature, business and culture, school and society. It really does not matter to which phase of our culture today we turn. The habit of simultaneous vision of all phases of process is what characterizes the articulate awareness in the field.

Thus, in the movement of information today by technological means we have by far the largest industry. American Telephone and Telegraph alone greatly exceeds the capitalization of General Motors. The production and consumption of information, that is, is the main business of our time. Culture has taken over commerce. Within industry itself the growth of the classroom for workers and for management receives a budget at least three times the $16 billion budget of formal education in North America. And for research, also, the trend and ratios are similar.

The movement of information round-the-clock and round-the-globe is now a matter of instantaneous configuration. Decision-making in business and in education as much as in diplomacy is now a matter of grasping these configurations. They have a language and a syntax of their own as much as does the iconology of pictorial advertisement. So that it is not only the business of education today to teach these new languages but to teach how we can in our previously achieved configurations of culture be enriched by these new powers and not merely dissolved by them. There is a classic definition of science originating in the Academie Française after the death of Descartes: "The certain and evident knowledge of things by their causes." Survival indicates that we grasp by anticipation the inherent causes and not the effects of the electronic media in all their cultural configurations and make a fully conscious choice of strategy in education accordingly.

The eminent French anthropologist, Claude Lévi-Strauss, in

an analysis of "The Structural Study of Myth" (*Journal of American Folklore,* October-December, 1955), presents us with a typical configurational insight: "we define myth as consisting of all its versions . . . therefore, not only Sophocles, but Freud himself, should be included among the recorded versions of the Oedipus myth on a par with earlier or seemingly more 'authentic' versions." Applied to the study of media in education, the Lévi-Strauss insight, which is characteristic of the approaches of the arts and sciences in our time, means that we have to regard our media as mythic structures, as massive codifications of group experience and social realities. And just as print profoundly altered the structure of the phonetic alphabet and repatterned the educational processes of the Western world, so did the telegraph reshape print, as did the movie and radio and television. These structural changes in media myth coexist in an ever-live model of the learning and teaching process. The changing configurations of this massive structure inevitably alter the bias of sight, sound, and sense in each one of us, predisposing us now to one pattern of preference, and now to another. Today, *via* electronic means, the coexistence of cultures and of all phases of process in media development offers to mankind, for the first time, a means of liberation from the sensory enslavement of particular media in specialized phases of their development.

What Harold Innis well called *The Bias of Communication* concerned not only the forms in which men have chosen to codify information but the causal effects of stone, papyrus, and print on the changing structures of decision-making.

Mr. Parkinson has recently entertained us with an analysis of bureaucratic decision-making as it exists in the written mode of the memorandum syndrome. The written forms of information movement begin to look quaint after a few decades of electronic information pattern. At present the co-pilots of Canadian jet fighters have to make decisions in quite another configuration; namely, that of the instantaneous. Before being assigned to their common task, they undergo a long phase of what is called *going steady*. When finally assigned to their plane they are publicly *married* by the commanding officer in a sober ceremony. Today, it is felt, only *marriage* can connote the degree of togetherness, tolerance, sympathy, and so on, necessary for decision-making in the use of new technology. This new pattern is the subliminal but overwhelming *message* of the media since the telegraph. Yet nowhere in our educational establishment have we made provision for the study of these profound messages which impose their configurations on the sensory equipment of children from their first days of existence. Yet some such provision would seem to be indicated against the persistent effects of media fall-out, as it were.

One effect of the commercial movement of information in many media is that today we live in classrooms without walls. The printed book created the classroom as we know it by making available exactly repeatable information. Even if the manuscript or handmade book had been cheap enough for all, it could never have been uniform or repeatable. Moreover, the best manuscripts are slow to read and create a totally different feeling for language in the student—a feeling for the multiple layers of meaning. Such a feeling has returned today, especially since television, with its light *through,* rather than light *on* the image. In a word, the printed page was no more a cheaper manuscript than the motorcar was a horseless carriage. And the repeatable character of print had consequences in science and industry which we are still working out.

But all previous configurations, including that of print from movable type, undergo a sort of alchemical change when they meet a heavy new stress or pull from a new type of configuration.

I have called the electronic age, which began with the telegraph, the post-mechanical age. For now that which moves in our new structures is no longer wheels and shafts (except incidentally), but light itself. We can now see in depth, as it were, the shape of the Gutenberg myth and technology. Our knowledge of the causal operation of the Gutenberg configuration might now save the Indians and the Chinese a great deal of needless liquidation of many elements of their cultures which we have come to value in the West. But even more urgently we need prescience of the full causal powers latent in our new media in order that we may do for our own print-culture what we could also do to save Chinese ideogrammic calligraphy and education. A kind of alchemical foreknowledge of all the future effects of any new medium is possible. Under electronic conditions, when all effects are accelerated in their mutual collision and emergence, such anticipation of consequence is basic need, as well as new possibility.

For example, our present concern about closed-circuit television in education is parallel to the sixteenth-century concern about whether print and the vernaculars could do a serious educational job. It is actually asking whether the car can ever supplant the horse. We are losing precious time in such static retrospection.

Let me mention one central feature of the electronic configuration; namely, its strong tendency to reverse producer-consumer relationships. Print over the centuries had stabilized a pattern of producer-consumer relations. But with the telegraph a century ago the reader of the press had to assume an editorial function unknown to the reader of the pre-telegraph press.

When news moves slowly, the paper has time to provide perspectives, background, and interrelations for the news, and the reader is given a consumer package. When the news comes at high speed, there is no possibility of such literary processing, and the reader is given a do-it-yourself kit. This telegraph pattern was soon transferred to poetry, painting, and music, to the bewilderment of consumer-oriented people. When John Dewey attempted to transfer the same electronic or do-it-yourself pattern to in-school education, he failed. He had not analyzed the situation adequately nor had he any glimpse of the media factors operative on his own enterprise. But had he merely turned the do-it-yourself bias towards the training of the young in the perception and judgment of the out-of-school media, he would have succeeded, and we would all of us be in a much stronger position educationally today. Because that is precisely the task we must now tackle—the training of the young in mastery of the new global media.

Most of the space in this paper has gone to pointing out the mere nature of the technological causes which, past and present, produce change in educational patterns. These causes are mainly subliminal and nonverbal. And may it not be that the new importance that is now accorded to the arts, both in education and in industry, is owing to our awakened sense of the role of art and artists in raising subliminal and nonverbal factors of experience to the level of conscious articulation?

In a simultaneous information structure such as the electronic global community we cannot afford subliminal factors, since their operation is haphazard. The simultaneous compels us to make a social order that, like a poem or painting, is totally realized in its interrelations, and in which each factor has total relevance.

To record briefly some basic educational changes which are now discernible and may well foreshadow major lines of development, let me suggest the following:

We have, in the age of literacy, educated more and more members of society. In the electronic age we shall educate more of each person. We now move from educational extension to even greater extension, but in *depth,* as well.

Is not this the drift of our new concern with the gifted child?

The meaning of the New Criticism today is not just literacy but a shift to reading in depth with total awareness rather than the single-plane approach of the older literacy.

As we extend our educational operation by television and video tape we shall find that the teacher is no longer the source of data but of insight. More and more teachers will be needed for the type of depth instruction that goes naturally with television, with light *through,* rather than light *on.*

The need for more and more profound teachers because of the very medium of television is shadowed in the panel show, at least to the extent that it seems more natural, even since radio, than a single source of comment and information. Two or more teachers in dialogue with each other and with class or audience create exactly that sense of light *through* rather than light *on,* which is the nature of television image or mosaic, as compared with movie or print. In the same way, with the panel, the voice comes, as it were, through the audience, rather than to the audience.

In the same way that industry now makes the consumer the producer by means of motivation research, do not educators now recognize the education problems to be motivation, rather than consumption, of packaged information? The fully motivated student is creative in his consumption and cognition. He is coauthor and coproducer, so that the new teaching must increasingly cast the student in coteacher roles. And, indeed, he is already potentially in such a position because of his vast intake of information in out-of-classroom experience, which is only in part shared by the teacher.

Increasingly the business of education will be discovery and interrelation. And just as industrial production now depends entirely on higher education, and as culture has become the main business of the globe, so learning and not teaching may well become the most highly paid profession. As we begin to learn for participation, rather than for specialist, applied knowledge patterns of action, we can look back and see how the growing habit of conferences already forecasts this change in the roles of teacher and learner. Applied knowledge for production is now taken for granted and knowledge shifts to the global role of community and participation in a way commensurate with the roles of the new media.

X

1959

Academic Rigor

Stanley J. Idzerda

❀❀❀❀❀❀❀❀❀❀❀❀❀❀❀❀❀❀❀❀❀❀❀❀❀❀❀❀❀

Before asking about the presumed effects of the new rigor upon
general education, perhaps it might be best to look into the origins
and means and ends of both general education and the current
stress upon educational rigor. For instance, it may be that the principles of general education have some significance for the current
stress upon educational rigor.

The history of general education in the twentieth century
has a rather Topsy-like quality, with all the overtones of illegitimacy that we usually connect with persons and institutions of uncertain or mixed origins. Generally speaking, I think that general

education was a response to four problems created by institutions of higher education.

First, there was the intellectual smorgasbord of the free elective system. Regardless of its merits, the system gave no guarantee that the student would be exposed to a balanced academic fare. Second, there is the obvious increase in the cash register approach to higher education. Many students enter college simply to be trained in some vocation or profession. Whether the student is seeking expertise in marketing, or in the trade of teaching physics in college, the vocational emphasis comes to the same thing. For those who think the last citadel of liberal education is the small liberal arts college, I refer to Earl McGrath's study of these colleges, *Are Liberal Arts Colleges Becoming Professional Schools?* (New York, 1958), showing that vocational offerings are just about as common there as elsewhere.

Closely related to the professional emphasis is the third factor: intellectual Teutonism at the undergraduate level. Intellectual Teutonism assumes that the student is preparing for an academic specialty in graduate school; each discipline must have its own department, and each student must take a major in a narrow field, as a precursor to graduate work in the same field.

Finally, the comprehensive urban high school, sending enormous numbers of students on to college, has changed drastically the social composition of the collegiate body. For a long time now it has not been safe to assume that all students enter college with the same cultural furniture possessed by a constituency derived almost exclusively from prep schools and the upper middle classes.

Since we are not born with an education, it is safe to say that we are born barbarians. Through a variety of persons, media, and institutions, and finally through our own efforts, we move to a stage which has the attributes of civilization. Formal education is not supposed to be a process by which we exchange one form of barbarism for another, but there is considerable evidence that quite often this is precisely what occurs for the hapless college student.

Whatever may be said of the student who enters college, it seems safe to say that even if his pre-college educational experience was of the best kind available, he still is not an educated person. If he enters college and pursues either an intellectual smorgasbord, intellectual Teutonism, or the cash register, his education will have advanced very little, if at all; the odds are quite good that he will simply have exchanged one form of barbarism for another. The distinguishing feature of the new barbarian is that he probably will possess talents making him more dangerous and more confused than he was before. Certainly there is no incompatibility between being well-informed and being stupid; such a condition makes the student a danger to himself and society.

Among the chief responses to the danger of a new barbarism were the various educational plans at the undergraduate level lumped under the heading of *general education*. We need not consider as general education those plans in which a student must have a distribution of courses in a variety of fields outside his major. A student majoring in business administration takes a course in genetics, inorganic chemistry, the philosophy of Immanuel Kant, and in rural sociology; this may satisfy a distribution, but any connection it has with general education is accidental.

Another response was to provide survey courses which were general enough to give the student a smattering of knowledge in several fields outside his major. The survey course has always been difficult to define. If one attempts to place it in the mainstream of education, one finds that the stream has dried up and all that is left is flotsam and jetsam. To be sure, survey courses have merits: they provide entertainment or soporifics for undergraduates, coin of the realm for authors of texts, and countless jobs for those unrebellious proletarians of academe, the graduate students.

To be sure, distribution and survey are key ideas in any program of general education. However, taken singly or together, and pursued for their own sake, they do not make general education. I would suggest that a viable general education program is based upon a number of considerations which go beyond administrative devices arranged to handle undergraduates before they are ready to take advanced courses.

What are some of these considerations? That man's first vocation is to become what he is—a human being—and that higher education ought to reflect this fact; that the fulfillment of our human vocation in college involves a development of the intellectual virtues: understanding, wisdom, science, prudence, and art. That the pursuit or development of these virtues includes both formal and material elements: the function of the student is not merely to assimilate knowledge as defined by the school; he must be aware that selection, organization, analysis, synthesis, and communication have some significance as well. The curse of a second-rate education is the undiscriminating mind, a mind which assumes all details to be of equal relevance as long as they are facts.

In detail, such considerations mean that the college will see to it that the student's curriculum includes a course or series of courses that enable the student to attempt an integration of what he knows or can know about God, man, and nature. Very simply put, general education is that education which enables the student to know his past, his place in the present, and enables him to communicate with himself and others concerning the questions that should move us all.

This means that the courses are not merely introductions to or surveys of something or other. It means that those involved with a general education program have to do some things quite unusual for a college faculty: instead of assuming that mastery of a subject matter is the first and last prerequisite for the college teacher, the faculty member interested in general education must ask himself the significance of every element in the course being taught, its relationship to other subjects or areas, and, most radical of all, he pays some attention to the quality of his teaching.

Now, what of educational rigor? The new stress upon it has several possible origins. First, nostalgia; a rigorous education is almost always the kind that the last generation got. An important element in this nostalgia is that rigor is identified with the content of the curriculum; the classical curriculum of the genteel tradition is often thought to be more rigorous than any other since that time. Second, it may be that both high school and college have alternate periods of expansion and reexamination. After democratizing educational opportunity, perhaps the educational system must then examine the effects of democratization: Did it mean a broader curriculum or a flabbier one?

Finally, there is the national interest. The Russian schools stand for no nonsense; we are told that we must imitate the Russian emphasis in education or be doomed to defeat by the Russians. We are told also that the technological and scientific needs of the next fifty years are such that we must train many, many more people in the rigorous sciences and mathematics. Manpower and defense needs mean more educational rigor is necessary. If this seems an overstatement, read the National Defense Education Act. I know it seems unpatriotic of me, but the justification of national interest is one of the weakest of all possible arguments when we seek educational change or improvement. It tends to identify the interests of the individual and society with that of the state, or it tends to say that the interests of the state are preeminent.

It also seems to assume that the interests of the state are going to remain stable long enough for educational changes to follow them. If the Russians are as shrewd as everyone seems to think, it is perfectly possible that they have a whole string of secret schools behind the Urals, where they are trying to produce poets and theologians. When our spies discover this, Congress will doubtless decide that poetry and theology are just as important for the survival of a civilization as technology and science. This is not entirely improbable; when we discovered the Russians were interested in piano players as well as missile makers, we gave a rousing national response to Van Cliburn.

As for the specific details of a program stressing educational rigor, they usually run somewhat as follows: a standard curriculum including much more work in mathematics, science, and foreign languages. In what ways these areas will help in the pursuit of the intellectual virtues is not quite clear. All I can see at the moment is that math, science, and language are difficult, and if we stress difficult courses, we are being rigorous; and we should emphasize the subject matter, the content, over any or all other considerations. I submit that the stress upon educational rigor has not been thought out very carefully. Too often it is a mindless reaction to public or official criticism, saying, in effect, if we punish ourselves with things that we do not like or that are difficult, then we are producing the necessary rigor.

I submit further, that the current re-examination may lead the rigorists to the better general education programs. If the stress upon rigor is effective within general education programs, it might eventuate in a renewed emphasis in the field of communications.

What I have in mind is quite simple. I am suggesting that in few courses anywhere is the student taught or required to express himself effectively. It might be well for those in general education to give up the luxury of the specialists, who complain that no one has ever taught their students to write. Second, the emphasis upon rigor might lead those in general education to seek a closer relationship between the work the student takes in general education and the rest of the curriculum. Ideally speaking, all the student's experience in college should contribute to or relate to his general education. If the stress upon rigor does not result in rigor mortis, we may see the values and methods of general education infiltrating every classroom.

XI

1960
Progressive
Philosophy

Harold Taylor

❀❀❀❀❀❀❀❀❀❀❀❀❀❀❀❀❀❀❀❀❀❀❀❀❀❀❀❀

There are two fundamental weaknesses in contemporary American society, a lack of purpose and an overconcern with security. The two weaknesses are directly related to each other and mark a degeneration of American democratic philosophy into a doctrine of hedonism and laissez-faire. Where everything successful is approved, each must decide upon his own satisfactions and his own obligations, and, as Mill says, men "addict themselves to inferior pleasures, not because

111

they deliberately prefer them, but because they are either the only ones to which they have access, or the only ones which they are any longer capable of enjoying." In the absence of constraint, and, as of late, in the absence of leadership, the personal choice of the citizen is conditioned more by what is convenient and materially gratifying than by what is honest, good, and true.

In place of the bold line of progressive thinking, we are content to forsake our own tradition and to establish, without thought, an equilibrium of economic and political forces by simply allowing events to happen as they please and accommodating ourselves to their results. We therefore find ourselves alternately amazed and alarmed as we move from one crisis to the next with improvised policies to meet each one as it comes along.

Nowhere is this seen more clearly than in our public debates about education. Yet the public debates on education reflect the aimlessness of our national policy, the same impulsive jumps from crisis to crisis, the same tendency to run from problems and talk in empty abstractions, the same refusal to come to terms with the real issues of the world of the twentieth century.

The real issues are not ideological. They are practical, and they have to do with establishing means of disarmament, feeding the hungry, teaching the ignorant, building schools, housing the destitute, giving productive work to the unemployed, using science for human welfare, and doing all these things on a world scale.

On the other hand, we do have a philosophy which lies at the heart of our social system, one which not only provides the working plan for a system of government, but which provides the moral and social energy which has made this country great. It has taught us how to deal with practical issues, how to establish a society based on justice, generosity of spirit, equality, and mutual respect. It is a progressive philosophy which broke with the social ideas of the old world and set itself the task of building a new society on truly equalitarian lines. It is pragmatic, experienced, empirical, evolutionary, pluralistic, liberal, and democratic. Emerson was giving it a voice when he asked his famous question, "If there is any period one would desire to be born in, is it not the age of Revolution? When the old and the new stand side by side and admit of being compared; when the energies of all men are searched by fear and hope; when the historic glories of the old can be compensated by the rich possibilities of the new era?"

This is the authentic sound of America. I suggest that we return to our roots in the American tradition and enjoy the possibilities of the new era. I suggest that the optimism of progressive thought is at the center of American achievement, and the old and the new do stand side by side and do admit of being compared. When we compare them we can be proud of the fact that we have a national system of free and democratic education, free from authoritarian control either by church or state, operated by our citizens, and dedicated not only to the intellectual development of American youth, but to their moral and social welfare. We can be proud that this system has invented new forms of education previously unknown in Europe or anywhere else and that it stands as a monument to the democratic ideals of a new society founded in a new world.

There are those who now tell us that progressive philosophy in social and educational matters has weakened our society, that we must turn back to conservative doctrines as we enter the new era. The first thing we must do in education, we are told, is to return to European concepts, separate the sheep from the goats at an earlier age, put some to work with their hands, the others with their heads, select the gifted, stiffen the examinations, raise the requirements, stop trying to educate the whole man and the whole country and concentrate on the intellect and those who possess it.

But what then is our national aim in education? To compete with the Russians in their terms? It is clearly not this. It is to give to every child the education his talents deserve. The purpose in doing that is to open up his life to everything that is possible in the world, and thus to allow him to add his gifts to the total life of his community.

This philosophy is strong, active, and understood among educators. When we say we mean to educate *all* American youth, we mean just that and nothing less. All American youth are not the same; they vary in talent, motivation, and interest; some of them are poor, others rich, some of them city boys, others from the country, some of them are quick to learn, others slow; some of them are boys, some are girls. The progressive idea is to build an education which takes account of who the children are and what they can become. If they are ignorant, what they need is knowledge, not exclusion from further education; if they have not yet learned to learn, if their environment has crushed their curiosity, if they are culturally under-nourished, if their vocabulary is underdeveloped, what they need is teaching which is lively, vigorous, informed, and productive; they need a chance to get started, not more hours of textbook material which they cannot yet handle. If their test scores are low, what they need is a teacher who can find out why and can set about raising them, not someone who classifies them as stupid on the basis of circumstantial evidence. If their teachers are incompetent, what they need is better teaching, not a storm of rhetoric against American education.

The progressive says, education is for everyone; let us have all the students in our colleges who can qualify, let us seek them out. Let us use our universities to raise higher the level of intelligence of our whole population, not looking down at them from a height as if the educated minority were a separate breed possessing the innate virtues of the higher learning.

The progressive says, they are better than you think. The conservative says, they are not what they should be. The progressive says, the child is at a stage in his development, give him a chance to grow; the conservative says, he is not good enough to be promoted. The progressive says, human nature is malleable, mankind is perfectible; the conservative says, human nature is everywhere the same, afflicted with sloth and original sin.

Progressive philosophy rejects, as a start, the idea that there are two separate realms, the mind and the body, one for thought and another for action, one for the liberal arts, another for science and the vocations, or that the intellectual and the ordinary citizen live in different worlds.

To be specific, the philosophy which I am advocating is the philosophy of those practical-minded democrats who founded the state universities, not as sanctuaries for the liberal arts nor as the special preserve of intellectuals, but as institutions of learning which could meet the needs of the people of the state. The natural sciences were obviously important since they provided the knowledge on which agriculture, industry, and the expansion of modern society rested; the social sciences were important because they gave to the people the facts and the insight by which the state could write its tax bills, organize its social welfare, build its communities; the arts were important because they fulfilled the need of the people for experience with aesthetic and cultural values in their daily lives.

For the student with a purpose, at a university which recognizes what that purpose is, there can be no conflict between vocational training and liberal education. The curriculum will contain those studies and will foster those experiences which are significant in the individual lives of the students and are at the same time relevant to the needs of society in which the students will live. Some of them will be scientists, others lawyers, others businessmen, others nurses, teachers, dietitians, doctors, salesmen, farmers. But if their university education has been successful, they will be prepared to take the role in society for which their talents are best suited, and they will at the same time be liberally educated, that is to say, they will be interested in the arts, in ideas, in thinking critically and creatively about their society, in forming standards of taste and of judgment about the culture which surrounds them.

We must rescue the idea of *vocation* from the disrepute into which it has fallen and the misuse to which it has been put. Training in the techniques of fly-fishing, basketball playing, business practice, radio repair, or personal charm is not the responsibility of the scholars and teachers of a university. Such training where needed can best be given in institutions designed for that purpose, and we need make no apology for such institutions if they do what they are intended to do. On the other hand, the essence of the liberal arts is not that they are nonvocational. They are directly related to one's vocation. A vocation is a calling, something to which the individual is drawn by talent and interest, something to which he is called. The liberal arts furnish the forms of experience through which the individual can learn to make discriminating judgments about himself and his world, and the truly educated man is one who has learned to use what he has in ways which are productive both to himself and to his society.

It is for this reason that the progressive philosophy advocates the fusion of the liberal and the vocational, the practical and the theoretical, in one curriculum. It puts its emphasis on the practice of the creative arts rather than on textbooks about them, but in so doing does not intend to ignore the study of those works of art which are classics in history. Similarly, a progressive philosophy urges the use of contemporary materials in the curriculum of politics and social studies, the use of direct experience with political and social phenomena, but not at the expense of the wider views to be obtained through the study of history and the literature of the past.

How then is education related to the national purpose? What do we have to do with establishing a national purpose? Certainly we must take account of the national need for scientists, engineers, linguists, and skilled workers of all kinds to strengthen the national defense. Certainly we must improve the range and quality of the high school curriculum by enriching the content of our courses in science, mathematics, history, and languages. The students are ready for it whenever we are. But the purpose in doing so is not merely to maintain American prosperity and military security by recruiting technically trained manpower. The national purpose is to establish a just and peaceful world order in which we as the greatest democratic power take the leadership in democracy. We therefore need to concentrate our national attention on the proposition that a free society in a free world can only be achieved when our educational system has not only taught its citizens the skills and techniques necessary to run a modern industrial society, but has taught them to believe in the generosity of heart, the boldness of imagination, and the liberal ideals of a truly democratic philosophy.

XII

1961
The Happy Crisis

Charles Frankel

❀❀❀❀❀❀❀❀❀❀❀❀❀❀❀❀❀❀❀❀❀❀❀❀❀❀❀❀❀❀

The permanent business of higher education is almost always mis-defined, it seems to me. Almost every approach to higher education in the United States begins by pointing to the existence of certain problems and asking whether our educational institutions can solve these problems. I do not mean to imply that we do not have problems. I certainly do not mean to imply that colleges and universities have no responsibility to solve them, if they can. But the proper function of higher education, broadly speaking, is not to solve problems; it is to create them. In any free civilization, the college or the university is not simply an instrument of the society to which it belongs; it is one of the special places where we find the meaning of that society. Higher learning is the meaning of a civilization or a considerable part of the meaning or function of the civilization. It represents a society's efforts at self-consciousness. It is an attempt to know the world around it, to know itself, and to stand back and appraise its condition and its commitments.

If higher education does its job, the society will be aware of problems otherwise unknown. More, the society will have problems, proud problems, the problems of civilized men which it would not have had if higher learning did not exist. For insofar as institutions of learning raise questions about standards and ideals, they ask men to consider their own conscience. Insofar as universities produce new knowledge, they invite and encourage and cause a collision with traditional pieties, with old institutions. Higher learning in a society means that that society is in a permanent state of disequilibrium, and it is for that reason that higher learning has so often been suspected.

It is the barest of commonplaces that American higher education today is in a condition of crisis; but the commonplace is an ancient one, at any rate as Americans measure time. Those who have been associated with American higher education have almost always thought that our colleges and universities were in a condition of crisis, and they have been right. For higher education, which in most countries has an inherently conservative and backward-looking orientation, has had to be in the United States an instrument for regulating and stabilizing an explosive movement into modernity.

Almost all our problems in higher education, past and present, have arisen out of the fact that the American—the new man, as de Crèvecoeur called him—is the exponent and apostle of modernity, and the problems that our educational systems have rehearsed and are still rehearsing are rapidly becoming today the problems of most educational systems throughout the world. The problems with which we are now concerned, the problems which we seem to think have exploded in our faces, are not in fact new problems. They are old problems simply brought to sharper focus, and they are the

problems that are peculiar to a modern culture, a permanently un-
settled, heterogeneous, and impious culture: The problem is that of
training young men and women in highly specialized skills needed
by a modern society while at the same time opening their eyes to
what lies outside their specialties; the problem is that of retaining
and rebuilding the essentially aristocratic tradition of liberal learning in a democratic climate; the problem is that of connecting technology to the ideals of liberal civilization; and finally, the problem
is that of negotiating and mitigating the extraordinary tensions between traditional elements in our culture and the scientific elements.

Let us briefly examine each of these problems. In the first
place, we have as part of our unfinished business a kind of chronic
disease with which we have to live, the problem of trying to bring
together specialized training and broad general education. The problem is aggravated in the United States because our educational system
is, in large part, the product of a mismarriage. At the undergraduate
level, most of our educational institutions were conceived and created
in the Anglo-Saxon mold. At the graduate and professional level
most of our educational institutions were conceived in the mold of
continental education in France or Germany. Anglo-Saxon education is not, perhaps, a theory of education; it is something even
deeper, an inbred habit of thought. I recall the first time that I
visited Oxford. I had just left France where I was residing and
where I knew a good many teachers and students at the Sorbonne.
At Oxford I dropped into a bookstore and among other things
bought a little guidebook. The first sentence said, "The University
of Oxford exists to train character." I could not have imagined finding such a sentence in any book in France on French education.

Anglo-Saxon education is intended to be, as American education is intended, too, not simply a training of the mind but of that
impalpable and not easy to locate entity known as character. Anglo-
Saxon education had tried to do this in a special way. The differences between John Dewey and his opponents are very slim indeed
when looked at against the background of other systems of education. Almost all American schools from the grade school on up have
tried to provide the individual student with a special little microcosm
of the adult world. They have tried to provide the student with something like a planned and total environment. In this environment, the

student is expected to rehearse, to practice the skills which he will have to have as an adult. So, he must learn how to get along with the group; he must, of course, learn to read and write, go in for dramatics, journalism, regular exercise, and all the rest.

The American college is student oriented, it is a home away from home. It is, indeed, more than a home. In its intent it is a community, a sheltered community where people will be hurt, but not hurt very badly, where they can practice most of the skills they will need later on, but not on issues that are really serious or final. So American students are tremendously interested in politics. They are by no means apathetic, but you must see them in their student governments to see their interest in politics. They are not as interested, or at any rate they are not as active, in politics on the streets of great cities as are students in Paris or Cairo. As a result, very often American students show a good deal more practical know-how about political organizations than their Continental counterparts. They know a great deal less, however, about ideology, which may or may not be a good thing.

On the other hand, however, the graduate or professional school brings a different temper and a different spirit into the university atmosphere. It exists not to train individuals as individuals, but to treat individuals as instruments for maintaining a discipline. The graduate school has the attitude of the specialist. A graduate professor looks upon his students as apprentices in his own discipline, as targets for his ideas, as aides in his research. The problem of specialization versus general education, therefore, is a peculiarly difficult problem to solve. It is difficult because we occupy houses that are divided against themselves. The spirit and temper of our universities and our colleges are, as it were, self-alienated. People look in two directions at once, and so it is extremely difficult to come up with any coherent program.

I am not at all sure that this is entirely bad. Like many chronic diseases it probably produced a state of siege, an attitude of sorts. It is a very serious and difficult problem. I think the issue is frequently misstated when it is conceived to be an issue between practical or vocational or professional training on the one side and liberal education on the other. Liberal education is not the same thing as general education. Nor for that matter is general education incompatible with a high degree of specialization in some disciplines. A liberal education is not, in fact, a specific group of subjects; it is not any definite curriculum or program of study. A liberal education is an education conducted in a certain way with a certain purpose from a certain point of view.

The heart of the matter is this. We train people liberally in a subject when at all times we try to expose the working of the human mind in that subject, when we try to show how it is an achievement of mind, when we try to expose the elements of logic, of imagination, of historical perspective, or moral meaning in any subject. To do so is an extraordinarily difficult thing to do, but one can teach chemistry liberally, and one can teach English and even philosophy vocationally, professionally, narrowly. The distinction between liberal education and specialized education is not a real distinction. The important distinction is between liberal education and purely vocational education. There are some subjects that have to be vocational and can only be that. Typewriting is an example, but there are very few subjects in college or university curricula that are vocational—doomed as it were to be vocational subjects. If there are, it is the teacher who makes them so. So in a large part the problem is not going to be solved by great, sweeping programs. It is going to be solved by getting educated, liberal teachers.

If we can take the specialized discipline, train people in it, but open the windows and the walls of that discipline so, from a given point of view, they can look out on the gardens that are adjacent, we have done what we should do, giving them a solid, civilized education in a specialty and at the same time substantial general or generalizing education.

The second great problem—another problem of unfinished education in America—has to do with the domestication of the liberal arts tradition as a tradition of liberal learning in an essentially democratic environment. This is an extraordinarily difficult thing to do for a number of reasons. The first reason I have already suggested: To teach people liberally requires that we try to fix their minds and imaginations not on what is immediately in front of them, not on some specific practical objective, but on ideas and ideals. The second reason that we have a very difficult problem here is that the tradition of liberal education is an essentially aristocratic tradition, aristocratic by nature and aristocratic also by historical pedigree. It is aristocratic by nature simply because learning is an arduous thing. No one has really got the spirit of an education, the spirit of learning, unless he has seen the kind of self-mastery and self-discipline that any achievement in the arts and sciences requires.

At the same time, however, we live in an impatient, mobile, restless, democratic environment. I am not sorry about it, and unlike a good many of my colleagues I do not think there is an iron law which says that democracy kills liberal learning. On the contrary, I am rather aware of the fact that in many, many societies, higher education has broken down into a kind of esotericism, a kind of preciosity which is of no service to society and is not very good higher learning either. So I rather like a society which looks upon intellectuals with a certain measure of skepticism. I live with intellectuals, and with bitter experience I know I look at them with a certain measured and sometimes unmeasured skepticism, myself included. I sometimes think it would be nice to live in a society in which it was habitual to think that a man with a title of professor was really a distinguished man, but I have seen what that habit does to the professor who enjoys it. He thinks he is very distinguished, too, and sometimes without any supporting evidence. A serving of skepticism and even a tiny soupçon of anti-intellectualism is helpful to keep intellectuals on their mettle.

Accordingly, I rather like the tension between democratic tradition and the special aristocratic tradition of liberal learning. There are, of course, very great problems here. In a democratic society higher education comes to serve very special functions. One of them is that higher education becomes the principal social escalator. The reason most young people are in schools in America is that they hope to get more money as a result, or else to have somewhat higher social positions than their parents did. I do not think that is dishonorable. I think it is not less dishonorable, or no less honorable, than the motive that brought the children of aristocracy to schools a century ago. Wanting money is as honorable as wanting to ride after the hounds. After all, the desires for money and for social position are strong desires and may help students to apply themselves. If we did not do so much to distract them and perhaps to cushion them, perhaps they would do it. But more important, it is a remarkable evolution in the history of mankind that the major pathway to social advancement should be higher education. That is the problem with which we are faced. I think every professor ought to rejoice, and I think it is one of the reasons we are in the midst of quite a happy crisis in higher education.

At the same time, however, the problem is a serious one. If we try to satisfy all the consumers without erecting very careful safeguards, we will be going in for a species of democratic demagoguery. Very careful safeguards have to be erected if the standards of liberal learning are to be maintained. There has always been a tendency in the United States to survey broadly, to cheapen, to turn learning into the hobby of the dilettante—the democratic dilettante, which almost is a contradiction in its term—and I think that our universities and colleges have to take severe steps to prevent this cheapening process from taking place.

Moreover, there is another issue involved here, that of shifting the perspective of traditional liberal education. No liberal education in a democratic environment can have quite the perspective it once did. In the past, the graduates of a great university went into the elite positions in the nations. They knew they were members of the elite when they entered and they knew they had a steady and secure position, if they wanted it, when they left. Moreover, they came from backgrounds which had already acquainted them with the world of learning, as such. In contrast, in a democratic environment, most of the young men and young women who go through our schools are going back to relatively modest positions in life. The women in particular are going to spend their most vigorous years largely doing manual work, and we must reflect on the fact that we are now giving collegiate education, and sometimes even graduate education, to people who are then going to go out the next twenty years and be hewers of wood and drawers of water. Now, poverty is one of the indispensable conditions in life. But we are an affluent society and it is harder for many of us to be gentlemen. How can we give a kind of education which will cling and will stick? How can we give a kind of education that will change the perspective of young people when they get it and give them one which will stay with them after they have left?

The problem is a problem of seduction. It is not a problem

of fitting their motives, but of using the motives they have and luring them into an appreciation of the broader world of learning.

A third issue is the great problem of maintaining the traditions of higher education in a society that is in love with technology. We have all sorts of contradictory images of ourselves these days, we Americans that do not fuse at all. They tell us we are undisciplined and conformists, sodden with materialism and aching for a cause, and all the rest. The images do not fuse. In particular, we tell ourselves that we are materialists and we point to our booming technology as one of the illustrations or proofs of this point. But American technology is in its own way not a proof of materialism or even a love of gadgetry. It provides a curiously moral, aesthetic, and almost religious sense of proportion to our society and to our institutions of higher learning. In order to provide that civilizing sense of proportion, however, technologists have to be able to keep first things first, to know what their main business is. I do not mean to suggest that specialized research, in space, for example, is not worth doing. It is worth doing in the interest of national defense; it is worth doing in the interest of science. But the most important reason for wanting to do such research is that it contributes to the long-range purposes of science.

This brings us to the final great problem. In the United States, the greatest danger to our conception of the intellectual life comes from our preoccupation with technology. As a result of that preoccupation, we have absorbed the image of science and the image of technology. Until recently, and perhaps even today, most Americans confuse Thomas Edison with a scientist. He was an inventor, but only a scientist of sorts. Science is not organized gadgetry; it exists to provide knowledge for its own sake, to give us some understanding of the order of things insofar as is given to us to understand that order.

For this point of view, we come to a fundamentally difficult problem, perhaps not acute in America, but a problem in Western civilization. The college or university that carries on its activity in a climate of freedom is not just an instrument of a free civilization; it is one of the special places where we find the meaning of that civilization. So it is perhaps natural that the deepest intellectual and moral division in our civilization is felt with peculiar intensity on our college and university campuses. I refer to the conflict between means and ends, techniques and values, or science and the humanities. The mere form in which this issue is stated is a reflection of that conflict, a reinforcement of it, and, I think, the expression of a dangerous and exhausting illusion.

The argument, properly construed, is not between those who are engaged in expanding human powers on one side and those on the other who are guardians of the heritage of the human spirit. Science is part of that heritage—an unwelcome part, because it overthrows a good many other parts of the heritage. It is perfectly true that science gives no authoritative or final answer to questions about human values, but then do the humanities? Despite the differences between science and the humanities, both are, or ought to be, examples of disciplined intelligence, of refined analysis, of sober respect for evidence, of taste in the selection of problems, and in the organization of them. The real argument is not between subjects. It is between two rather different conceptions of what is the meaning of evidence, what is the nature of intelligence. The source of that argument is the challenge which the scientific style and spirit have presented to those who have traditionally occupied special positions of authority as arbiters of cultural, moral, and social knowledge. The scientific philosopher makes life hard for the metaphysician; the sociologist breaks into the conversation of the teacher of literature and asks for evidence to support the producer of literature's association with our culture.

But the main issue is the question of the nature of intellectual authority, the kind of answer which a society is going to regard as a good answer. The problem that science creates for all of us is a very complicated one. It has two essential features which illustrate its discomfort. The first is that science almost never answers the question the ordinary man and the humanities want answered. So science seemingly is an evasion. But it is not; it is a triumph over ignorant questions. It is a reformulation of the question. There are some questions, indeed most questions, of common sense which we cannot answer, and we cannot answer them because they are foolish questions. That hurts, and that is part of the problem.

The second part of the problem is that science almost never gives us an answer that really says something definitely because it

does not say yes or no. It says "yes, but . . ." or "no, in this respect. . . ." It is really a complicated problem, and it is a dozen
problems, and we will have to go after them one by one. We stand
by while science is subordinated to the humanities. Science does not
answer the mystery of life—it has told a lot more about that mystery
than it told us one hundred years before, but it has not solved the
mystery. It has insulted our traditional culture in a sense. It would
not pay attention to *the* mystery but would look into the mysteries.
This is the abominable snowman which Sir Charles Snow has called
the conflict between the two cultures. I have considerable sympathy
with the view he expressed. Although I am a professor in what con-
ventionally is thought to be one of the new mystic disciplines, I have
noted that on the whole my colleagues in the department of literature regard themselves as highly educated men because they read
novels and regard scientists as illiterate because they only read books
in physics. Whereas, I have noticed that most scientists actually read
novels, and they know a good deal beyond the discipline which the
average professor of literature thinks is a civilized learning discipline.
There is a conflict between two cultures. However, unlike Sir
Charles, I do not think that our ability to win the cold war, or even to
give aid to underdeveloped nations, depends on our ability to solve
this problem. That would be a depressing view of our situation. I
think it is unjustified. I do not think the arguments between the
scientists and the humanists are going to die in our time. I do not
know when, if ever, they are going to die. I rather suspect they will
die when men conquer the tendency to go in for wishful thinking
and quick answers. Until that happens, I think the conflict will remain.

As long as the argument remains in its present form, however, there is one thing we probably will not do very well. We will
not do liberal education very well. We will not do university education very well. As long as the discussion continues to be surrounded
by eagerness for the easy, sweeping answer, by arrogance and by a
kind of stubborn ignorance, there is very little likelihood that we are
going to get very far in dealing with the fundamental issue in liberal
education. At the very least, a substantive education in one of the
sciences is a prerequisite for any educated man in our society. To
give him less than that is to shut the door to his appreciation of

some of the most majestic achievements of our culture. In the Middle Ages, things were there for everyone to see. Most people who had experience putting one stone on top of another could understand the kind of achievement the cathedral represented. They could not do it, they did not know how the architect conceived it. But they understood it was quite a glorious achievement. That elementary kind of appreciation is denied to the great majority of educated men in our civilization. The sciences are not more important than the other disciplines, but substantive education in the sciences, education for its own sake in the sciences, is a very high priority matter in the coming decade. And, education ought to begin where most education should begin—with the education of the college and university faculties.

The trouble with the scientists is that life has been so good to them recently that they are no longer interested in teaching. They get better-paying jobs, or they can do something else and look as though they are teaching. Scientists have a habit, like other professional groups, of saying they are not popular. The self-image of professors in America is lower than the image that the outside world has. Sociologists show that the professor is one of the most highly respected people in America. It is the professors who think they are not. We must not worry about that, because doctors have a deplorable image of themselves, and lawyers. The members of every group think we do not like them. We are a very self-conscious society. So, scientists complain they are looked upon with suspicion, and, in view of the loud bang some of them are responsible for making, I suppose they are looked upon with mixed feelings. I look upon them, too, with mixed feelings. They have a major job of education to do. The great imaginative task in the coming decade is that task of liberal education for the laymen in the sciences. Unless a good many scientists make this a major part of their professional commitment, the job is unlikely to be done very well.

Now, let us look briefly at two new issues which I think have not been located or perhaps quite properly defined. A modernist in a society like ours is always in danger of becoming a kind of split personality. This is particularly true when his work becomes more highly specialized in its demands and when on the other side the habit of consuming goes up and up. What is that split personality?

On one side, our work sinks into routine. On the other side, our play, our leisure, or what we choose to call our "culture" becomes increasingly disorganized and frivolous. But the sharp division between work and play, machinery and culture, science and the humanities, is itself a sign of man's age-old battle with scarcity—a hangover from that battle. In a society as wealthy as ours, such divisions are increasingly anachronistic. The problem is to unite discipline and spontaneity, usefulness and culture, work and play.

One of the fundamental problems waged by every society moving toward modernity has been the struggle against illiteracy. The colleges and universities of the United States have in the past been part of that struggle. In the coming decade I think they are going to wage a battle against a new kind of illiteracy—creeping illiteracy of adult human beings in a world in which they have been turned loose with more leisure than before, illiteracy about the uses of leisure or the meaning of leisure. To call the process in which our colleges and universities engage adult education is a misnomer, for education suggests preparation for something and I am not thinking of preparation. I am thinking of an invitation, as it were, to a consuming and concentrated task. Our society is rich enough and, in terms of its best and most traditional culture, it ought to offer its members a challenge for the kind of play that is the best kind, the kind that is like work or at any rate the best work, disciplined, cumulative, with a chance to perform and to achieve. The colleges and universities are the agencies to perform this task, and they are in the years to come going to have to change themselves over increasingly. Instead of being merely an exclusive training ground for the young, instead of going in for adult education as a form of advertising or an easy form for raising money, they are going to have to take it for granted that they are in America, and have been what the medieval church was in its day—a great shelter for human culture and human achievement.

The process for transforming the lost weekends and lost leisure hours of Americans into something that will help them to demonstrate and find themselves is a process to which I should like to see our colleges and universities commit themselves.

The second new issue is this: The democratic process depends on the state of communication, but communications in our society are warped by the pressures of the marketplace, burdened by the difficulties of the matters to be communicated, and inherently complicated by the fact that today just to report the news is to make news. An event is not simply what happens, it is what is reported. That plays back on the event, expanding its area and transmuting it into something other than it would have been if it were allowed to play out its career in private. I do not mean to say that the newspapers create events or make them important. I mean to say only that in an open society, in a society in which people want news, the fact that they get the news expands the area of conflict. It is, therefore, terribly important that those who get brought into the conflict by way of communications be reasonably well prepared to understand what is going on. That, of course, is terribly difficult, but it is particularly difficult in a society in which most of our news services, most of our public affairs services, are geared to the moment, the shock, the sensational. Bad news, from a journalist's point of view, is good news; good news is no news. And long-range news is a bore. One cannot understand the nature of the world he inhabits so long as information comes to him in that form and only in that form every day.

I do not know quite how to produce a revolution in this area, but I do think that once again a society as diversified, as plural, as ours ought to be able to provide those citizens who care with other media of communication—media of information that offer an alternative, a standard, a way of judging what they are getting as daily fare. Once again, the colleges and universities have an extraordinary opportunity and responsibility in this area—in radio, in television, in magazines, and in communicating with a large and eager general audience. I do not know whether they can do this individually or regionally or through an association like the Association for Higher Education, but there is a long-range job to be done if the level of communications in the United States is to be raised, and once more it looks to me as if the obvious candidate for the job is the higher educational system.

We do, then, have a burdensome, difficult set of issues to deal with, but they are old issues. It is fortunate, it is a happy crisis when we are aware, as we are now aware, that we have these problems. It is also fortunate that, for the first time in the history of American higher education, a very large and broad public is looking upon all of us with considerable curiosity and interest. If we do badly, we will hear about it.

XIII

1962
The Goal of
Individual
Development

Nevitt Sanford

꙳꙳꙳꙳꙳꙳꙳꙳꙳꙳꙳꙳꙳꙳꙳꙳꙳꙳꙳꙳꙳꙳꙳꙳꙳

The development of the individual personality must be a major objective of societies such as ours.

How may we conceive of a highly developed person? How may he be recognized and understood? How is change in the direction of higher levels of development to be brought about? How does the aim of optimal personality development interact with other basic aims, and how and to what extent do means adopted for one purpose favor or hamper the achievement of others? In discussing these questions I shall limit myself to youth of college age, and inquire into some of the conditions and processes of developmental change in this age range.

The ideal of the fullest possible development of the individual is an ancient one to which men have rededicated themselves many times during the past two thousand years. Yet it is an ideal that is continuously in need of clarification and reformulation. What we value in individuals is bound to be influenced by our times and circumstances. And our conception of the highest development is bound to be shaped by our knowledge of what is possible. The limits of human potentiality are still unknown; hence any conception of the ideally developed person must be open-ended. Nevertheless, it is possible, and desirable, to achieve a conception that is consistent with existing theoretical and empirical knowledge.

From the point of view of psychology, a high level of development in personality is characterized most essentially by complexity and by wholeness. There is a high degree of *differentiation,* a large number of different parts or features having different and specialized functions; and a high degree of *integration,* a state of affairs in which communication among parts is great enough so that different parts may, without losing their essential identity, become organized into larger wholes in order to serve the larger purposes of the person. In the highly developed person there is a rich and varied impulse life—feelings and emotions having become differentiated and civilized; conscience has been broadened and refined, and it is enlightened and individualized, operating in accord with the individual's best thought and judgment; the processes by which the person judges events and manages actions are strong and flexible, being adaptively responsive to the multitudinous aspects of the environment, and at the same time in close enough touch with the deeper sources of emotion and will so that there is freedom of imagination and an enduring capacity to be fully alive. This highly developed structure underlies the individual's sense of direction, his freedom of thought and action, and his capacity to carry out commitments to others and to himself. But the structure is not fixed once and for all. The highly developed individual is always open to new experience and capable of further learning; his stability is fundamental in the sense that he can go on developing while remaining essentially himself.

We appreciate the goal of optimal individual development best when we think of our own children and what we want for them; other people's children can have their talents discovered, processed, and put to work in the interest of purposes they do not necessarily share. All the resources of society should be utilized for the development of children and youth. This is mainly what a society is for. If suitable agencies and institutions do not exist, they will have to be created.

The school of hard knocks will not do. Perhaps there was a time when it was reasonable to believe that critical events at an early age, such as taking a man's job at fourteen or getting married at sixteen, had a maturing effect. I believe we know better today. Deeply challenging experiences are necessary to development all right, but their benefits depend heavily upon readiness for them. Taking a responsible job is by no means the same experience for a fourteen-year-old that it is for a twenty-one-year-old; and if it were postponed for a few more years, it might be even more meaningful. The same thing may be said of leaving home, going abroad, getting married. There is an optimum time for such experiences— a time when they are not so threatening as to lead to regression or so long delayed as to hold little promise; a time when they are richly meaningful because they can be connected with a broad background of other experiences and a wide range of capabilities for response.

Another great disadvantage of the early assumption of adult roles, and of premature commitment to the later assumption of a particular role, such as a vocational one, is that the individual is thus prevented from having experiences that could be vital in his development. He is restricted not only in his freedom of movement but in respect to possible ways of looking at things. The rate of development slows down sharply when men and women leave college and take on adult responsibilities. We should not expect more when people have to do this before they finish high school.

Probably these considerations hold cross-culturally. There

are relatively underdeveloped countries in which boys go to work at ten and girls get married at twelve. Perhaps they become in some sense adapted to their relatively simple societies, but no one would claim that they realize their human potentialities. It seems that some kind of social wisdom has decreed that as societies become more complex and affluent, they postpone longer and longer the time of the young person's full participation in adult life. The European aristocracies expected little of men before they were thirty.

There is wisdom, and psychological theory, to support the notion that the longer the period of preparation for adult life, the richer and more productive that life will be. In this country, at this time in our history, we can afford to make this period of waiting as long as we like, and we cannot in our democracy restrict its benefits to any privileged group. As in the early 1930's, but for quite different reasons, these are great times for focusing on the development of youth. Actually we are bound to. The vast armies of unemployed youth will swell as automation continues to increase the efficiency of our production. It is no good training youth for jobs that do not exist, or that will not exist by the time their training is complete. And jails and reformatories are not by any means the least expensive institutions that can be contrived. One of the great benefits of personality development, from the point of view of society's needs, is that it generates taste for things—and for services—that cannot be produced by automated devices, just as it generates productive activities that cannot be duplicated by machines.

If the school of hard knocks is out, what about psychotherapy and counseling? Here we have another means for developing the individual. Freud, it may be recalled, envisioned an army of social workers who would practice psychoanalysis or psychoanalytically oriented therapy for all who needed it. And today, enlightened practitioners of the psychological healing arts state their goals in developmental terms. Curing symptoms or relieving suffering is secondary to the development of autonomy and wholeness. But the ideal of an army of social workers or other professionals who could by means of individual or group psychotherapy take care of all failures in development seems a bit impractical. More than that, we have to say on theoretical grounds that psychotherapy as a means for inducing development is severely limited. It can indeed remove barriers to development, but it is no substitute for all those experiences, mostly vicarious ones, that expand the range of stimuli that have relevance for the individual, and that increase the power and diversity of his capacities for response.

It appears that the kind of institution that is needed will have to be very much like a college. If colleges did not exist, they would have to be invented. Even if we should set up youth reservations, or work camps, or overseas projects, or kinds of facilities or organizations for which no models yet exist, it would be necessary to offer instruction and exercises of a more or less intellectual nature.

Development after the age of about two, after the acquisition of language, is in considerable part a cognitive—one might even say "intellectual"—matter. It involves in a crucial way the use of symbols—words, images, thoughts. Development is largely a matter of expanding the range of things that can be appreciated, and the range of responses—largely involving the use of symbols—that can be made. Books, with their gift of boundless vicariousness, are a great benefit to parents or teachers who would develop personalities. It is through utilizing the symbols of this culture, in the life of the imagination, that the individual may most appropriately, and most joyfully, express his deepest impulses and feelings. It is through solving problems with the use of his intelligence—typically in the manipulation of symbols—and through being held to the requirement of seeking, and being guided by, the truth, that the individual develops, through exercise, the functions that enable him to control himself, in accord with the demands of reality. And it is largely through confrontation by a wide range of value systems and ethical dilemmas that conscience becomes enlightened and therefore stabilized.

What I am arguing is that the human individual is all of a piece. He functions as a unit, and his diverse features develop in interaction one with another. Intelligence, feeling, emotion, action can be separated conceptually, but no one of them functions independently of the others.

We know this from our own experience. *Our* productive work is a very passionate affair; creative endeavor leaves us limp with emotional exhaustion, and the hot pursuit of truth keeps us jumping with excitement. And for *us* to learn anything new, to have our minds changed, we have first to be practically shattered as personalities and then put together again. Why then should students be regarded as cool and well-oiled machines for storing and retrieving information? There is something to be said for teaching machines, for they may spare the teacher some machine-like work, but there is nothing to be said for a learning machine.

It is frequently said that the proper concern of higher education is with the intellect only. But the notion that the intellect is somehow disembodied, or separated from the rest of the personality, is not only unintelligent, in that it favors no legitimate educational aim, it is actually perverse in its implications, in that it encourages the assumption that if one takes it upon himself to be a student he cannot at the same time be a human being. I would go so far as to say that those who talk the most about training the cognitive, as if they were the sole guardians of these functions, are far from being successful in their efforts to promote cognitive development. They attempt the impossible; for the cognitive normally develops in pace with the rest of the personality, just as development of the whole person, as I believe I have shown, depends heavily upon exercise of the cognitive functions.

Just as nothing is truly learned until it has been integrated with the purposes of the individual, so no facts and principles that have been learned can serve any worthy human purpose unless they are restrained and guided by character. Intellect without humane feeling can be monstrous, while feeling without intelligence is childish; intelligence and feeling are at their highest and in the best relation one to the other where there is a taste for art and beauty as well as an appreciation of logic and of knowledge.

We may wonder where some educators and educational spokesmen got the idea of the disembodied intellect that is to be developed through the intake, storing, and reproduction of data. Certainly not from the observation of what goes on when learning occurs in college. I am afraid they got it from psychology. Psychologists not only abstract processes such as cognition and learning from their living context, as I have indicated, but they commonly seek to isolate these processes experimentally, in the hope of obtaining precise information and demonstrating general laws. In consequence there is a vast literature—and even a vast, indigestible undergraduate curriculum—in which perception is treated independently of the perceiver and learning independently of the learner. Apparently this kind of psychology still has influence upon education. The abstractions of the psychological experimenter have been reified, and are used to rationalize current practices. There is irony in the fact that the vaunted general laws derived from laboratory experiments are not really general. They break down as soon as a new variable is introduced into the situation; and since in real life numerous additional variables are at work, it is impossible to go directly from the laboratory to applications in school.

But we should not blame too much the present generation of psychological experimenters. They were probably taught by college professors who thought they could train the intellect without touching the rest of the personality. Such professors very probably were under the influence of the know-nothing behaviorism of the 1920's, and this could be understood as an outgrowth of a long tradition in which the narrowly cognitive or mentalistic has dominated in Western approaches to knowledge.

I do not want to suggest that there is no psychology that is applicable to learning in college. There is a fair amount. Of particular relevance are studies of the modification of belief systems, of attitude change, or development over time of social perception. Indeed I rely upon such studies for the argument being made here.

The argument that development in intellectual functioning goes with development in other features of the personality is based on evidence such as the following. When personality tests are given to entering freshmen, and then to sophomores, juniors, and seniors, it is found that such basic characteristics as freedom in the expression of impulse, independence of pressures toward conformity, sense of social responsibility, and sensitivity to ethical issues increase on the average with length of time in college—that is, in a good liberal arts college like Vassar. Obviously such changes are far more pronounced in some students than in others. Some actually go backward. Now ask faculty members, as Donald Brown did, to identify those students who most resemble the "ideal" college product. It turns out that, in general, students who are thus singled out are those who stand highest on the measured personality traits. We may be sure that college teachers in expressing their conception

of the ideal student put the stress on intellectual characteristics—
though not necessarily, as the data show, on the fact of earning
high grades.

Again, a great deal of research—at the Institute of Personality Assessment and Research at Berkeley, and elsewhere—has
been directed to the determination of what personality traits are
associated with creativity. Creativity in students is rated by their
teachers, in professionals by their peers, and personality traits are
estimated by a variety of assessment techniques. Here the basic
fact is that the traits that distinguish the creative from the noncre-
ative are essentially the same as those that distinguish college seniors
from freshmen. The picture of the creative person that emerges
then is that of a relatively highly developed person.

But now we come to a serious complication. Certainly not
all creative people are of the type described. I have known creative
artists and musicians who were spoiled, difficult and, far from being
mature, actually infantile in psychological make-up. And I have
seen ten-year-old boys who could solve, like lightning, mathematical
puzzles that completely frustrated a group of distinguished behavioral scientists. We are talking now about talent. And we must
admit that it may exist in a wide variety of psychological house-
holds, including some that are pretty unattractive by conventional
standards. Creative performance by some people, in some areas
of activity, it must be admitted, cannot be regarded as all of a piece
with the development of the total personality.

Some time ago I took part in a symposium on creativity,
and in advance of our meeting I sent in some rough notes on what
I had planned to talk about. I mentioned rather cryptically "the
Nobel prize winner with a ten-year-old mentality." Of course, I
was merely trying to be dramatic, and I was expressing an old prejudice against the physical scientist so distinguished that he is asked
to speak on any subject under the sun, and who is so unwise as to
participate in the popular image of his authority; being easily in-
duced to get beyond his depth, he reveals primitive tastes, social
insensitivity, and narrow, parochial, or even jingoist values. What
was my surprise then to discover, on arriving at the conference,
that my colleagues had been discussing which Nobel prize winner
I was talking about.

Of course, the value of a contribution does not depend on the personality of the man who makes it. From the point of view of society's needs and wants, it does not matter how immature its artists, musicians, mathematicians, and natural scientists might be. It does matter in the case of other fields of endeavor. Certainly it is hard to see how a man can create anything in social science or psychology or certain kinds of literature without first having much deep experience and undergoing much development in his personality. And in the case of the special or God-given talents for music, mathematics, and so on, there is nothing to suggest that immaturity is a necessary condition for their display. We could safely bring our hypothetical Nobel prize winner up to, say, the age of eighteen without endangering his creative potential.

When we consider society's obligation to the individual, we can see good reasons why it should be at special pains to develop the personalities of its talented people. Such people are very likely to be exploited by society. Historically, natural scientists have been set to making gun powder, artists to entertaining their masters. Natural science and art have flourished under the older tyrannies and under modern ones. One may wonder if the practitioners of these specialties, who became pliable tools of the powerful, had any way of knowing what was happening to them.

Talent belongs to the individual—not to society and not, let us constantly remind ourselves, to his family. It is, of course, a shame when talent is not developed. It is a shame when *any* constructive human potentiality is not developed.

However, higher education has other goals besides that of individual development, and it is possible to debate the relative importance of these goals. I put individual development first because in my view it is the most important goal in its own right. If you were to say it is more important that the individual be adjusted to his society, I would reply that it is more important that he be able to transform society. But I also argue that individual development should have first attention because it is favorable to the achievement of all other legitimate goals. Is it our aim to preserve culture? This can best be done by individuals who have been developed to a point where they can appreciate it. Do we wish to create culture? This is mainly done by highly developed individuals, though I have admitted some important exceptions. Is it our desire to train people for vocations that require technical skills? If this can be done at all in college, it is through the development of qualities that are valuable in a great variety of jobs. Preparation for a high-level profession? Good performance in any profession depends heavily upon qualities found only in highly developed individuals. Ask professors of engineering to characterize a good engineer, and they will list such qualities as leadership, capacity to make wise decisions, flexibility of thinking, and so on. They ask how such characteristics are to be produced and, receiving no answer, they go back to teaching mechanics and thermodynamics.

The question is: If professors of engineering did know how to produce the desired personal qualities, would they take the necessary steps, or permit others to take them? This is the main point here: Where we are dealing with human beings, means adopted for one purpose have implications for other purposes, and the close study of means-ends relationships leads to criticism of the ends as well as of the means. This is why natural scientists often oppose, and with much political skill, the scientific study of their educational activities.

There is, of course, something to the idea that the job of science is to produce facts, which can then be applied by policy-makers and practitioners in the interest of their particular goals. Probably psychology has something to contribute to the effective teaching of thermodynamics, and most psychologists would hesitate to take a stand on whether or not this subject ought to be taught. But the question of how a particular mode of teaching this subject affects individual development is an empirical one. And so is the question of what bearing procedures introduced with individual development in mind have upon the learning of engineering subjects.

Given the entering college student as he is, a relatively undeveloped human specimen, everything that happens to him in college is relevant to his development, either favoring or hampering it. Settling upon a career, or choosing a major field of study may be favorable to the development of a stable personal identity. On the other hand, early specialization can close off sources of developmentally potent stimuli. Losing oneself in the exploration of an academic discipline can be highly favorable to the development of an autonomous self. But note that it is one thing to argue for encouraging this kind of absorption with problems on the ground that it is good for the discipline or academic subject; it is something else to say that it develops the individual. If the latter is being argued, then it is necessary to say how the experience does its work, at what stage of development it is most to be desired, and why it is to be preferred to other developmentally potent experiences.

The other side of the picture, how development in the personality interacts with other desired outcomes—usually favorably—has been sufficiently emphasized above.

In sum, the scientific study of education means the continuing examination of innumerable means-ends relationships, and of the origins and consequences of ends, so that our means may become increasingly effective and our ends ever more intelligently chosen.

Once we have decided upon individual development as a major goal, we have to think of how all the conditions and processes of the college may be brought into its service. The curriculum, modes of teaching, the social organization of the college community, the behavior of the president—all must be considered as means for the attainment of this goal without neglecting the ways in which these things may promote the achievement of other goals.

With respect to curriculum, let it be stressed that there is nothing in the present approach to suggest that subject matter does not count. On the contrary, students who are to develop need culture in almost the same way that they need food. We should, if necessary, ram it down their throats, or feed it to them in the form of sugar-coated pills. But let us continuously ask ourselves why we use the ingredients we do.

This concern with curriculum applies to disciplines or major subjects as well as to specific materials within them. Happily, it is possible to say that all the major subjects usually taught in colleges can be taught in ways that are developmental. This includes vocational subjects. Not that any known vocation, at the technical level, can be prepared for in college, but vocational courses might provide the means for introducing students to valuable developmental experiences. But the great liberal arts subjects are the easiest to support on the ground of developmental theory. History is a great instrument for showing students, quickly and inexpensively, the joys of more or less independent inquiry; philosophy, and especially ethics, is probably still the standby for challenging unexamined belief systems and for giving the student his necessary introduction to relativism of values; and literature is the great means for acquainting the student with his own feelings—through showing him something of the variety and depth of what is humanly possible. And so on. It would seem to me an interesting exercise for any teacher to ask himself just how his subject, as he teaches it, contributes to the development of the individual.

Nearly everybody agrees that the teacher is the heart and soul of the educational process. But it is not always agreed why this is so, or what the teacher actually does, to influence the student, or what are the processes by which students develop under the teacher's guidance. What is it that he does and that cannot be done by machines or by libraries or by TV? The whole phenomenon of the teacher-student relationship is much in need of further study and analysis, with attention to both developmental and antidevelopmental modes of teaching. Let it be said at once that there is nothing in the general theory of personality development in college to suggest that all teachers should be interested in students as persons, or have any special knowledge of them as developing individuals. Indeed, teachers—or administrators—who try to be one of the boys, try to participate vicariously in the student's adolescent trials and errors, can be positively harmful. It is enough for a teacher to teach his subject and to convey his enthusiasm for it. But if this is the heart of the teacher's work he should not be called upon, or feel called upon, to assign grades, or to teach something just because it appears to be needed to fill out the department's offerings, or to serve as a prerequisite to something else. A college faculty could be made up very largely of dedicated teachers of subjects. But somebody would have to be responsible for an overall plan in which such teaching had a place. And if a teacher wished to do something more, something that would be very likely to contribute to the students' development, the most fruitful thing for him to do, probably, would be to exhibit for students, not just what he knows, but also the way he goes about seeking to discover truth. This means that he himself must be a student, in some sense of the word. He must create situations in which his own learning may be observed. One way to do this might be to let students in on his own research or scholarly activities. In some fields this is not easy to do. Another way to show how he learns would be simply to teach a subject that he knows little about—perhaps in cooperation with a colleague who knows some more about it. This, as Joseph Katz has pointed out, is one of the ways to avoid becoming deadwood. The other major way, of course, is to become intellectually interested in students as developing individuals. Why not? Students are so sadly in need of development and, at the same time, in most cases show so much potential for development, that it is hard to understand how so many teachers can remain essentially indifferent on this score.

When we come to the general social organization of the college, our main concern—from the developmental point of view—should be to arrange things so that teachers can get at the students and vice versa. College graduates a few years out of college tend to remember very little of what was offered in their courses, but they do remember a few of their teachers. (Which supports at least one claim of the psychologists: that people are more interesting than anything else.) In many, perhaps most, of these cases of the remembered teacher not a great deal of the teacher's time was involved—he was not a tutor or counselor, or companion or a man with a great taste for desserts at fraternity houses. Quite likely he is remembered for some brief encounter, in which something that he said or did struck something that was in a special state of readiness in the student. The point is, that in planning campus arrangements to bring faculty and students together in ways that are favorable to the student's development it is not necessary to assume that a great deal of the teacher's time will be involved. The thing is to have the right kinds of encounters. It is a task of social psychology to discover what these are and how they might be favored by planned arrangements.

With respect to the organization of student life, it should be our aim to bring about a maximal integration of living and learning. Students learn from each other, like lightning it seems, and where they live apart, geographically or psychologically, from the academic centers of the college, they may actually acquire a culture that is in many respects in opposition to the intellectual culture that the faculty would like to introduce them to. We must find ways to bring the intellectual life of the college into the establishments where students live. We must create campus-wide student-faculty or faculty-student communities in which the social needs of students, far from being suppressed, are brought into the service of the intellectual aims of the college.

The administration, and particularly the top administration, must not be left out of account. It has a critical role in the development of the student's personality. College presidents are bound to represent much of what it is that students are supposed to become. As leaders of the whole enterprise, they must embody aims and ideals, and cannot be merely the engineers who keep the machinery turning. They may overlook this and it may appear at times when things are running smoothly that the students are overlooking it, too. But let the president make a mistake, act in violation of some ethical norm, compromise once too often with the forces that oppose the true aims of the college, or display some measure of hypocrisy or "phoniness," and the effect upon students is immediate and profound: They feel betrayed and lapse into cynicism or passivity. It would be a fine thing if college presidents could be heroes. If they cannot be that, what with all the shopping, housekeeping, and trouble shooting they have to do, they must at the least behave so consistently with our basic values that they can be ignored, or taken for granted by students on the assumption that all is well. College presidents have to be wise and just and good men without expecting, or getting, any credit for it.

If the examples that I have given represent well what must be done in college in order to promote individual development, and if this should be our major aim, then it follows that colleges must change many of their practices—perhaps in radical ways.

But how do colleges change? I mean: How do they change in desired ways and according to plan? The situation is serious but not hopeless. All social institutions are difficult to change, and educational institutions are probably more difficult than most. The public seems generally satisfied with things as they are, and the colleges—though not many are complacent—are by no means convinced that they should change in the ways here recommended. But there is hope in enlightened public criticism, and I should like to see this encouraged by informing the public about the colleges. Professions benefit from occasional public examination. Probably most college professors would agree that health is too important to be left to the doctors. It is time that college educators had their turn.

There is hope in the new institutions that are being founded now and that will be founded in the years immediately ahead. We know more about education for individual development than is being applied, and innovation is far easier when we start from scratch than it is within an existing system.

There is hope of progress in the professional schools. I mean hope that the scientific study of education in these settings will greatly expand our knowledge of means-ends relationships in higher education. These schools are accustomed to applying science to practical problems, and as compared with the liberal arts colleges, they are clear about what they want to do—for their purposes are explicitly occupational. The liberal arts colleges have unstated, even unrecognized, aims and hence the scientific study of their workings could be quite upsetting, for it could lead to painful revelations.

The existing liberal arts colleges probably hold the key to improvement in higher education for some time to come. Here we have to put our faith in the further advance of educational knowledge. The inarticulateness of these colleges about their aims is often baffling and so is their failure to understand the real sources of their difficulties. In many of these colleges there is grave concern about such problems as raising standards and getting students to work harder. Generally speaking, the liberal arts colleges are certainly trying to do *something*. It is remarkable, as Santayana noted, how we redouble our efforts as we lose sight of our goals. What the colleges need most of all, it would seem, is knowledge, knowledge of themselves—of what they do and of what they should do. They should acquire this knowledge for themselves—with help from psychology and the other social sciences. They should study themselves; focusing upon goals of individual student development and asking with respect to each practice how it favors or hampers progress toward these goals. Each teacher should ask this question about his own work. There should be continuing and genuine experimentation with new programs, including colleges within colleges, with careful appraisals of results. This can make knowledge of higher education cumulative at last; and the inquiry itself will serve students directly, by displaying for them, and involving them in, the excitement of the quest.

If our colleges would do all these things they would be providing the kind of leadership which many nations expect of us today, and they would provide inspiration for us all, for they would be acting to further major ideals of the American tradition: the value of the individual as an end in himself, and the belief in the power of intelligent experimentation to improve him and his society.

XIV

1963
Critical Decisions

W. H. Cowley

❀❀❀❀❀❀❀❀❀❀❀❀❀❀❀❀❀❀❀❀❀❀❀❀❀❀❀❀❀❀❀❀

The practical problems of today come out of the past, and those who are unaware of history struggle with them, unaware of many of their complexities. Thus to describe decision-making in American higher education, I shall mention about a dozen dates on which major decisions were made, and I shall try to answer two questions about each date: what was the decision, and who made it?

I am not going as far back in this discussion as Genesis and the three momentous decisions that had to be made once God had decided to create Eve. The third chapter identifies the serpent as the most subtle of the beasts of the field which had to decide whether to proposition Eve or Adam. It chose Eve, and then Eve had to decide whether or not she was going to accept; then Adam had to decide whether or not he would eat the apple. These were momentous decisions, but I begin much later with the founding of the first American college.

1636: The Founding of Harvard. Two very important decisions had to be made about Harvard College. Most people do not know about the first one: that Harvard was established not by academics, not by clerics, but by laymen. Harvard arose from the decision that academics would not alone control it but that laymen would participate in its government, its decision-making. Laymen have been involved in the government of American colleges and universities ever since.

This was not an American innovation, incidentally. The Puritans who established the Massachusetts Bay Colony were Calvinists, and one of the fundamental tenets of Calvinism is that laymen must participate in the decisions of all social institutions. In creating Harvard, the Massachusetts Puritans took its governmental pattern from Trinity College, Dublin. Trinity got it from the University of Edinburgh, which got it from the University of Leyden. Leyden got it from Calvin's Academy at Geneva, and Calvin got it from the Italian universities, where lay boards of trustees were orignally established in the fourteenth century.

Lay participation in the government of Harvard was a basic decision, since the creation of a lay governing board meant that in all fundamental decisions laymen would be involved. It also meant that American colleges would be institutions serving societal purposes and would not be the private syndicalistic preserves of scholars which, like Oxford and Cambridge, would often operate in complete disregard of the public interest and be largely incapable of self-reform. And who made this basic decision? The General Court of the colony and Governor John Winthrop, a Cambridge graduate.

A second decision made in 1636 or thereabouts concerned the type of institution Harvard would be. What evolved was a uniquely American institution: the unitary four-year liberal arts college. The founders of Harvard, however, had no intention of creating a unitary college. Like the founders of William and Mary, America's second college, they intended instead that Harvard would be the first of a cluster of small residential colleges like those which make up the universities of Oxford and Cambridge. That turned out to be visionary. Sparsity of population, scarcity of learned men, and the economic conditions of the country made their hoped-for institution impossible until the twentieth century, when Harvard and Yale moved in that direction. We now have seven hundred examples of the unitary liberal arts college, not because of historical plans and decisions, but because social forces favored their development. In American higher education, decisions are often made not by intention but by the dice of destiny.

1648: The First Alumni Gift. This event may seem unimportant, but in fact it is tremendously significant. In 1648, four graduates of Harvard's first class bought a piece of land near the college yard and gave it to their alma mater. It is now the site of the Widener Library. This was the beginning of alumni giving, which last year totaled over one hundred million dollars and which permits American colleges to make decisions to do things that would otherwise be beyond their grasp.

1725: Faculty Organization. In this year Harvard's small faculty began to keep and preserve its minutes. It is an important date in the controversy about who should control colleges and universities—professors, the faculty as a group, presidents, or trustees. The general impression seems to be that presidents and trustees have been monstrous tyrants and that professors have had to fight them for their rights. Admittedly, this sometimes has been true. Eliphalet Nott, the president of Union College for sixty-two years and record-holder for American college presidents, was asked late in his career about faculty meetings at Union. "We had a faculty meeting fifty years or so ago," he said. "But I hope we never have another."

This attitude may still prevail in some retarded institutions, but it has not been true of our educational institutions in general. Harvard has had an organized faculty since at least 1725; the Yale faculty has participated in promotion and advancement decisions since at least 1839; Cornell opened with an organized faculty in 1868, as did Stanford in 1891; and all institutions of any real stature in this country have similarly long histories of organized faculty participation in institutional decisions.

1805: Annual Subventions for State Universities. Both

Pennsylvania and North Carolina provided in their constitutions for the establishment of state universities, and we generally consider that the University of North Carolina and the University of Georgia, which opened first, are our earliest state universities. But in my book a university cannot properly be called a state university until it has continuing support from the state, and this began with the creation of South Carolina College in 1805. It may seem strange that a southern state should have begun state subventions, but before the Civil War the southern states ardently supported higher education. Until then they alone provided annual support for their state universities, for although the northern states were providing land endowments for buildings, none made annual grants until Michigan began them in 1867.

Who made the decision that the University of South Carolina should have an annual subvention? John Drayton, the governor of the state. Drayton, like his fellow Jeffersonians, believed that the state should participate in the support and control of education from the common schools through the universities, and his address advocating the annual grants is one of the most decisive documents in American higher educational history.

1819: The Dartmouth College Case. In six states, the Jeffersonians sought more than public support of higher education: they fought for complete state domination of it. For example, they closed the private University of Pennsylvania and established a new state university in Philadelphia. They closed King's College in New York City, which later reopened as Columbia College, and they made similar efforts at Harvard and at Yale. In 1816, they attempted to take over Dartmouth and to convert it into a state university. The Dartmouth trustees divided on the issue, and this led to legal battles which ended in the United States Supreme Court.

Daniel Webster, a Dartmouth alumnus, represented the loyal college trustees before the Court and argued that the New Hampshire legislature could not abrogate the charter granted by George III. In his plea he held that a charter is a contract, and the Court upheld this point of view. Incidentally, three Supreme Court justices wrote opinions favoring Dartmouth—Joseph Story, Bushrod Washington (the nephew of George Washington), and John Marshall, whose decision is the one usually quoted—but each favored Dartmouth on different grounds.

The Jeffersonians' defeat in the Dartmouth College Case ended their efforts to control higher education and resulted in the American distinction between public and private colleges. Until the decision this distinction was not clearly made. Harvard, Williams, and Bowdoin, for example, were all receiving subventions from Massachusetts, but the Dartmouth decision forced them to choose between state and private support. Thus since 1824, when its ten-year state grant came to an end, Harvard has received no funds from Massachusetts. Somewhat later, when Harvard was in financial trouble, its then president Edward Everett suggested that it seek legislative support; but happily for Harvard and, I think, for the rest of the country, Massachusetts turned Harvard down.

In addition to making this distinction between public and private institutions, the Dartmouth decision stimulated both state legislatures and religious denominations to organize new colleges, particularly in the new Middle Western states. The competition and diversity which resulted in American higher education has proved one of its greatest strengths.

1815: The Trek to Germany. Three American students made an important decision in 1815. They decided that since no opportunity for advanced study existed in this country, they had to go to Germany. Over ten thousand American students followed them during the next ninety-nine years. They brought back not only their Ph.D.'s, but also German concepts of university education. (The first American to earn a Ph.D., incidentally, was a scoundrel. He was Nathaniel Eaton, the first head of Harvard, who was dismissed after twenty-two months for being corrupt in almost every way you can imagine, and who then left the colonies to take his degree at Padua.)

One of the trio was Edward Everett, whom I mentioned above. He later served as congressman and governor of Massachusetts, president of Harvard, and Secretary of State under Fillmore, and is best remembered as the man who gave the two-hour oration before Lincoln's Gettysburg Address. The second was Edward Cogswell, who introduced progressive education to America in his

school in Northampton, Massachusetts. The third was George Ticknor, by all odds the most important. He came back to teach the
modern languages at Harvard, but he found that in comparison
with the German universities, Harvard was no more than a high
school. He therefore petitioned Harvard's governing boards to
reform the curriculum.

He had no success until a new group entered the decision-
making scene: the students. True, students had controlled the universities of medieval Italy, but in northern Europe and in America
they had influenced policy decisions only indirectly. Harvard's class
of 1823, however, were such hell raisers that a third of them, including the son of John Quincy Adams, then Secretary of State,
were dismissed outright in their senior year. Despite Adams' appeals
from Washington, the Harvard governing boards refused to rein-
state the seniors. Faced with continuing student unrest as well as
Ticknor's proposals for reform, they decided on a self-study.

1825: The First Self-Study.   Many college self-studies have
been recently undertaken, but in my judgment the original self-study
initiated by Harvard's governing boards must be called the most
successful, because it accomplished the most effective reformation
ever made of an American college. The Harvard Corporation, the
Board of Overseers, and the faculty all appointed committees which
met for two years. They redefined the functions of the president,
they established instructional departments, they instituted a primitive
elective system, they sectioned classes in the modern languages on
the basis of ability, they revised the college statutes, and they abandoned money fines for student misdemeanors. And who made the
decision? The governing boards, stimulated by Professor Ticknor's
petitions and precipitated by student unrest.

1828: The Yale Report.   Two years after the Harvard self-
study, Yale's governing board made a decision which had far-reach-
ing effects. Reforms were altering not only Harvard. Amherst had
opened in 1823, and its faculty soon thereafter had proposed that
technological subjects and teacher training should be included in the
liberal arts curriculum; the University of Virginia had opened in
1825 offering the experimental sciences; in the wilderness of western
Massachusetts, Williams had added the modern languages; and in

Schenectady, Union College was preparing to introduce the quite unrespectable subject of engineering.

All these developments stimulated the Yale Corporation to petition the president and the faculty to report to them whether and how Yale should change. Notice the initiative here: the governing board decided to ask the faculty to look at what it was doing. In 1828 the Yale faculty made its report, the most reactionary document ever written in American higher education. Only three subjects were worthy of study in a liberal arts college, claimed President Day, who taught mathematics, and Professor Kingsley, who taught classics. The three? Mathematics, Greek, and Latin. The function of the college was to turn out intellectually disciplined minds; and only these studies, they insisted, gave intellectual discipline. This attitude that the liberal arts college should stay pure and undefiled by the modern world around it influenced not merely Yale but the curricula of most American colleges into the twentieth century. One reason lay in the fact that more college presidents during the nineteenth century had graduated from Yale than from any other institution, and they took with them the rationale of the 1828 report. Five Yale alumni, for example, had preceded me as president of Hamilton College, and in my judgment Hamilton has never recovered from them.

Yale is a great institution, but it had to await the collapse of the doctrine of intellectual discipline before it could advance very far beyond its faculty report of 1828. The country at large, however, could not wait for reform. It was outgrowing the old classical college, and two memorable decisions were necessary to create the institutions it needed.

1862: The Land-Grant College Act. The decision behind this legislation ranks, in my opinion, as the most important ever made in American higher education—and all because of seven words. The Act established state institutions supported by endowments of land from the federal government, and it provided that the new institutions must teach agriculture and the mechanical arts or engineering. Most important, however, it required that these subjects be taught—and here are the seven words—"without excluding other scientific and classical studies." May I repeat these words:

"without excluding other scientific and classical studies." Their inclusion produced the most influential institution in American higher education—the comprehensive university.

By "comprehensive university" I mean an institution which combines the historic academic disciplines with the modern subjects and with professional or occupational education. Remember that the European university had four faculties—law, medicine, divinity, and the arts or philosophy. It had no place for experimental science and no place for professional education in engineering, agriculture, or commerce. Yet the idea of the comprehensive university came from Europe. Leibniz proposed it at the end of the seventeenth century in advocating the establishment of a fifth faculty which would teach economics, engineering, technology, and agriculture. In 1776 Denis Diderot, the great French encyclopedist, also proposed a comprehensive university when Catherine the Great asked him to design a new university for St. Petersburg.

In America, Benjamin Franklin at the University of Pennsylvania and Thomas Jefferson at the University of Virginia made attempts to create comprehensive institutions, and a number of colleges began to establish parallel curricula and to adopt the elective principle in order to expand their offerings. But the Land-Grant College Act securely established American higher education on the comprehensive pattern.

Who wrote the decisive seven words? It may seem that the author of the Act, Justin Smith Morrill, wrote them. I do not think so. There is nothing in his background to suggest that he knew that much about educational thinking. Yet I do not know who made this decision, and so I propose that someone should be given a small research grant to find out who did. In any case, whoever wrote those words made more American higher educational history than any other person I know of.

You may not like the modern comprehensive university. Many people do not. Thorstein Veblen did not; Abraham Flexner did not; Robert Hutchins does not. But like it or not, because of the Land-Grant College Act, the comprehensive university is today the most characteristic and the most powerful institution in American higher education.

1876: The Recognition of Research. Twelve years after

the passing of the Land-Grant College Act and one hundred years after the founding of the nation, the first American institution opened worthy of the name of university. What do I mean by worthy of the name? In the judgment of most people, an institution cannot properly be called a university unless it undertakes research, and no American institution honored the function until Johns Hopkins opened in 1876.

A few professors had done research previously, but they did it on their own time. America's first professor who gave any time to research was Isaac Greenwood, who taught at Harvard during the middle of the eighteenth century, but he had been dismissed for drunkenness and, being a bachelor, for coming back from Europe with three pairs of silk stockings. As late even as 1909 Edwin E. Slosson could report after visiting the University of Minnesota that "the regents generally regarded research as a private fad of a professor, like collecting etchings or playing the piano."

We do not know who decided on the seven words in the Land-Grant College Act, but we do know who decided to make research a basic function of American universities. His name was Daniel Coit Gilman, in my book the greatest American college or university educator of the nineteenth century. He alone saw that the country needed a research-oriented university. Eliot did not see it at Harvard. White did not see it at Cornell. Angell did not see it at Michigan. They all, however, recognized Gilman's brilliance, and they all recommended that he be made president of the new Johns Hopkins University.

Gilman had been considered for the presidency of Yale, but the Yale Corporation had elected instead a broken-down clergyman, Noah Porter, who looked resolutely to the past and denounced his reform-minded colleagues as quacks and charlatans. Johns Hopkins' Board of Trustees were more far-sighted: they brought Gilman to Baltimore to learn about his ideas, elected him president, and accepted his proposal that a research university be established under their government and his leadership.

1890: The Graduate School Begins To Dominate Undergraduate Education. Gilman foresaw that if graduate education and research were added to the existing American liberal arts college, general education would be overwhelmed. Hence he proposed that Johns Hopkins be entirely a graduate school with no under-graduate college. His board of trustees rejected this proposal, how-ever, and Johns Hopkins opened with a three-year undergraduate curriculum.

Had Gilman succeeded in this plan, general education today might not be crippled by graduate education and research as it is at most American universities. We would have the teachers respon-sible for general undergraduate education administratively separate from the teachers concerned with graduate education and research. In a history-making reorganization of Harvard in 1890, however, President Eliot and his associates made the Harvard Faculty of Arts and Sciences responsible for all nonprofessional education from the beginning of the freshman year through the Ph.D. degree. This put undergraduate education at Harvard under the control of professors interested primarily in research, and general education in American universities has been shackled ever since. The other Eastern colleges which were also remodeling themselves into universities all followed Harvard's leadership, and the state universities followed the ex-ample of the older Eastern institutions. Being new and with no funds to speak of, they could not go to their legislatures and plead for two separate faculties, one for general education and one for ad-vanced education and research. Consequently, the research point of view has come to dominate undergraduate education and has created the most serious conflict in American higher education.

No other weakness of our colleges and universities seems to me so flagrant as their failure in general education. They push it into neglected corners by leaving it to junior members of the faculty and to graduate assistants, and they undermine it by delaying or denying promotions to its teachers. Thus, despite the concern about general education that gave such promise just after World War II, our undergraduate colleges are rapidly becoming prep schools for the professional schools and the graduate schools.

1921: The Two-Year College Comes of Age. To avoid the conflict of general education with graduate education and research, Gilman wanted to create a separate graduate university. Other uni-versity presidents tried to bisect the existing four-year college and turn over its first two years to the secondary school and add the upper two years to the graduate school.

Henry Philip Tappan, the first president of the University of Michigan, proposed this plan in 1852. Enamored of the German system of education, he held that American education should be reorganized into a system having an eight- or ten-year elementary school, a six-year high school, and a university beginning at the present junior year. In the 1870's, William W. Folwell actually got the University of Minnesota to operate under this plan for five or six years, and in the 1890's William Rainey Harper at Chicago supported the plan and established several six-year high schools. For want of a better term, he called their top two years "junior colleges." Finally, Robert Maynard Hutchins unsuccessfully resurrected Harper's plan at Chicago in 1942 and awarded what came to be called the "bastard of arts" degree at the end of the historic sophomore year.

There are still people who believe that we should bisect the four-year college. I do too, logically. The four-year college is a very illogical institution, but I have long pointed out to my students that we do not make social policy in terms of logic, we make it in terms of history. Logic cannot dispose of vested interests, and in this case the vested interests were the existing liberal arts colleges which quite naturally refused to accept an invitation to commit suicide.

As a result, in the interplay of forces between the proponents of the six-year high school and the defenders of the liberal arts college, there emerged the two-year junior college. By 1921 the American Association of Junior Colleges came into being. The two-year college had achieved recognition and was here to stay. But its emergence was an historical accident. I do not mean this invidiously. I simply mean that nobody intended the two-year college. Instead, the proponents of what developed into the junior college originally planned to create the six-year high school.

The other significant dates of this century are probably familiar. In general education, for example, there are the decisions at Amherst in 1914, Columbia in 1919, Chicago in 1931, and Harvard in 1945. In federal support, the G.I. Bill of Rights in 1945 and the National Science Foundation in 1952. Let me move on now very briefly to a discussion of how we make decisions in higher education.

The general notion is that tyrannical presidents force decisions on their institutions. But look at the major decisions I have listed. Of the thirteen, only two—Gilman's in 1876 and Eliot's in 1890—were initiated by presidents. Trustees initiated the Harvard self-study of 1825 and the Yale Report of 1828; students made the 1648 and 1815 decisions; and faculty members undertook Harvard's 1725 reorganization and, with student help, precipitated the 1825 reforms. In contrast, at least four of the decisions were made outside these groups: by the General Court of the Massachusetts Bay Colony in 1636, the governor of South Carolina in 1805, the Supreme Court in 1819, and Congress in 1862. And two decisions were actually historical accidents—the creation of America's unitary liberal arts colleges and its two-year junior colleges.

Thus, not only faculty members, students, alumni, administrators, and trustees all participate in institutional decisions, but so do professional organizations, accreditation bodies, governmental agencies, and the American public at large.

I believe we are more and more coming to recognize that the way to make decisions in higher education is through participation of all interested groups, not only those inside our colleges and universities, but many outside. No group, in my opinion, should monopolize the decisions of social institutions. The history of academic government seems to be clearly against monopoly by either the general public or by professors, by students or by alumni, by administrators or by trustees. It demonstrates that the most successful system involves all interest groups—the general public, the faculty, the administrators, the alumni, the students. This system of academic government prevents monopoly; and since the essence of democracy is the power of participation in decision-making, it represents democracy in action.

I am a little worried about the American Association of University Professors, however, because it seems to have recently taken a new position on academic government. When Joseph A. Leighton, professor of philosophy at Ohio State, and the other members of AAUP's Committee T established the Association's principles for academic government in 1920, they clearly declared that governing boards should be the partners of faculty members in making policy. But a year ago in his AAUP presidential address Dean Fuchs of Indiana University took the position that primacy in decision-making belongs with the faculty. I disagree, and believe that the participation of lay trustees is essential to the effective operation of American higher education. The skills, the knowledge, the wisdom necessary to make decisions in higher education today require, I strongly believe, the intelligent cooperation of all interested parties.

I have not yet mentioned computers. Some people seem to believe that these machines can and will be the preeminent decision-makers of the future. I recall, however, a doggerel poem that was surreptitiously distributed during my New England prep school days when the typewriter had not been around very long, the automobile was not very old, and the airplane had just been invented. A verse was devoted to each of these great inventions, and each one ended with the line, "But thank God we're making babies in the good old-fashioned way." Regardless of computers, we are going to continue to make decisions in the good old-fashioned way.

XV

1964
Viability of
Liberal Arts

Lloyd J. Averill

❀❀❀❀❀❀❀❀❀❀❀❀❀❀❀❀❀❀❀❀❀❀❀❀❀❀❀❀❀❀

In an article on Japanese drama, James A. Michener wrote some time ago:

I once boned up on a play whose synopsis read, "Two lonely men meet in a lonely gorge and are about to kill one another when from a distance a strange man cries, 'Wait a minute,' and tells them how foolish they are to fight." I went to the play, but it wasn't in a lonely gorge, it was a luxurious palace. It wasn't two lonely men, it was three bullies, each with eight retainers. They weren't stopped by a man; it was a woman. She didn't preach peace; she killed eighteen servants. I went back to the synopsis and read in fine print, "Sometimes local companies adapt this play to their own actors."

With malice toward none, but with apologies to Michener, we might undertake a paraphrase of that to describe an experience some of us may have had:

I once picked up a college catalog whose introductory statement read, "Here you will find a community of scholarship engaged in liberal learning conducted in a Christian atmosphere and directed toward responsible participation in the contemporary world." I went to the college, but it wasn't a community; it was a collection of individual teachers and students held together by a common grievance against required chapel. What they were engaged in wasn't liberal learning; it was the academic numbers game, requiring a combined College Board score of 1100 or better for admission, a grade-point average of 2.0 for good standing, 120 hours to graduate, and an annual contribution of $100.00 to the alumni fund in order for the president of the college to remember your name. The atmosphere didn't exactly give comfort to the Christians; it more, like, encouraged the lions. And what the whole thing was directed toward wasn't responsible participation in the contemporary world but successful admission to graduate school. I went back to the catalog and read in fine print, "This program is subject to change without notice."

There is much honest concern among us about the discrepant aspects of the education we sponsor. There is widespread uneasiness and uncertainty about the special vocation—the "margin of uniqueness," as some of us are likely to put it—of the private liberal arts college, especially of such colleges under Protestant auspices; and there are many signs that we are unsure of our identity in the general community of American higher education.

There is no doubt that the pressures and threats to liberal education are dangerously real. It is by no means clear, however, that we no longer have an important educational and cultural role to play. On the contrary, as I shall try to show, our importance to sound learning and to a meaningful culture is as great now as it has ever been; and it is high time the liberal arts colleges, whether under private or public auspices, whether on small campuses or in comprehensive universities, stopped giving hostage to intimidation and developed a sound strategy for survival.

Liberal education is intended to serve genuinely humanizing ends. For this reason, educational concern is directed toward the student as a person rather than simply as a function. The college seeks to enable him to become a more complete man and not just a more efficient technician.

Liberal education seeks an appreciation of the unity and interrelation of human knowledge. In the presence of cultural and academic forces which tend toward the fragmentation of knowledge, the liberal arts college seeks to foster an awareness of the interdependence and complementarity of the several intellectual methods and disciplines, and it does this as a means of inculcating intellectual humility and intellectual wholeness in student and teacher alike.

Perhaps it may be useful to go beyond formal definition by attempting to draw a profile of the liberally educated man: He is intellectual rather than bookish. He is competent rather than competitive. He is committed rather than captured. He is informed rather than opinionated. He is discriminating rather than prejudiced. He is compassionate rather than condescending.

If it is true that liberal education now faces the threat of rapid extinction, as some observers confidently predict, is that because men in contemporary society no longer need what the liberal arts and sciences have traditionally sought to supply? On the contrary, I am persuaded that men in our contemporary society need to be liberally educated as much as men ever did, and I see no evidence that we have now reached that level of human evolution which confers upon us the maturity which in former days was hard-won. Without beginning to exhaust the reasons, simply consider these:

Some would tell us that the incredible acceleration of knowledge now makes liberal education—in the sense of general education —impossible. My reply is that it is precisely the acceleration of knowledge which makes a larger liberalizing of education essential. The acceleration of knowledge will threaten increasingly to disorient and to destory the equilibrium of the man whose education is set in technical knowledge and skills which may soon be outdated.

The acceleration of knowledge will increasingly pose an unprecedented moral problem. At the 1963 meeting of the Association for Higher Education, Glenn Seaborg, chairman of the Atomic Energy Commission, made a sobering prediction: "The biologist will not, as in the past, merely observe and describe, but will modify and direct and create, for example, with the chemical drugs which change personality." In the face of this kind of power which is coming into man's hands, an educational system which trains the future scientists and makers of social and political policy and which nevertheless persists in giving them no explicit moral guidance can only be described as irresponsible. The prospect of future generations of scientists deficient in that quality of moral imagination which can sensitize them to the fateful responsibilities of their work is frightening to contemplate.

The narrowing of specialization which has accompanied the acceleration of knowledge promises to intensify an already existing spiritual problem. It is common for those who write about the current young generation to speak about the "crisis in self-identity" which seems to mark our young people. I am persuaded that a similar crisis also marks the adult culture; it is simply more visible in the young. One of the things which has created the crisis is the difficulty we have in entering into meaningful contact with each other. This contemporary loss of a meaningful world can only be intensified by a growth in specialization, which means also the growth of personal and professional isolation.

The technical developments which are mechanizing so much of our life, even to the invasion of the professions, face us with an unprecedented social problem. Automated procedures, in addition to a greater mechanical efficiency, have two practical human results: they increase routinization, and they increase leisure. And the danger is unprecedented boredom.

The educator who is persuaded, as I am, of the importance of liberal learning to our present personal and cultural situation must nevertheless admit that the problems the liberal tradition faces are formidable. Outside and inside the college a variety of pressures and influences are at work to modify, or even to take over, facets of the liberal arts program:

There is, for one thing, what *New York Times* Education

Editor Fred Hechinger describes as "a specialized technological economy which devours special skills and rejects unspecialized job seekers." Such an economy creates in prospective college students and their parents an ever-larger demand for the kind of training which is readily convertible into the high salaries awaiting technical specialists and makes them impatient with educational requirements which do not directly enhance earning power.

It has become fashionable for liberal arts colleges to complain of pressure from the graduate schools which seem intent upon a steady increase in the number of undergraduate courses they require before permitting a student to enter upon graduate level study. As Jacques Barzun has commented, although schools of law and medicine and engineering still profess to want "well-rounded" applicants, their admissions committees continue to give preference to those who show what he calls "a positive gluttony for science and mathematics."

It is not simply pressure from above which creates problems, however; it is also erosion from beneath. The upgrading of secondary education means, according to Jacques Barzun, that more and more of the work traditionally assigned to the first two years of college is now being done in the high schools. The result of this two-pronged invasion is that the liberal arts college is left without anything to do.

One of the most formidable internal problems lies in the fact that many teachers in liberal arts schools come from backgrounds which lack cultural depth; to put it bluntly, they are not themselves liberally educated. They reach their first teaching assignments by way of intensive years of study whose purpose is precisely that of specialization.

The young teacher, fresh out of graduate school, finds himself under pressure to do research. This pressure comes, not so much from the college as from the profession as the chief means of establishing his own credentials within his own discipline. The teacher may feel little by way of identification with the aims of the college and may even look on it as a professional way station to more important things. As an increasingly larger proportion of liberal arts faculties are staffed with men and women who have no commitment to liberal arts teaching, the task of maintaining the integrity of the liberal arts ideal becomes more and more difficult.

The result of this is that even the most traditional liberal arts departments become preprofessional, with the preoccupations of their teachers infecting their students. Students, to quote Barzun once more, "are treated as if everyone in the class were to become a professional, a duplicate of his own teacher."

Finally, there is the nagging question whether, even under the best of recent conditions, we have really succeeded in accomplishing what we set out to do. All of us are acquainted with embarrassingly large numbers of alumni from our own schools who could not, by any stretch of the imagination, be called liberally educated. They do not read, they do not go to museums or attend the theater, and their conversation may seldom go beyond the superficial and trivial. Perhaps then, we may sometimes be tempted to think, little will be lost if the present prophets of our doom turn out to be right.

That verdict is not yet in, and the jury is going to be out for a very long time. In the meanwhile, those of us who believe in the liberal arts need to get to work as unapologetic partisans in its behalf. The American liberal arts college, if vulnerable, is nevertheless viable; and I want to make some observations which may exhibit, and some proposals which may strengthen, its viability.

There is, I am convinced, a large reservoir of public good will and support for liberal education in the American community, but until now that support has been amorphous and undirected. Perhaps its largest single source is to be found in the business community. This is an alliance which some traditional academics would find incredible and even dangerous, but I think it is neither. David Riesman and Christopher Jencks have noted, in *College and Character,* how "The men at the top in business . . . increasingly insist that they prefer recruits initially trained in the liberal arts. They do so partly because this has become a fashion, but also because they realize that the scientific revolution has outdated technical skills almost as fast as it has required them." Similar support for the liberal arts is scattered through the professions and may be found as well in the labor movement, with its intense awareness of the human consequences of automation. From whatever source, such support awaits the effort to organize it and give it a voice.

I want therefore to propose, as of the first order of importance, the formation of a national organization of the Friends of
Liberal Education, with a membership drawn as widely as possible
from leadership in business and industry, the professions, and the
labor movement. Such an organization would serve frankly as a
public lobby for the liberal arts college. First, through the use of
educational and advertising means, it would seek a wider understanding of the importance of liberal education. Second, it would
use its influence to persuade those who hire college graduates that it
is sound policy to insist on men and women who have the intellectual
and personal resourcefulness and adaptability which are the finest
leverage on the graduate and professional schools in moderating
their inordinate specialist demands in the direction of an intellectual
breadth to complement intensity.

The movement of high schools into a level of work comparable to what has been taught in the first two college years in the past
is no threat to the colleges but the very opposite. It does not obviate
the importance of the college but permits it an importance it has
never been able to assume because of inadequate secondary instruction: it permits the college to engage in higher education. In
the past too much of our time has been spent at the elementary
levels of instruction, with the result that some of our students have
had little enough time left for study in depth.

We need seriously to reconsider what appears to be a growing movement toward undergraduate, and perhaps even secondary
school, acceleration. Liberal education needs a certain maturity in
the student for its effectiveness. Although most schools put their general education requirements in the first two years, I think an equally
good case could be made for putting them in the last two years.
Second, acceleration is very likely to take place under a strong preprofessional motivation and at the expense of the liberalizing elements of study. And third, given our present cultural and educational situation, we ought to be in the business of enriching rather
than denaturing the college experience.

Commonly we have required that every student take a certain minimum number of courses in each of the major divisions of
the curriculum, on the assumption that every student should have at
least minimal experience with each of the major ways in which men

interpret their experience. The student is introduced to the several areas of the curriculum, but this introduction scarcely adds up to liberal learning. Why should we not be prepared to admit that no student can be adequately introduced to all the major divisions of knowledge, and be satisfied instead with providing for him greater depth of study in a program which is less than totally comprehensive? I have proposed to my own faculty that, instead of requiring minimal work in all four of our curricular divisions, we allow the student to choose three and expect him to work at greater depth than before in each of them.

Two comments about faculty will suffice. One is that faculty recruitment has traditionally been a desultory and disorganized business, and it is little wonder that it has failed to bring us men and women who have a strong sense of vocation for liberal arts teaching. I see only two possibilities for the smaller college. One is to have a full-time faculty recruiter, just as we have a staff of full-time student recruiters. The other is to conduct faculty recruiting on a cooperative interinstitutional basis. But when the teacher, carefully recruited, arrives on the campus, he may find no clearly articulated or effectively utilized agreement on the liberal aims of the college, and no continuing medium through which teachers and administrators can reach each other with their educational concerns. When we proceed with day-by-day decisions, without any conceptual norm to guide the direction of the college, it is not surprising that we waken some day to find that subtle changes made piece by piece have moved the institution in directions no one desired but had no conceptual wisdom to foresee.

The viability of any social institution depends, in part, on its ability to transcend its own private good in serving the general welfare. Here I think we must speak quite plainly about the painfully marginal role the liberal arts colleges have played in the racial revolution of our time and the fact that we have contributed so little to the legitimate aspirations of the Negro in American life. Whatever we may have said about this issue, the almost total absence of Negro teachers and administrators and the merely token presence of Negro students on our campuses have spoken with unhappy eloquence.

There are at least two steps which ought to be taken. First, groups of colleges must provide facilities for supplementary instruc-

tion of potentially able students, Negro or any other, whose high
school backgrounds are inadequate to prepare them for the academic
competition on our campuses. Such summer institutes ought to be
held at a number of locations around the country and aimed at the
marginal but promising high school graduate in the summer immediately following his high school graduation. It might also be
aimed at the marginal but promising student who has just completed
his junior year. Second, joint intercollegiate efforts are needed to
identify able Negro college students who can help meet the growing
need for qualified college teachers; to encourage them through their
graduate preparation; and to assist them in finding teaching appointments among us when they have completed their training.

Mason W. Gross, president of Rutgers University, speaking
some time ago before the American Library Association, made an
appeal which those of us in the liberal arts colleges ought to hear. Said
he, "Information and information retrieval is the order of the day.
. . . Somewhere, somehow, we have got to let the shadows creep
back into the university, so that in mystery and privacy the human
soul can grope secretly on its way all by itself. All today is bright
and cheerful and optimistic and objective—all, that is, except the
ultimate problems of value with which each soul must wrestle. . . .
As we are coping with the problems of information retrieval, to
satisfy our insatiable appetite for fact, can we also devise a system
for value retrieval?" My reply is that we already have one, and it is
called the church-related liberal arts college.

But having said that, it must also be said of many church-
related colleges that they are religiously nondescript. Stop an administrator on the campus and ask him what it means, exactly, to call
the college Christian, and his answer may be vague, but he is persuaded nevertheless that it means something worth maintaining. Stop
a teacher on that same campus, and he is likely to be even less sure
of what it means but dislikes what he suspects the administrator
means by it. Stop a student, and you may discover he is on his way
to a student body mass meeting called to demand an end to required
chapel.

I have no intention of entering into a detailed discussion of
all that is entailed, educationally and theologically, in adding
"Christian" to the designation of a liberal arts college. I do want to

insist, however, that it means at least two things: first, that the college rejects any standard of competence which does not also include goodness; and second, that the college claims the freedom to take a position on the source of human good. And it is able to do both things without in any way subverting its primary intention to be a college. Let it be clear that I am far from saying only the Christian college can do these things; rather I am insisting that the Christian college must do them if its designation is to bear any more than mere historical significance. And it is precisely these things, in my view, which give special viability to learning which is both liberal and Christian.

We are living in a *de*moralized period of history, in which men have lost confidence in any objective definition of the good. They are learning to be hospitable to almost any statement of value, since values are only expressions of personal preference, in the presence of which any attempt at normative adjudication is out of place. I wonder if that is not a pretty fair description of the American college today? The *de*moralization of education—our refusal even to advocate goodness, as if it were out of fashion; our fear of commitments, as if we were somehow excused by academic immunity from the obligation to appropriate and to live by the truth once we recognize it to be true—has had two kinds of effect. It is responsible for the confused and uncertain state of the liberal arts. It is responsible as well for the religious nondescriptness of the church-related college. In recent years the Protestant college, with its passion for intellectual respectability, has taken for its standard of excellence the secular college, with its disdain for the institutional expression of value preferences.

If I have any understanding of human nature and any insight into the crisis of our contemporary culture, I cannot accept any educational system which is prepared to *de*moralize its graduates. Of course we ought to expose the student to the major forms of ethical response among us; that is a part of the liberal educational task of subjecting the whole of culture to a searching scrutiny. But it is assuredly not enough to assume that, exposed to the options, the student ought to be able to appropriate the one which seems to him to make the most sense, since the college, by the very fact of its own nondescriptness, suggests implicitly but quite clearly to the student that appropriation of any of the options is not really a very important business. So the result of this optional approach is not a well-rounded student, as we prefer to think, but a cipher.

So I am persuaded that we shall fail in our responsibility as colleges which seek to be both liberal and Christian if we do not seek as a matter of first importance to create in our students an intelligent awareness and appreciation of that meaningful and moral faith which claims us and which promises to give shape to individual life and direction to corporate life. And if that faith be Christian, then let us say so clearly and unequivocally; but if it be not Christian, then for God's sake let us find what is better and say that.

Certainly this is a perilous course, as faith is always perilous, for the evidence is never all in. But may it not serve our times and the task to which we are called better to "sin bravely" than to seek refuge in the empty security of noncommitment? This peril is precisely the special vulnerability of the Christian liberal arts college; but the promise of a faith which overcomes the *de*moralization of our times is precisely the special viability of the Christian liberal arts college.

XVI

1964
Future of
Liberal Arts

Richard P. McKeon

❀❀❀❀❀❀❀❀❀❀❀❀❀❀❀❀❀❀❀❀❀❀❀❀❀❀❀❀❀❀❀

The possibilities of the future are conditioned by existing views of the present. However the future of the liberal arts is conceived, the topic tends to merge today with topics like the plight of the liberal arts or the degradation of the liberal arts. We have been told that our times are anti-intellectual, antihumanistic, and even antiscientific; and right-minded men have pleaded for a future in which wisdom, culture, and science will be united in polity, community,

and cosmos. Much that has been written about the liberal arts—
from the controversies and schematisms of Alexandria and Rome to
those of the present—has been concerned with the plight of the
liberal arts or with the subversions of communities and degradations
of men consequent on their pursuit. Even before the technical learning and rhetorical pedantry of the Hellenistic Age, the Greeks of the
classical period, who were busy inventing the liberal arts which have
been used, modified, and turned upside down in the cultural and
educational history of the West, lamented the inauspiciousness of
their times for the use or development of the liberal arts. The bibli-
ography concerning what the liberal arts are and what they do when
they are not degraded is shorter. At present, after a long history of
continuity and change and a new list of revolutionary innovations
and returns, the ambiguity of the liberal arts is a problem antecedent
to any version of the plight of the liberal arts. That ambiguity will
continue to be the fruitful source of undecidable controversy unless
the nature of the arts that are liberal is examined on the basis of
some formulation of the modern problems which need liberal arts
for their consideration and treatment.

The true function of the liberal arts, as their name suggests, is
to liberate men. They have performed this function from time to time
in the past by adapting disciplines to the problems men have faced.
They have become obsolete and ineffective, at other times, by elabo-
rating old methods without consideration of new facts or problems.
The liberal arts are then the arts of the freeman, in the sense of his
possession and mark, which other men seek as symbols of status, and
which liberate only by facilitating ascension in the social scale; a
liberal education is the acquisition of polite and useful arts exhibited
for emulation by the successful and attained by rules set forth in
textbooks. In reaction, the liberal arts are thereafter adjusted to facts
and experience, to needs and purposes. The liberal arts have gone
through the three steps of this cycle a number of times during their
history. The etymologies proposed to explain the meaning of the
liberal arts in the Middle Ages reflect aspects of the evolution:
liberalis was derived from words meaning *free,* or *book,* or *child.* We
are at present in the third stage of evolution. New liberal arts must
be devised for the problems of the modern world. The liberal arts
which we associate with the names of liberal arts colleges and liberal

education are adaptations of the nineteenth-century liberal arts, modified by omitting some of the skills once inculcated, and by adding a broader scope of areas of the world and a diversified selection of aspects of life. The arts thus modified are better suited to acquaint men with problems than to provide them with means for understanding or action. Their irrelevance will not be remedied by returning to earlier unadjusted forms of the liberal arts, not even to the well-springs of the liberal arts of the Renaissance or of the liberal arts of the Middle Ages.

The liberal arts of the Middle Ages were the *disciplines* of the trivium and the quadrivium. They had become abstract and verbal when the revolt of the Renaissance sought enrichment in the study of literature, history, and science. After the Renaissance, the meaning of discipline changed from methods of inquiry, like grammar, logic, or geometry, to subject matters or areas of inquiry, like the multiplying departments of the natural sciences, the social sciences, and the humanities. The degradation of the modern liberal arts has consequently been in the opposite direction from the degradation of the medieval liberal arts. The methods had become abstract and technical; the subject matters have become subdivided and fragmented. We have sought interrelations and unifications. They cannot be found by simple addition of related subject matters or of supplementary methods, and the numerous experiments in cross-fertilization suggest that miscegenation is not the only factor in scientific breeding of livestock or of live thought.

The problem of the liberal arts today is to discover a new structure of disciplines constructed of the two kinds of disciplines. New disciplines or methods are needed to relate and advance new disciplines or subjects of knowledge and action. The liberal arts are instruments of activity. They liberate men from passivity by removing false problems which obstruct, and by clarifying true problems which open up inquiry and action. Such a false problem is the antithesis between science and the humanities, which is a modern revival of the medieval distinction between arts of things and arts of words. A "principle of indifference" was developed in the Middle Ages to relate scientific and humanistic disciplines. In its most inclusive formulation the principle recognizes that analysis of the structure of a statement is valid and pertinent only when it is also analysis of what is stated or signified. The use of the principle of indifference on the problems discussed as problems of teaching and learning, of inquiry and demonstration, shifts the perspective from unending controversies about forms and matters, separations and unifications, to ongoing inquiries concerning the applications of disciplines to encountered problems. Four liberal arts can be seen in process of formation today by abandoning dubious antitheses which mark points at which existing liberal arts have become impertinent to problems, and at which they have uncovered aspects of those problems to which new liberal arts must be adapted. As they are perfected, the new liberal arts will take over functions relative to the problems of our times similar to the functions performed by older liberal arts relative to the problems of earlier ages.

The structure of disciplines as a structure of facts. The concern for concreteness in the modern world has become an idolatry of facts. The adjectives which Alfred North Whitehead borrowed from William James to characterize facts as "stubborn" and "irreducible" express the underlying attitude aroused in most men by reference to facts. Such solidity as we find in the world is based on facts which are fixed and well grounded. Yet the learning processes in which the student encounters knowledge disturbs the fixity of attested facts at each stage of education by enshrining new and better-grounded facts. He preserves his conviction that the new facts are stubborn and irreducible by learning from the transition that no knowledge is certain and absolute.

We need an art to meet this situation. It must be an art which uses the principle of indifference to combine recognition of the familiar with discovery of the novel. The harmonious adjustment of these apparent contraries has always been an objective in learning and teaching. It has long been recognized that education is directed to both objectivity and creativity. This is a single aim, but it has been transformed in the growing literature on the character of our times into one more instance of the age-old controversial opposition between Tradition and Innovation.

The liberal art rhetoric was once concerned with the art of invention. Cicero's youthful work on rhetoric has probably been the most widely used textbook in the history of Western education—it was fundamental, directly and indirectly, during long periods of medieval education; it provided the crucial weapons of the revolt of the Renaissance against the medieval arts; it is the source of some of the basic critical devices which established the modern study of literature.The work was called *On Invention*. It influenced science as well as literature. When Francis Bacon constructed a new organum as a logic of discovery for the sciences, he adapted the places for the discovery of arguments in rhetoric to make the places for the discovery of things and of arts. The transition is an instance of the operation of the principle of indifference; and the phenomenon of degradation is illustrated in the semantic changes by which "commonplaces" moved from signifying means for the discovery of new ideas to signifying forms for the repetition of old ideas. The student is faced by a controversial choice between tradition and innovation; yet the novel is discovered only by starting from the familiar, and the familiar is recognized and takes on meaning only in the context of the novel.

Rhetoric has undergone degradations in the course of its history following the three-stage cycle of evolution of the liberal arts. It has been, from time to time, an art of persuasion by invention or discovery. It has become an art of persuasion by three devices, pleasing, moving, and "teaching," which have been analyzed with respect to audiences and to effects on audiences. It has finally been degraded to an art of persuasion by using arguments adapted to existing opinions, ascertained by polling methods, in order to induce unexamined, imposed attitudes on captive, passive audiences. Yet it is known, even when this is the received conception of rhetoric, or communication, or public relations, that great rhetoricians practice an art of rhetoric by which they change opinions rather than conform to them and that they induce new opinions by arguments that lead to agreement rather than to submission or hypnosis. It is known also that communication is a road that leads not only to consensus in shared illusion, preconception, and error, but also to critical insight, interpretation, and definition of what is the case and how it may be formulated. The art of communication is an art of achieving consensus about facts or actions by use of language: it is a technique of cajolement when its devices depend simply on the use of communication for desired effects; it is an instrument of satisfaction when the devices are adjusted to what is in fact wanted; it is an art of discovery when the devices relate agreement and aspiration to what is the case.

The idolatry of facts is often expressed as a conviction that the progress of science makes the practice of the liberal arts difficult, if not impossible: the sum of knowledge is now so great that no one man can encompass it; the universal genius of the Renaissance and the generally educated man of the Enlightenment who understood all the sciences and appreciated all the arts are now impossible. It was never possible, even in dark ages and in primitive societies, to grasp all the facts available concerning circumscribed objects and experiences or concerning the whole culture. The facts potentially available in any situation are infinite; those actually available are sufficiently numerous to provide the marks of an elite, or sage, or sacred class. We may question the facts of other ages, or cultures, or sciences; but their fault will not be found by counting them and finding them finite. The liberal arts provided disciplines applicable to facts by isolating structures of facts; those structures do not become more complex and difficult as facts become more numerous. A new rhetoric is developing as a liberal art to provide the discipline for investigating the structure of facts and the interrelations of facts. It examines inventions in the humanities and discoveries in the sciences, not as continuations of traditions nor as abrupt unprecedented innovations, but as originalities in which the construction of the new is built in faithful and assiduous imitation of nature and of men.

The structure of the disciplines as a structure of interpretations and of experiences. The concern for facts has become an idolatry of unadulterated, "value-free" facts. What is, must not be confused with what ought to be; and no insight can be gained into what ought to be by examining what is. Such values as we find in the world owe their authenticity and acceptability to their separation from what is the case. Yet the student's encounter with knowledge in his education finds the guidelines to facts in values and the determinations of values in facts. Values serve as criteria in inquiry and action. We have knowledge of facts only if what we profess to know is objective or true, relevant to something significant or good, and well constructed or beautiful. The student preserves his conviction that facts are value-free by making a dubious distinction between facts related to knowledge and values related to preferences.

The liberal art that is needed to meet this situation must use the principle of indifference to combine the interpretation of facts with the interpretation of values. It is indeed impossible to separate the two interpretations in fact, but it is possible to distinguish them in thought and then construct arts which make the distinction a separation and to formulate philosophic principles which provide theoretic grounds for the separation of the processes and the products of the arts distinguished in the single, common experience. Education is directed to both factual criticism and valuative appreciation, to understanding the assumptions which ground facts and the facts which ground assumptions. This is a single aim, but it has been split into a tiresome iteration of the age-old opposition between facts and values.

The liberal art grammar was once concerned with the art of interpretation. At times in antiquity and the Middle Ages it was practiced as an art of interpretation of texts which is also an interpretation of experience and the world. One medieval writer brings his description of grammar to a culmination by observing that it trains us not only in the use of language, but also in the use of our faculties of sight and hearing; that it guides us to writing correctly, and it sharpens our vision. In accord with current conceptions of the province of grammar, since the texts in which these statements are made present no philological difficulties, little grammatical ingenuity has been used to puzzle out what the author and his contemporaries might have meant by such statements. Yet, when grammar is used as an instrument of interpretation, it is seen that they are not vague formulae of praise. A student who learns to interpret and understand what a wise man or a poet says will have learned to see, and hear, and perceive things that he would not have noticed before.

Grammar has had three stages of degradation in which the concern with statements has been separated artificially from attention to what is said, and verbal forms or usages have been purified from requirements of facts or values. Grammar has been, from time to time, an art of interpreting language, experience, and nature by being an art of using language according to requirements set by what is meant and how and in respect to what it is meant. It has been narrowed to the art of interpreting what is said by becoming an art of using language according to rules calculated to achieve the various values discovered in interpretation of masterful instances of the use of language. It has finally been degraded to an art of interpreting actual verbal usages by becoming an art of describing language as it is used without intrusion of theoretic or normative considerations. Yet it is known—even when the received conception of grammar conforms to criteria provided by the description of the sounds and forms men do use in speech and the ways in which they do make themselves understood—that some forms of statement are more effective than others in communication with men, and that some are better adapted to the expression of what is true, what is good, and what is beautiful in facts, actions, and compositions. It is known also that the art of stating value-free facts may provide the model indifferently for the expression of vacuous inanities and for the expression of substantive values. The art of interpretation is an art of determining and using the senses and significances of language, of relating words to facts and meanings. It is descriptive when it is an art of the facts of language and of language use; it is normative or prescriptive when usage is made to conform to rules intended to go beyond linguistic facts to encompass intention of users and insight of hearers; it is interpretative when patterns of senses and meanings are explored in constructions of statement and expression.

The idolatry of value-free facts is often expressed as a conviction that statements of fact are subject to unambiguous interpretation, while statements of value impose a multiplicity of interpretations on the same facts, since they are expressions of emotional responses to facts and of preferences based on those emotions. On the basis of this dubious antithesis it is concluded that men in all parts of the world agree in their knowledge of facts but differ in their appreciation of values, and programs of study of other cultures than our own reflect the consequences of this premise. The connections between facts and values in a culture are closer than such a separation permits, for values enter into the determination of facts and facts into the determination of values: the discovery of facts is either by learning known facts or by uncovering unknown facts; the discovery of values is either by recovering values once recognized or uncovering values not yet expressed. The universality of art is not unlike the universality of science: one of the marks of great art is that it is recognized and appreciated by men of different backgrounds without need of explanation, and the use of footnotes to recover meanings familiar to the artist does not always contribute directly to uncovering of values in his art. A new grammar is developing as a liberal art to provide the discipline for interpreting the structure of statements and experiences in arts, sciences, and societies. It examines the structure constituted by facts and values which makes transition possible from statement to expectation to fact.

The structure of disciplines as a structure of methods of inquiry and proof. The concern for facts and values, for observation and interpretation, has become an idolatry of "unique" facts in their contexts and circumstance. What is, is always particular, and generalizations are subject to suspicion or rejection unless they are presented as generalizations used to order particulars rather than as generalizations about particulars. Such generalities as we recognize are the opinions of particular men or particular experts, or they are the structures of particular cultural or mathematical groups. Yet when the student learns, his encounter with knowledge is an exploration of universal connections and laws. He is encouraged to think of these sequences and consequences alternatively as interrelated causal chains and as unrelated and noncausal formulae of covariation.

The liberal art needed to relate the uniqueness of experience of particular occurrences to the regularity of knowledge of universal processes must use the principle of indifference to combine awareness of the consequences of processes with awareness of the consequences of arguments. Education is directed to both inquiry and proof, to description of the concrete and generalization of the universal. The two are aspects of a single aim, but it has been transformed into the age-old problem of universals and particulars, subjected to vast attention and ingenuity during the Middle Ages and revived again today, which works out puzzles about the grounds of generalities when they are considered apart from properties in particulars observed and thought about.

The liberal art logic was once concerned with the art of examining discursive, rational, and phenomenal consequences. Aristotle thought that logic deals with terms, propositions, and syllogisms whose characteristics depend on the language in which they are formed, the significances they express, and the things they denote. He criticized Plato for making things thought and Democritus for making thoughts movements of atoms. The Platonic dialectic as a result depends on a universe intrinsically intelligible, and the atomistic canonic avoids verbal forms to concentrate on rules of thought. Cicero thought that any systematic treatment of discourse must have two parts—one concerned with invention or the processes of inquiry and the other concerned with judgment or the processes of proof. Mill and Whewell engaged in lengthy and acrimonious controversy in the nineteenth century concerning the meaning and possibility of a logic of discovery distinct from the logic of proof.

The controversies of logic are as active and as impassioned as the controversies of grammar and rhetoric, and any list of degradations or purifications of logic bears the mark of partisanship in those controversies. We have purified logic of metaphysical commitments to the nature of things and of psychological commitments to the laws of thought; we have instituted logic on arbitrary undefined symbols and arbitrary rules in artificial languages constructed to avoid ambiguity, and we have discovered logic in the wisdom imbedded from long and multifarious experiences in ordinary language; we vary the formulation of logics of proof with excursions into the construction of symbolic logics, mathematical logics, logics of inquiry, and logics of discovery. We note, from time to time, that many philosophers, scientists, and cultures cultivate varieties of dialectics in preference to abstract verbal logics. The art of discourse or argument is an art of tracing consequences in statements, thoughts, and processes. It may place its emphasis on one or another of these sequences; it is a liberal art when it relates the three; it becomes technical knowledge when it is limited to an account of the facts or operations of symbols, ideas, or occurrences.

The idolatry of concrete facts in their contexts is often expressed as a conviction that the problems of the social sciences and the humanities will become intelligible and solvable when the scientific method is applied to them. A dubious antithesis emerges from this plausible hypothesis, for the particular in its determining context will be discovered by the scientific method, while the universal is recovered in the recognition that there is but one scientific method and there should be but one unified science. Yet the structures found in knowledge and science suggest that there are many methods of inquiry and there are many formulations of the one method of demonstration. The methods of inquiry and investigation and the method of argumentation and of discourse are more closely related than the separation of particular facts from formal statements permits, for the sequences of discourse must coincide at points with the sequences of occurrences, and the sequences of occurrences are apparent only when they are formulated for communication to determine whether others also recognize them. Logic is developing into a liberal art again to provide the discipline for examining the structure of consequences in processes and the structure of consequences in discourse.

The structure of disciplines as a structure of systems of knowledge and action. The concern for facts, values, and discursive sequences has become an idolatry of "coherent" relations of facts. What is contradictory is impossible, and what is unadjusted, disorderly, or chaotic must be modified to adjustment or disappear in destruction. Such order as we find in the world is an arrangement of definite facts in mutually consistent relations. Yet the student's encounter with knowledge, and inquiry, and discusssion throughout his education is a discovery that the very possibility of these enterprises, as well as progress in them when they are possible, depends on ambiguity and contradiction.

The liberal art needed to guide the student in his response to systems and in his essays at systematization must use the principle of indifference to combine definite literalness with productive ambiguity. Discussion would be impossible if the agreement on the issue to be discussed did not contain an ambiguity, for there is no need for discussion if the statement of the problem does not open ways to alternative hypotheses. Inquiry and progress in knowledge take their start in the same productive ambiguity and employ methods to arrive at unambiguous resolutions. It has long been recognized that education is concerned both with schemata and loci, with wholes which determine the character of the interrelated parts and with parts which determine the character of constructed wholes. This is a single aim, but it has been made into one more instance of the age-old dilemma of Part and Whole, in which the whole is and is not the sum of its parts.

The liberal art dialectic was once concerned with the art of systematization. The system it sought was not merely an ordering of things in a universe, but an ordering of things, thoughts, and symbols in a cosmos. It adjusted to fruitful progressive interactions the realms of necessity and freedom, of prediction and choice, of possibility and desirability, of statement of fact and expression of value, and many other realms which might seem antagonistic and mutually exclusive outside their systematic interrelations. Dialectic has been degraded to an ideological and schismatic device to advance the interests or to apply the preconceptions of materialistic, or spiritualistic, or verbalistic factions.

The idolatry of coherent facts is often expressed as a need for a common frame of reference for all men, all cultures, or all knowledge. Yet it is obvious from the history of cultures and of systems that the frame of reference for mankind must preserve the pluralism of frames that made possible the advances in knowledge, in culture, and in community which have constituted for mankind a common frame of reference. A new dialectic is developing from the contacts of cultures, and peoples, and disciplines to provide the discipline for investigating the systems of things, of experiences, and of discourses.

To summarize, ours is an age of concreteness. The liberal arts are the universal skills required to do particular tasks. They are disciplines both in the sense of methods of inquiry and in the sense of acquaintance with subjects. The disciplines as methods relate the disciplines as subjects. They are liberal arts in that they liberate man and equip him to be active in four respects—with respect to other men, with respect to the world about him, with respect to the achievements of men, and with respect to his own potentialities and actions.

The liberal arts liberate man with respect to men in communication. The dangers of conformity result from the use of the art of persuasion. Conformity is as great in revolution as in tradition. Whether or not it is called rhetoric, the new liberal art will combine tolerance and freedom, respect for the views of others with responsibility in expressing and advancing one's own.

The liberal arts liberate man with respect to the world in knowledge. The double and allied dangers of dogmatism in asserting fact and gullibility in accepting fact result from the use of the art of advancing the interpretation of fact and value advocated by one's faction, or sect, or pressure group. The dogmatism and gullibility are as great in statements of fact as in statements of value. They are interpretations which raise no questions about what is or what ought to be but only questions about how to translate what you think ought to be into what must be. Whether or not it is called grammar, the new liberal art will combine the descriptive with the normative, expression of the facts of the case with expression of the values of a culture.

The liberal arts liberate man with respect to the achievements of men in appreciation. The dangers of reductionism, of viewing everything as *merely* one form of something else which must be taken as basic, result from the use of one preferred method. The reduction is as rigid in inquiry into the unknown as in demonstration of the known. Whether or not it is called logic, the new liberal art will combine perception and criticism, insight into the consequences of particular things and application of the consequences of universal laws.

The liberal arts liberate man with respect to himself in individuality. The danger of yielding to illiberality because of the complexities of knowledge, the difficulties of human relations, and the pressures of interests in the modern world result from the use of divisive arts of systematization. The danger is as great when the system is pluralistic as when it is monolithic. This freedom is the summation of the other three freedoms in the freedom of the individual. Whether or not it is called dialetic, the new liberal art will combine increased individual spontaneity with increased complexity of environing circumstances. It is an art which focuses on the opportunities in the modern world which are uniquely threats and dangers without the liberal arts.

XVII

1964 Turbulence Among Students

F. Martin Erickson

I do not believe we have ever been very successful in channeling student energies toward any ends—constructive or otherwise. From time to time, we may establish appropriate boundaries for students, but essentially we cannot in any real sense channel the energies of the young. I believe that what has been termed the present climate of student criticism and desire for independence may be extremely misleading; what we are confronted with is essentially a question of values and the search for self-identity, a far more complex and challenging problem. I also believe it is necessary to develop a different relationship than we have traditionally sought with students. This relationship I would oversimplify and refer to as one of trust. This is a most difficult relationship to attain with anyone and is further complicated by the differences in status, role, and generation we experience when attempting to achieve it with members of the current college generation. I place a great value on an open and permissive relationship with students. The concept of channeling student energies toward any end seems to me a contradiction of what I believe is most important in working with students. To be anything else than open and free with students is to risk the possibility of manipulating and covertly directing student behavior.

As for my conclusion that the real issue is one of values and the search for self-identity, it is here that I have the greatest concern. Let us look at today's college population and note some of its characteristics. I believe there is some evidence that students begin resolving some of their basic feelings regarding authority at an earlier age than they have previously. It seems to me there is clear evidence today that high school students are actively engaged in resolving this authority issue, and this accounts for much of the aggressive behavior demonstrated by high school students both within and without the classroom. Therefore, attempts to deal with students in a nondirective fashion so traditional in our approach to relationships with students seem to be appropriate no longer. If the student has begun to resolve some of the critical issues in his personality development, he may look forward to some true confrontation with issues of life rather than nondirective reflections of those thoughts he has already expressed. I fear that we stand in danger of rationalizing the true significance of student action or protest under the guise that they are acting out the authority problem. Although many of the students, like all of us, are still coping with this critical issue, I do not believe that what has been termed student criticism and desire for independence can continue to be placed under the heading of the authority issue. Today's students are more mature and more knowledgeable when they enter the university; and there is every reason for us to believe that they come to us better prepared emotionally than they did ten years ago.

What is the college student really like? I am sure each of us has a different perception, but I believe that Kenneth Keniston, in his article on "Social Change and Youth in America," offers some penetrating insights into what may be going on:

One of the most outstanding . . . characteristics of young people today is their apparent lack of deep commitments to adult values and roles. An increasing number of young people . . . are alienated from their parents' conceptions of adulthood, disaffected from the mainstreams of traditional public life, and disaffiliated from many of the historical institutions of our society. This alienation is . . . one of the cardinal tenets of the Beat Generation; but it more subtly characterizes a great many other young people. . . . A surprising number of these young men and women, despite their efforts to get good scholarships and good grades so that they can get into a good medical school and have a good practice, nonetheless view the world they are entering with a deep mistrust. . . . The adult world into which they are headed is seen as a cold, mechanical, abstract, specialized, and emotionally meaningless place in which one simply goes through the motions, but without conviction that the motions are worthy, humane, dignified, relevant, or exciting. Thus, for many young people, it is essential to stay "cool"; and "coolness" involves detachment. . . .

This is a bleak picture, and it must be partially qualified. For few young people are deliberately cynical or calculating; rather, many feel forced into detachment and premature cynicism because society seems to offer them so little that is relevant, stable, and meaningful. They wish there were values, goals, or institutions to which they could be genuinely committed; they continue to search for them; and, given something like the Peace Corps, which promises challenge and a genuine expression of idealism, an extraordinary number of young people are prepared to drop everything to join. . . .

The members of this apparently irresponsible generation are surprisingly sane, realistic, and levelheaded. *They may not be given to vast enthusiasms, but neither are they given to fanaticism. They have a great, even an excessive, awareness of the complexities of the world around them; they are well-read and well-informed. . . . The sanity of young people today is partly manifest in their aware-*

ness that their world is very different from that of their parents. They know that rash commitments may prove outmoded tomorrow; they know that most viewpoints are rapidly shifting; they therefore find it difficult to locate a fixed position on which to stand.

Furthermore, many young men and women sense that their parents are poor models for the kinds of lives they themselves will lead in their mature years: that is, poor exemplars for what they should and should not be. Or perhaps it would be more accurate to say, not that their parents are poor models (for a poor model is still a model of what not to be), but that parents are increasingly irrelevant as models for their children. Many young people are at a real loss as to what they should seek to become: no valid models exist for the as-yet-to-be-imagined world in which they will live. Not surprisingly, their very sanity and realism sometimes leads them to be disaffected from the values of their elders.

I agree with Keniston that many of our youth are at a real loss as to what they should seek to become. Participation in the Peace Corps, Student Nonviolent Coordinating Committee, Freedom Riders, Literacy Education, and other social movements where we find a significant number of students involved are in reality not so much a reflection of student criticism or a desire for independence, but rather a seeking after a fixed position upon which they may take a stand and be better ready to meet whatever change this "yet-to-be-imagined world" may offer. It is my belief that we must, as responsible educators, develop a relationship with the students that enables them to explore with us our beliefs and values as well as our sources. If we cannot serve as exemplars, we can at least share with them what we do believe and why. In order to do this we must begin, then, to cope with a relationship of trust. Each one may approach this in his own way. It seems to be clear, however, that there are some characteristics that all of us can strive for in developing this relationship. We must provide acceptance and in turn ask the student to accept us. There must be a climate created in which there is a high degree of awareness and spontaneity so that we and the student may give and take in an honest fashion. We must share in working toward a common goal. And lastly, in order to obtain trust, awareness, spontaneity, and shared goals, we must have an interdependent relationship.

Very simply, then, the values that are important in developing this climate are love, trust, faith, honesty, integrity, and genuine freedom. If we can join in this open way of relating to students, we may significantly help them in the process of self-identity. They may learn from us whence we came and why and, from this panorama, project the goals and the future that they envision. They then may emerge with a set of personal goals which will help them achieve a maturity in their criticism of the world around them and a real sense of freedom far greater than that to be found in independence. I am sure that, for many of us, joining with students in their search for values is an anxious and threatening thought, but I am convinced that neither our generation nor theirs knows exactly what will be right for them tomorrow. All we can do is share with one another in such a way that the values with which they emerge are appropriate to the challenges they will face.

XVIII

1964
Abolishing the Grading System

Paul Goodman

❀❀❀❀❀❀❀❀❀❀❀❀❀❀❀❀❀❀❀❀❀❀❀❀❀❀❀❀❀❀❀

The retaining of grading in the colleges is an interesting case of bureaucratic inertia and subservience to the social climate. Almost a consensus of teachers says that grading hurts teaching and learning and the spirit of the community but is inevitable, apparently because of extramural pressures. Yet the colleges are fairly autonomous and could do what they want in such a respect, and indeed some colleges do not have grading without disastrous results.

It is said, "Without grading, how will corporations, graduate schools, or foundations know whom to select?" They can select by admissions testing, just as the student was first admitted to the college. Why should the college test and grade for these extramural persons? Furthermore, each employer or graduate department has its own specific requirements for which it can test far more efficiently than it can rely on college grades, often outdated. In fact, civil service, accounting, medicine, and others do test specifically for licensing, apart from college grades. It is absurd when the dean of a leading university praises the high predictive value of the aptitude-and-achievement tests for entrance and then condones the unnecessary grading system in the school itself.

We need a clear and distinct idea of examining. We properly examine a candidate to see if he is acceptable *into* an enterprise or community. Once he is in, why distinguish one from another in the class, like first- and second-class citizens? If a student is not performing, it is more courageous and sensible to fire him out of the class than to downgrade him. A second proper kind of examination is to see if the youth has now grown up to be a peer. In medieval times, he proved his entry into the guild by a masterpiece—academically, a lecture and disputation. The point, however, is to do something that wins respect—not to pass somebody else's questions, which would maintain him precisely in his condition of inferiority and immaturity.

Perhaps the chief objectors to the abolition of grading would be parents and the students themselves. The parents would object because of their anxiety and insecure competitiveness; but these attitudes have already done too much damage to their children and should be rebuffed. The students would feel at a loss and unstructured, because they have been used to nothing else. But it is the duty of the college to make them grow up in this, as in other respects, to become self-reliant, self-initiating. With the grading and the tutelage on sexual and other moral matters, how do we expect the young suddenly to be independent and make important choices at twenty-one?

The worst defect of grading is that it destroys the use of testing. The pedagogic use of a test is to help the student structure what he knows and discover what he does not know. It is contradictory to punish him, by downgrading, for revealing his ignorance, rather than encouraging him to place himself at the level where he really is. Inevitably grading invites faking. Testing is a good diagnostic for the teacher, both of the student and of the teaching. But what does a grade mean? If out of five questions in algebra, the student misses two, what does 60 per cent mean? It is particularly logarithms and permutations that the student does not know, not 40 per cent of the subject.

Consider the important case of science teaching. According to the colleagues of Jerome S. Bruner (professor of psychology at Harvard University) in *The Process of Education,* the young creative scientist must be taught not facts but the basic ideas and methods; and he should be encouraged to guess and make wild hypotheses. *The Process* explicitly warns against grading. For the average youngster who will not become a scientist, it is the humanistic and moral value of science, and the meaning of science altogether, that are important. For instance, it is most instructive if the student spends the whole term checking up why his chemistry experiment did *not* work—his carelessness, dirty test tube, and so on; this is more profitable than repeating the table of the elements or memorizing formulas. But is such an activity really gradable?

Many students are lazy and do not do the work, and it is said that grading is a necessary extrinsic spur. By and large, laziness is a character neurosis: for example, it may be a way of avoiding failing, or it may be a way of proving one is superior and does not need to (will not) learn anything more. In such cases it is certainly unwise to repeat the traumatic demand which caused the neurotic pattern in the beginning. Most often, however, not doing the work means exactly what it says: that the work does not really suit—either not that subject, or not at that time, or maybe not in a school setting at all at that time. Then the terrible thing is that the bright student, threatened by failure, *will* cram and pass—and at once forget what he has learned; he has given up his own instinctive demand and wasted the teacher's time. In an atmosphere of ungraded testing, he might discover what he really wants to do. Conversely, some students who fail and are flunked out are really fit for the subject but have not quite found themselves. The teacher might guess this, but the computer is inexorable.

The competitive grading, the credits, the lock-step scheduling, and speed-up are all part of the cash accounting and logistic mentality that is exactly what we do not need in the automated future, when most of the serious work in life will, or should, be concerned with community culture, citizenly initiative, worthwhile leisure, and social service. These are not gradable and cannot be subdivided into credits.

Needless to say, the present emphasis and reliance on grading is partly a consequence of the incredible overcrowding of the schools by many who are not academically talented at all. But this should be faced as a separate problem, and it would be salutary indeed if the Association for Higher Education would resolve somewhat as follows: Very many young people—including many who are bright— ought to be educated in ways other than under academic administration in high schools and colleges. To subject them to long schooling is a misuse of their time of life, or society's money, and of the efforts of teachers. Therefore, we urge society and government to find out and provide numerous other ways to solve some of the present problems of technical training and unemployment, rather than putting a disproportionate burden on the schools. Further, almost all youth need experiences other than twelve to twenty years of uninterrupted school lessons to grow up and find themselves; and many people profit by schooling when they are more mature. Therefore, let us devise and provide more flexible and open opportunities for quitting and returning to academic life than the present system allows.

XIX

1964
Universities and
Social Order

William Sloane Coffin, Jr.

❀❀❀❀❀❀❀❀❀❀❀❀❀❀❀❀❀❀❀❀❀❀❀❀❀❀❀❀❀❀❀❀

Here is a text from the late Whitney Griswold: "Every basic institution bears a direct responsibility for society's moral health. The university bears a large and exceptionally important part of this responsibility." What can we say of our moral health? Not long ago a
foreign observer remarked, "You Americans are so obsessed with the
luxuries of life that you are forgetting the necessities." What he had
in mind might have been what *Newsweek* recently termed the "good

nonlife" in America, the way our culture makes the middle class safe, polite, obedient, and sterile.

A couple of centuries ago most college graduates went into the service of the church or state. Since then the range of vocational choices has widened, and properly so. Still, is it not disturbing to recall that, at the founding of our nation when we had a total population less than Los Angeles County today, we turned out a generation of statesmen named Washington, Hamilton, Franklin, Jefferson, Adams—and you could name a list as long as your arm? Yet today, with population sixty times as great and with statesmanship needed as never before, how many people can you name of the caliber of our first generation of statesmen? And why are there not more? Because, as Plato said, "What is honored in the country will be cultivated there."

"Cease to do evil, learn to do good. Seek justice, correct oppression." So said the Prophet Isaiah. But how many of our graduates are actively seeking justice, actively correcting oppression? Our society is organized with a view first and foremost to business— profits first, people afterward. You have heard the civil rights debate: what is more real, real people or real estate?

There is an increasing number of people for whom the affluent society is neither a reality nor even a hope: most Negroes, and millions of whites. And while a few months ago these millions were as wailing orphans on the doorstep, now they are finding their strength and finding the structures of society strangely vulnerable. So, if things do not change radically, soon, Samsonlike, they are going to strive to bring the structures of society crashing down in a cloud of dust. And woe to the privileged who judge them, for surely it is the role of society's leaders that they should bring forth the captives out of bondage.

Traditionally, two institutions—the church and the state— have transcended society. But I suggest that the problem of both is ineffectiveness. In the churches with breath-taking regularity Sunday after Sunday the wine is turned into water. And the university seems equally ineffective. Never before have we had a level of attendance so high, never a level of performance so high, and yet never before have we had a level of influence so low. Our problem is not that we are incompetent, only that we are somehow insignificant; not that what we say is not impressive intellectually, only somehow unimportant historically.

Why does our teaching lack consequence? I suggest we look in four areas of university life. The first is ourselves. Teachers are not a committed lot and are in danger of becoming even less so as their intellectual competence increases. Our fear of being naive prohibits the possibility of being moved, so that increasingly we end up going through the motions but not the emotions. If you want to assess the degree of timidity of an academic community, assess the degree of risk in what follows whenever a professor says, "Now I am really going to stick my neck out." The poet Heine wrote in a letter: "When I lately stood with a friend before the Cathedral Amiens, he asked me why we can no longer build such piles. I replied, 'Dear Alphonse, men in those days had convictions. We moderns have opinions, and it requires something more than an opinion to build a Gothic cathedral.' "

For instance, in November, 1954, when public hearings were held in Virginia as to whether the public schools should remain open and public, 143 people testified. When Jeffersonian principles were at stake, how many professors from Mr. Jefferson's own university raised their voices? Not one. How many raised their voices during the McCarthy era? And how many college presidents have spoken out in support of the Civil Rights Bill, or in opposition to the mindless militancy of the right?

"The teacher as pedagogue has an obligation to stand up and be counted, if only for the sake of stimulating thought and debate. But as preceptor, he also has the duty to set an example of moral and intellectual courage." So said Kingman Brewster. Too often safety is treasured above truth, and our students know it. And they know you cannot talk about love of truth if you fear to take a stand, for love and fear cannot be mated. Of course there are prudential considerations that are real, particularly for college presidents. But let them find others to say for them what they cannot say themselves. And let them back up these individuals with the simple statement that the university guarantees members of the faculty no less freedom than that guaranteed them by the nation. If they do not do at least this much, then let them make no judgments on the cynicism of their students regarding the power of money, for the students know they are bought.

A second area where I think our teaching lacks consequence concerns the curriculum. Albert Camus, in his play *Caligula,* has Cherea say: "To lose one's life is a little thing, and I will have the courage when necessary. But to see the sense of this life dissipated, to see our reason for existence disappear, that is intolerable. A man cannot live without meaning." It was Socrates who said, "To philosophize is to learn how to die." He knew where to look for meaning. But how many philosophers consider death the burning business of philosophy? How many educators are concerned with the great implacables of life? Is it not melancholy fact that most are paid to avoid these issues as we educate, not to make a life but to make a living; and that even those not paid to avoid them still manage to sidestep them with an agility that is positively breathtaking? Small wonder, then, that our students find so little of higher education meaningful; we are not dealing with areas where meaning is to be found.

A third area concerns vocational decision. Not long ago a great trial lawyer addressed a class at Harvard Law School and asked, "How many are going to become criminal lawyers?" One hand in front, and one in the back of the room. Then he asked, "How many are going to become corporation lawyers?" A forest of hands. "So," said he, "you all want to enter the guiltless society."

There is a distinction between an attractive job and an important one, and it runs through all our professions today. If a man is going to become a teacher, where is he going to teach? In Chicago, New York City, in the slums—or in some nice preparatory school? And if he is going to be a minister, is he going to be the pastor of a well-to-do suburban church, or a slum priest? A man can join something a little more controversial than the Heart Fund. Among all the people for whom I have voted as a school or college trustee, never have I found one who has listed the Urban League, or the NAACP, or the Human Relations Council, or any of the civil rights groups as an extracurricular vocation—and in a day when this is the number one problem of the nation.

While universities and churches are concerned with how

people spend their money, they are not concerned with how they make it in the first place. Universities know that the acquisition of knowledge is second to its use, yet still allow public relations aspects to dictate which moral concerns they will make their own; so in every college I know sexual morality is considered far more important than vocational morality.

The last area is the extracurricular. I recently went to lunch with a law student who had just decided to join the civil rights section of the Justice Department. He pointed out a teacher at a neighboring table. "On account of that man I am going into the Justice Department." My heart leaped with joy: a teacher with influence! He explained, "He was my twelfth-grade teacher, and on the first day of class said, 'Fellows, there are things in this world on which you cannot turn your backs, and this year is going to be devoted to finding out what they are.' What happened in class was nothing. But he dragged us into town, into the slums. He dragged us through the court so we could see the whores, and drunks, and all the other lost people in the society who get judged at 9 A.M. in what constitutes an exercise in futility. It was at that time I pledged myself to do something for the poor."

In other words, are values taught or caught? Are they learned abstractly in the classroom, or are they experienced concretely outside?

From all sides we are urged not to self-sacrifice, but to self-preservation. Don't give, take. Don't climb out on a limb, cling close to the trunk. Look out for every bit of self-advantage you possibly can. We absorb these values on the deep emotional level, and it is naive of the academic community to think that in the classroom, on a purely intellectual level, these values can be confronted and overcome.

Take, for instance, the issue of civil rights. Everybody says all men are created equal, but who feels the monstrosity of inequality? Usually only those who become concretely involved in the civil rights struggle. Let us open the gates and let more experience come in, open the gates and encourage our students to go out. We cannot allow ourselves to be caught in the contradiction of having an extracurricular life on a residential campus enhance values which are opposed to the very values we are trying to stimulate in the classroom. Yet this happens all the time. Fraternities, for instance, are monuments to irrelevance; and yet how many colleges have done much about them? Rushing could be put off till the sophomore year. Better yet, the junior year. By that time many have seen the light. Or one can take the bottom quarter of all fraternities and put them automatically on social probation.

And what of the summer vacations? College students should not be lifeguards to get suntans. To stimulate them to do something else, colleges ought to have one full-time man, a live wire to play a brokerage role in collecting all the interesting kinds of experiences students could have at home and abroad, during and after college, that would enhance the values the college is trying to stand for. For values, once again, are caught as well as taught and therefore must be deeply experienced so they become part of the whole person.

The relationship I would like to see between university and society is that of a lovers' quarrel, with the accent equally on lover and quarrel. For there are two things neither society nor the university can risk: alienation or identification.

PART *Three*

After 1964

This generation of students is going to produce enormous changes in our social, political, ethical, and religious life, both in and out of our universities. It is not going to be easy. In fact, I think we have some pretty rough years ahead; but if any organization is responsible for this transition—and it is a frightening one—it is the university. As a member of a university, I feel a little scared by my responsibility.

On the other hand, I am afraid it is no good to be frightened. We have to take our courage in both hands and go on; because there is no way back to Eden. The angel stands at its gate with the flaming sword, and once you have lost innocence, you have lost it. Once you wise up you can never wise down. There is no way to go but on to Zion, wherever and whatever it is.

from the address of Kenneth E. Boulding
before the 1966 National Conference on Higher Education

1965
Challenge of
Civil Rights

Whitney M. Young, Jr.

❀❀❀❀❀❀❀❀❀❀❀❀❀❀❀❀❀❀❀❀❀❀❀❀❀❀❀❀❀❀

The events in Selma, Alabama, have made this essay a frightening necessity. The fact that we have a civil rights revolution is a credit to education. But the fact that there is a need for a revolution is to the everlasting shame of American education. Education has failed to teach what democracy is all about.

To assume that what happened in Selma is a tragedy only for the people in Selma is a mistake. If the events that happened in

Selma do not convince the American people that the government at the federal level must step in to protect the rights of American citizens, then nothing will. The federal government cannot expect to keep peace in the Congo or win in Viet Nam if it will do nothing in Alabama. We have to send in troops to Viet Nam because we have not been able to sell other people on our ideologies. Our men have to die in Viet Nam, therefore; but no Russian soldiers have to die in Viet Nam. Yesterday's headlines in Selma are today's headlines in Viet Nam, to our disgrace.

At stake is not just the rights of Negroes, but at stake is American education and American society. We will either inculcate people with the idea of standing up and being counted, or our entire society will eventually fail. I am far less concerned with the demagoguery or the rantings and actions of a Sheriff Clark or a Governor Wallace than I am with the thunderous silence of the nice, quiet, genteel, Christian masses. When people question whether the Negroes in Selma are pushing too fast, it is a challenge to all of American education to set the facts straight. What the Negroes in Selma are fighting for is more than just the right to march peaceably; it is the right for *one* Constitution and *one* Bill of Rights, instead of one for whites and one for Negroes. The federal government is going to have to step in. And this is no time to take an opinion poll to find out whether it is the expedient thing to do; this is the time to take courageous steps.

For this generation of Americans the opportunity is clear and challenging. It is to make civilization a stage of social advancement where human beings must combine their diverse resources, talents, and abilities to remove racial, religious, and ethnic barriers on the one hand, while rehabilitating the disadvantaged on the other hand.

I believe the twentieth century will not be remembered primarily by the historians as the age which saw the greatest advancement of technology, automation, Sputnik, or wonder drugs. Nor will historians make heroes out of those whose sole contribution to mankind was their escalade up the walls of an affluent middle-class society. The heroes in this history will be those who cared enough to become the voice of the voiceless people and the hope of hopeless people. It was Washington Irving who said, "The idol of today pushes the hero of yesterday out of our recollection and will, in turn, be supplanted by his successor of tomorrow." The heroes will be those who recognized that the poverty and discrimination of the rural Anglo-Saxon, of the overcrowded Puerto Rican, of the trapped Negro, of the naked Indian, of the migrating Mexican-American, of the Oriental, is not comic. Some people are being auctioned off cheap in our society because others cannot look beneath the veneer of skin or even be aware of the heart beneath.

One of the strengths of the American system has been the mingling of Anglo-Saxon, Afro-Asian, and European strains. Ours is a hybrid system. It is a blend of individualism and collection which reflects both the Yankee's distrust of government and the immigrant's reliance on government to broaden opportunities. As the late President Kennedy once said, "We are a nation of immigrants." Education obviously lies at the foundation of this American system.

Robert Hutchins said education may not save the world but it is our last best hope. But I view with concern certain forces that will catapult the American schools of higher education toward new conceptualizations of philosophy, orientation, and structure. These problems are part and parcel of our efforts to remove the barriers and rehabilitate the disadvantaged. Five to eight years from now, approximately 50 per cent more students should be on the American college campuses as a result of the wave of youngsters born during the baby boom following World War II. One of the first consequences will be a drastic increase in the cost of education.

Since the advent of the printed book, nothing has had such an impact as the technological revolution which is hitting American education simultaneously with the population boom. Peter Drucker believes that programed learning will be the first major technological change in teaching and learning which results from the force of this revolution. But there is still another force that the thinkers and planners of higher education cannot afford to overlook. In 1900, nine-tenths of all Negroes lived in the South. Of this number, four-fifths lived in rural areas where 60 per cent derived their income from agriculture. Today, less than 6 per cent have remained on the Southern farm, and the Negro's economic, social, and political power is being felt in our cities.

The Negro contributes more proportionately to the baby

boom than any other single minority. It is estimated, given the present rate of growth, that in forty-two years the world population will double itself. In forty years the American population will double itself. But the United States Negro population will double itself in thirty-three years.

It is inevitable that we will spend skyrocketing totals on education at the federal as well as state and local levels in the coming years. Under the circumstances, we have made heartening progress since we started setting priorities on education. But we have only begun. Still, over 100,000 of our brightest high school graduates each year will not go to college. Still, only 5.5 per cent of the young Negroes between the ages of 25–29 will complete high school against 75 per cent for white. In other words, the Negro, who constitutes 11 per cent of the population, supplies 21 per cent of the high school dropouts but only 7 per cent of the graduates. Still, two-thirds of Negro college students are women—just the reverse of whites. In a matriarchal unit, mothers make sure that if one of their children has a chance for higher education, the daughter is the one to pursue it.

Clearly, with the Negro student certain handicaps are to be expected, recognized, and overcome. The Negro freshman is usually less well prepared for college life than his white counterpart. His achievement level may be at the tenth-grade level. He is unfamiliar with taking tests, and the tests are not fair measurements of his background and environment. He may be unaware of the handicap of his inferior high school education, and the full realization may strike him with possible traumatic effect. He may not realize the standards of excellence he will have to maintain and how these compare nationally with other colleges. He is generally less well informed about the nation and the world than his white counterpart. He will require more counseling and special help in catching up, keeping up, directing himself toward, and preparing himself for, a career.

The colleges, however, should keep in mind certain facts.

One is that a follow-up study of college records indicates that Negro students are likely to be better achievers than their aptitude tests predict. Such tests tend to reflect not what they can learn but what they have learned. This again indicates the urgent need for proper counseling and special efforts by the institution. Still, out of four million college students enrolled, only 220,000 are Negroes, and 90,000 of these are on campuses of the Negro colleges, where the major course study emphasis, by necessity, is on the social sciences as contrasted with other universities, which are preparing for the age of automation and technology by emphasizing the natural sciences.

I am unimpressed by the college administrator who says he cannot get Negro students or Negro faculty on his campus. If we can get our colleges to work as hard at *in*cluding as they have in the past at *ex*cluding, we could change the situation. It took real genius to keep our college faculties all white over the years. It will take even greater genius now to get them integrated.

Many schools of higher education in the South, labeled for so long as "Negro colleges," will continue to play a significant role in the education of young people in spite of the miserly amounts of money appropriated by federal, state, and local agencies and foundation grants. Many of these schools today represent the major, if not the only, centers of cultural influence existing in some communities for white as well as Negro citizens. Their educational value is expected to expand. It is, therefore, unreasonable to suppose that these institutions will disappear at a time when the nation is faced with an enormous shortage of classroom facilities. But the inadequacies of past training are reflected in the faculties of today. Fifty-one per cent of the faculty in institutions with white students have earned a Ph.D. or equivalent, compared with 28 per cent in institutions with predominantly Negro students. Furthermore, the professor in the Negro college frequently must devote more time to bringing his students up to college-level work than he can devote to pushing them to the frontiers of knowledge.

Therefore, those institutions which desire to be helpful can provide fellowship grants for college teachers in service; can recruit staff without regard to race, sex, religion, or national origin, thus increasing professional incentive among Negro college faculty; can establish staff arrangements with accredited schools in other sections of the country; and can share staffing among small schools and establish cooperative programing.

There is federal support for this special effort. Under the Civil Rights Act of 1964 the U.S. Office of Education has established an Equal Educational Opportunities Program. One phase of this program includes financial and technical support for college and university institutes at which teachers will be specifically trained in solving educational programs occasioned by desegregation. Similarly, under the newly enacted Title XI of the National Defense Education Act, the Office has launched a program to assist colleges and universities in organizing special institutes for those who teach in schools largely populated by deprived youth and for training persons entering the teaching field.

There is higher educational support for this special effort. Indiana University and Stillman College (a predominantly Negro liberal arts college in Tuscaloosa, Alabama) have just concluded a cooperative pact which will include exchange students, faculty, and curriculum experimentation. Similar agreements entered into during the past year include the University of Michigan and Tuskegee Institute; Brown University and Tougaloo College; Florida State University and Florida A and M; The University of Tennessee and Knoxville College; The University of Wisconsin and Texas Southern University; and Cornell and Hampton Institute. Last summer 235 teachers from Negro colleges in the South attended five institutes at Princeton, Indiana University, The University of North Carolina, The University of Wisconsin, and Carnegie Institute of Technology. This was part of the academic upgrading initiated by the late President Kennedy in a special White House meeting in June of 1963 and followed up by the American Council on Education. Next summer a larger number of teachers will attend ten such institutes.

Just what is the American Negro's chance in an affluent society which passed the 1964 Civil Rights Bill?

The Negro begins life with higher odds against him. He is more likely to die in infancy than other babies. In fact, the death rate recently was 92 per cent above that for white infants, a rise from 66 per cent above the whites in 1950. This is largely because Negro women receive less prenatal care, more Negro babies are born prematurely or without hospital care, and are more likely to be delivered by midwives rather than doctors. (And it is up to the educator to interpret the statistics about social problems. When someone throws up the question of Negroes and illegitimacy, let us interpret the facts correctly: in 1962 there were 262,000 illegitimate births in the United States, with 60 per cent of them to Negro women who only comprised 14 per cent of the population. But in the same year there were an estimated one million abortions, 95 per cent of which were performed on white women.)

If the Negro baby lives, the chances of losing his mother in childbirth are relatively high; the maternal mortality rate was four times as high as for white mothers in the last three years. The Negro baby comes into a family that in 72 per cent of cases lives in the city in the Negro ghetto. It is usually a family that is larger than its white counterpart and is jammed into housing that is dilapidated, with quarters structurally unsound or unable to keep out cold, rain, snow, wind, rats, or pests. In other words, it is housing that is a danger to life and limb. Half of all Negro rented dwellings are dilapidated or lack adequate plumbing. Nothing more fundamentally dramatizes this condition than what I witnessed recently in Brooklyn. Disadvantaged Negro youngsters were seen picketing the school board with signs that read: "Ghettos are a crime." "De facto segregation is inhuman." "Keep the cold out." And one sign portrayed an oversize picture of a rat with the inscription, "Stop the rats."

With more mouths to feed, more babies to clothe, and more needs to satisfy, the Negro family is forced to exist on a median income of $62 per week, just 55 per cent of white family income. This proportion has actually slipped since 1952, when Negro family income was 57 per cent of the white family's. Negro men now earn 40 per cent less than white men, and Negro women earn 50 per cent less than white women. One reason for this is that three out of four urban Negroes are in low-skill jobs—those at the bottom of the pay scale—which automation is gobbling up at the rate of 35,000 per week.

Another limitation is that one out of ten Negro workers is illiterate as contrasted with one out of forty white workers. But if the breadwinner is working, the Negro youngster is truly fortunate, for in every fourth Negro home, the worker is jobless, compared with about one white worker out of twenty. In Detroit, 60 per cent of the unemployed are Negroes. So it often happens that the Negro family has to depend on welfare. In many urban centers, the welfare roles consist largely of Negroes. In Chicago, welfare costs the city more than $15.3 million a month, with 266,000 on relief, of which 85 per cent are Negroes. Every fourth Negro family is on re-

lief, some for the third generation. In New York City, where welfare
department expenditures have risen from $182 million a year to
$500 million, 20 per cent of the city's Negro and Puerto Rican pop-
ulations are on welfare as compared with 5.8 per cent of the city's
total population.

When the Negro youngster goes to school, often segregated
in the South and separated in the North, he starts down a path that
has proven no avenue to adequate living, much less to fame or for-
tune. He averages three and a half years less education than white
children. And because Negro children are generally taught in slum
schools with inferior teachers, equipment, and facilities, the real gap
is closer to five or six years. In Chicago and New York City, 90
per cent of the teachers in so-called Negro schools are either new,
problem, or probationary teachers. So the Negro youth is likely to
be a dropout or a "pushout"—pushed out of school, out of work,
out of the home, and out of a future. On street corners and in
alleys in cities across the country one million youths are idling away
their time. Half of these youths are Negroes, more than three times
as many as there should be, in relation to population.

But if the Negro baby survives these vicious barriers and com-
pletes his college work, what can he anticipate?

His lifetime income will be less than that of whites who have
just finished the eighth grade. There are two reasons: Nonwhites are
concentrated in the lower-paid professions, and nonwhite professionals are paid less than their counterparts in the same profession.
Thirty-three per cent of nonwhite male college graduates who are in
professional employment are in the low-paid teaching profession
versus 16 per cent for whites. Eight per cent of nonwhite male college graduates are in the high-paid engineering profession versus 21
per cent whites. Six per cent of nonwhite male college graduates are
lawyers or accountants versus 14 per cent of the whites. There are
proportionately as many nonwhite doctors as white, but the average
earnings of nonwhites are only half that received by whites. In the
highest-paying professions, Negroes are virtually absent. They make
up .5 per cent of all employed engineers, 1 per cent of all salaried
managers, 2.5 per cent of all professional and technical workers, and
40 per cent in the lowest-paying professions as Negro clergymen and
teachers.

History has handed us an irony. The same decade that has seen the virtual collapse of the elaborate legal structure of segregation and discrimination has also seen a widening of the gap between white and Negro in income status, unemployment, housing, and schooling conditions. And many white people have never seen this gap.

The invisible barriers exist, and their effects are more devastating than normal because Negroes are likely not to see them. For example, for three centuries five great European powers—the Dutch, the Belgians, the Portuguese, the French, and the British— ruled Africa and Asia. Africans and Asiatics came to look on colonial rule as the root, tree, and limbs of everything that was primitive and oppressive about Afro-Asian life. "Independence Now," "Freedom Now," "Africa for Africans" became the cry of the people. When legal barriers to independence fell, India was still plagued with the invisible barrier of population density and limited natural resources. African countries faced an explosive series of technological, financial, educational, social, and political problems that have led some to revolts, others to despotism, and still others to Communism.

One can easily understand why Indians, Africans, and Negroes have demanded their freedom, their civil rights, now. We can also understand a James Baldwin's passionate desire to batter down the walls of segregation regardless of what may lie behind the walls. Still, there is a grave danger in any number believing passionately in desegregation itself as a single all-encompassing goal of racial progress. It should be the first goal.

There must also be the opportunity to be equal. The Negro cannot win complete equality in the absence of crash programs for full employment, abolition of slums, the reconstruction of our educational system, and new definitions of work and leisure. This would not be out of character for Americans. From 1820–1830 Americans established special programs for the public school system in the lower grades. It was no less true at the vigorous turn of the twentieth century, when high schools were developed for the millions.

The situation of the Negro today in America to a great extent parallels a similar experience in Europe in 1840, where in every major city on that continent there was a revolution. In a frantic attempt to bring about peace, the surface desires of the people were technically met. But because what had been dealt with was the *symbol* and not the *substance* of the people's concern, the peace was only temporary. And in subsequent years we witnessed a variety of tyrannies with such tragic developments as Russia turning to Communism, Italy turning to Fascism, Germany to Nazism, and Spain to continuous revolt.

If this story of history teaches us anything, it is that community leaders—government and private, lay and clergy, faculty or administrator—cannot sit smugly by, thinking that because there is a crescendo of legal victories against discriminatory practices, the Negro citizen is now on the final threshold of equal participation in American life.

If, as we learned in the European revolutions and in Asia and Africa, peace is more than the absence of war, so it is in human relations. Good race relations are not the absence of conflict, tensions, or even riots. They are the presence of justice and equal opportunity to share in the rewards as well as the opportunities of a truly great society.

Once 90 per cent of our population earned its living from the land. A wise Congress enacted the Morrill Act of 1862 and the Hatch Act of 1887, which helped the state universities help the American people. With the aid of the land-grant colleges, American agriculture produced overwhelming abundance. Today 70 per cent of our people live in urban communities. They are confronted by problems of poverty, residential blight, polluted air and water, inadequate mass transportation and health services, strained human relations, and overburdened municipal services. President Johnson has said, "Our great universities have the skills and knowledge to match these mountainous problems. They can offer expert guidance in community planning, research and development in pressing educational problems, economic and job market studies, continuing education of the community's professional and business leadership, and programs for the disadvantaged. The role of the university must extend far beyond the ordinary extension-type operation. Its research findings and talents must be made available to the community."

In facing these challenges, the National Urban League is poised to make the greatest contribution in its half-century of service to disadvantaged minorities through special efforts with many colleges and universities. Toward this end, we have been providing consistent leadership. The Urban League vocational opportunity campaigns at the community level go back to 1930, and the pace-setting back-to-school campaigns were the forerunner of the U.S. Chamber of Commerce's current stay-in-school campaign. Consultations with school administrators, in-service institutes on minority youth guidance, parent clinics, career conferences at both the secondary and college levels, and the production of audiovisual aids for youth and their parents have all been part of this effort. The Talent Bank Youth Incentive Program is the League's nationally projected equivalent to New York City's Higher Horizons. The League's motion picture "A Morning for Jimmy" has been viewed by a television audience of more than eight million persons in two years and has become a permanent addition to the film collections of many schools and public libraries. Over the years, we have striven to motivate youngsters with such programs as Tomorrow's Scientists and Technicians, Success Centers Career Clubs, cultural enrichment projects, and vocational counseling and placement service. But the League's resources and staff have unfortunately been inadequate to the dimension of the problem.

This is no time for colleges and universities to adopt a posture of fine impartiality and simply announce: "We are now open to Negroes." After these institutions have for scores of years consistently rejected Negroes, extraordinary courage would be required for Negro youngsters to entertain thoughts of sending in an application.

Negroes are not likely to seek out colleges at which they are unsure of their reception. Therefore, the institutions that are serious about wanting Negro students must develop techniques of going out, seeking Negroes with potential, preparing them to meet the qualifications, and helping them over the financial hurdles. None of these factors is so mysterious as to defy solution by the aggregation of brains in American higher education. Some notable efforts are already being made. Northwestern University is recruiting promising Negro students with a $150,000 grant from the Fund for the Advancement of Education. The program will enroll twenty Negro students for each of the next three years. Recently the National Scholarship Service and Fund for Negro Students announced that teams of admission officers from twenty-one colleges in the New York metropolitan area will visit the City's high schools to help disadvantaged youngsters find their way into college. Representatives of the American Society for Engineering Education, the University of Illinois, and the nation's seven predominantly Negro colleges of engineering met to consider an expansion of educational opportunities for Negroes in engineering. In medicine and dentistry, special grants to Negro students have been stepped up. A committee for the development of art in Negro colleges has been founded under the direction of Albert Eisen, art historian at the University of Indiana, and Jack Jordan, chairman of Southern University's Department of Fine Arts. The Association of American Law Schools has created a Minority Groups Project to counteract the factors which have permitted only a few Negroes and Puerto Ricans to enter the legal profession. Wesleyan University and Pomona College have started tutorial programs. Typical of what is being done to help children of ghetto school areas is the University of Chicago Student Woodlawn Area Project. Today SWAP has 400 tutors working at least two hours each week with an equal number of Negro youngsters.

Manifestly, higher education has a great burden to discharge in helping disadvantaged children develop their abilities to the fullest extent possible. A causal relationship has been demonstrated between our needs and our practices. Countless proposals are being offered to remove the invisible barriers and close the educational gap.

I subscribe to the need for our textbooks and instructional materials not to reflect an all-white image of history and culture. Indoctrination for white supremacy took place for years. Now, somewhere in the course of college, the American student, white and Negro, *must* learn more about what the Negro has contributed to our society.

The first act of civil disobedience did not begin with CORE; it began with the Boston Tea Party, whose members are now national heroes. We must realize that women's suffrage demonstrations were markedly similar to the civil rights demonstrations, with exasperating (but good) ladies throwing themselves all over the voting booths and smashing in saloon windows with hatchets. And we must remember that the labor movement conducted its strikes and sit-ins, many with much more violence than seen in today's civil rights demonstrations. And all these past groups have become American heroes. They engaged in activities that would make the civil rights events look like a picnic. Students ought to know all this, so as not to deplore the civil rights movement but to laud it.

Today's students have not learned that it was a Negro who discovered the process of refining steel, that it was a Negro who invented the half-soling of shoes, that it was a Negro who invented watches, and that it was a Negro who first set foot on the North Pole—he was pushed to the front when it was dangerous, but he was not counted later on when it was safe.

I subscribe to the need for free four-year universities and two-year colleges to be built in all our major cities within reach of burgeoning urban populations, especially where Negroes make up 50 per cent of the school enrollment in Detroit, Cleveland, and Chicago; 52 per cent in Philadelphia; 54 per cent in Baltimore; 51 per cent in St. Louis; 70 per cent in New York City (Manhattan); and 85 per cent in Washington, D.C. Ironically, except for California, the heaviest Negro migration in recent years has been into states which have been losing industry to the South. Between 1950 and 1960, the eight Northern states with the highest Negro numbers—Illinois, Maryland, Michigan, New Jersey, New York, Ohio, Pennsylvania, and California—increased Negro population by 53 per cent while the number of nonmanufacturing jobs rose only 16 per cent. The Southern states, during this same period and while losing Negro population, were able to raise the number of their nonagricultural jobs 32 per cent.

I subscribe to a vast program of expansion of teachers colleges and teacher training programs.

I subscribe to a payment plan for those high school and college students now being driven from the classroom by the need to support their families.

I began by suggesting that we must use our creativeness to discern the dangers and exploit the opportunities implicit in the contemporary racial crisis. May I close by suggesting that just equalizing objective educational factors in universities and colleges will not wipe out the enormous disability of living in a slum and in a society that, despite a whole barrage of constitutional amendments and antidiscrimination statutes, still subjects the Negro to an inferior status—an inferiority he often accepts as his lot.

Unlike any ethnic group in the United States, the Negro is the only one whose entire group was split apart. Only Negroes had their families broken apart when they landed in America. Slave owners knew that if you wanted to keep any group weak, the best way was to keep the families broken up. All our other ethnic groups, even though they might have been poverty-stricken, at least had their close family groups to give them support, to keep them going. But the Negro could not change his name, or have an operation on his face; the port of entry for him became a prison.

All these civil rights difficulties did not happen overnight in the 1960's; it took great genius to create and maintain such a situation, and it will take great genius to correct.

Recently, a white professor in Alabama said that after fourteen years he finally had to speak out on the racial question. I maintain that the thunderous silence of many, many people has helped make our college students cynical today. And as to students taking part in civil rights activities, I maintain that all this is far better than crowding telephone booths, or conducting panty raids, or swallowing goldfish.

Education is no longer an option. People will either be educated or they will be nothing, they will become embittered, and many will become criminal.

Education has performed magnificently in helping individuals vault barriers such as race. What is needed now is for higher education to take the leadership in clearing away the barriers themselves.

XXI

1965 Measuring University Productivity

❀❀❀❀❀❀❀❀❀❀❀❀❀❀❀❀❀❀❀❀❀❀❀❀❀❀❀❀❀❀

Productivity may be defined as the output per unit of effort. It is a useful concept in discussing the economics of manufacturing and agricultural enterprises. Applied to such enterprises, where the product is usually physical, productivity seems to be a relatively simple, noncontroversial concept. Educational productivity, however, is neither a simple nor a noncontroversial concept.

A university exists for the purposes of conserving and disseminating knowledge, of seeking and discovering knowledge, and of performing various public services. In pursuit of these purposes, a university admits students, appoints faculty members to teach and to engage in research, and maintains a wide variety of institutes, centers, and bureaus to illuminate, to cure the ills, and to entertain its many publics. In presenting its case for increased financial support, a university can translate these activities into numbers of students served and to be served, additional faculty members needed, new equipment and new buildings needed, and dollars spent and additional dollars needed. At this point, a university might wish it could stop and rest its case.

But this is not its lot. By having become an indispensable partner of government and industry and by having attained indisputable popularity in the hearts of citizens, especially the young, the university faces unprecedented problems of expansion. But as seldom before, the university is being pressured to become more efficient, to economize, and in a sense to demonstrate its productivity.

For a commercial enterprise, increase in sales or increase in clients normally spells financial success. For an institution of higher education, increase in students and increase in demands for its services spell financial problems, some bordering on crisis. But these are problems that an institution should welcome. For they spell success of a different but very important sort—the success of the idea of higher education.

The literature on social institutions and formal organizations contains numerous references to similarities between colleges and universities and other organizations committed to the idea of service —the army and navy, penal institutions, welfare agencies, and police and other regulatory agencies. They are all nonprofit, and their products are equally difficult to define. But there is an important difference that should not be overlooked. Increase, either in the form of staff or clients, for such service agencies is no cause for societal rejoicing. Increase in demand for the services of our institutions of higher education, especially in the form of more students, speaks well of our society. In short, the current financial problems of our colleges stem from their success.

The doubts concerning the usefulness of measures of educational productivity center mainly on the difficulty of quantifying the output or products of a collegiate institution. As yet we do not have the techniques or instruments that can measure the learning that occurs in a student during a college year. We can speak of the great increase in knowledge stemming from the research activities of scholars, but to identify and quantify how much knowledge a group of scholars produces during a given year or two is quite another matter. We can speak confidently of expansion in services performed by a given college or university, but the precise (or even approximate) identification and quantification is again another matter. But interestingly enough, colleges and universities are being criticized for having failed to increase their productivity at a rate comparable to that experienced by many other segments of our society.

What is it then that those who speak of lack of increase in educational productivity really mean? What the critics generally have in mind is the number of students that can be dealt with by an instructor or a group of faculty members. They are not speaking of increments of learning per an input factor, or of research productivity, or of service productivity. The more careful writers are quick to point out the difficulty of obtaining these other measures but justify their use of number of students as the output, because it is the most readily available figure that suggests productivity.

There are two major ways by which number of students has been used to suggest output. One is to compute the number of student-credit-hours produced per faculty member. The other is the number of degrees granted. A variant of this second is the number of engineers, mathematicians, physicists, teachers, and so forth, produced.

The frequency with which the words *produce* and *productivity* occur in the conference rooms and reports of colleges and universities suggests that academics have internalized to a considerable degree both the language and perspectives of the business community. A dean who says, "We must be prepared to produce more Ph.D.'s," is no longer likely to be corrected by another and urged to say, "We must be prepared to educate more people so that they might qualify for the doctorate degree." And faculty members are less likely to protest loudly if the annual report for an institution speaks of "degrees produced" instead of "degrees awarded." Faculty members really cannot take too pious a position toward such administrative lapses, for they themselves speak of "research productivity" and "scholarly productivity" in appraising each other's worth. The use of numbers of articles and books published as quantitative measures of scholarly productivity is no better nor worse than the administrators' use of degrees produced and number of student-credit-hours produced per faculty member as measures of instructional productivity.

Thus my thesis, simply stated, is this: Colleges and universities do not, as of now, possess valid measures of "educational productivity," "instructional productivity," "research productivity," and "scholarly productivity."

I question whether higher education has a choice any longer whether or not to use productivity terms in describing its operations. The trap has been sprung. Publicly supported institutions are harassed by legislative committees, state budget offices, and coordinating agencies to increase class size, lower the rate of increase in unit costs, increase student-faculty ratios, increase space utilization rates, and so on, which are all parts of the productivity trap. For many private colleges the need to increase productivity, especially as suggested by the student-faculty ratio, has become tied to the question of survival. Within those private institutions where the struggle for survival is acute, administrative pressures on faculties to produce more student-credit-hours of instruction per faculty member are sometimes more intense, direct, and overt than in publicly controlled colleges. Both public and private institutions are being exhorted and tempted by foundations to experiment with devices that will permit a faculty member to deal with larger numbers of students. Professional associations and federal agencies speak of the need to devote more funds to higher education so that more engineers, more scientists, more doctors, dentists, nurses, and teachers of technical education or of modern languages can be produced. Faculty members in seeking grants for research occasionally speak of the anticipated "products" of their projects. More significantly, it is no secret that for faculty members, promotion, tenure, salary increases, and professional prestige rest on their capacity to respond to pressures to be "productive scholars." This last no less than the external pressures on the institutions is part of the productivity trap.

The only choice left appears to be between permitting ourselves to be evaluated and governed by confusion, or launching a concerted effort to obtain measures by which we are willing to live and educating both ourselves and others in their proper usage. It is in the latter that colleges and universities will find rationality. There is no promise, however, that this rationality will eventually lead to salvation from the productivity trap. That salvation may well require another people of another time.

XXII

1965
Abuses in
Undergraduate
Teaching

Bruce Dearing

❀❀❀❀❀❀❀❀❀❀❀❀❀❀❀❀❀❀❀❀❀❀❀❀❀❀❀❀

It is ironical that in our fortunate time in the long history of higher education when resources, facilities, and highly qualified faculty are available in richer profusion than ever before, very few voices are raised to assert that "undergraduate teaching is better than ever."

Instead, there appears to be general agreement with John Gardner's somber and eloquent essay on "The Flight from Teaching," Logan Wilson's pungently expressed fears that the college student is becoming a "forgotten man," and other widely circulated expressions of dismay and concern over the ways in which quality in undergraduate education has not kept pace with either traditional standards or expanding needs and opportunities.

Undergraduate education is said to be a victim of the preoccupation of the best-qualified teachers with research instead of teaching. Such a preoccupation has multiple origins. In the European ideal the professor is primarily a research scholar and only incidentally and minimally responsible for offering courses of lectures to those who wish to share at firsthand the fruits of his investigations. There seems little doubt that a situation has developed partly out of competition for prestige and visibility, among scholars and institutions, where status is measured by professional reputation of individual scholars, departments, and institutions. Such reputations are normally established on the basis of publication and interaction with specialist colleagues (including protégés among the Ph.D.'s one has prepared), rather than by devoting energy to excellence in undergraduate teaching of the nonspecialist or the prespecialist. Visibility beyond one's immediate campus is very difficult to obtain through undergraduate teaching. Some institutions have exacerbated this problem by imposing some version of the doctrine of "publish or perish." In my view the usual wars over this doctrine are essentially unproductive, since many who are loudest in denunciation of a preoccupation with publication are merely expressing an inverted snobbery and are all too rarely justified in the implication that since they do not publish they must instead be magnificent teachers.

Several further ills flow from this overemphasis upon research. One of them is a tendency on the part of ambitious professors to devote more of their teaching time and attention to graduate students than to undergraduate students. There are many reasons for this. It is usually more agreeable to work with a highly motivated, usually deferential graduate student well grounded in one's specialty than with a mixed bag of ill-prepared, apathetic, or even initially hostile undergraduates. A graduate professor can often learn something from his students and can hope to extend his reputation and improve his prestige and status through original work by his graduate students, either independently or in collaboration with his mentor.

A third abuse in undergraduate instruction which has been increasingly concerning the students themselves is the assignment of a great portion of undergraduate instruction to the least experienced neophyte instructors and to graduate assistants, often with little preparation and little supervision. More and more students, especially in the larger institutions, lament that they experience the distinguished professors they had come to study under only as glowing reputations and legendary presences, or at best in occasional mass lectures; their immediate teachers turn out often to be doctoral candidates, or sometimes even master's degree candidates in their first year of graduate study. I hasten to add that in my opinion this situation is not wholly evil. A gifted and conscientious graduate student who is one day going to be a distinguished professor may very well do some of the best teaching of his career as a graduate assistant. He knows how much he has to learn, understands from his own immediate experience some of the problems of the undergraduate student, and consciously does his best to make up for his inexperience by careful planning and self-critical examination of his teaching techniques. Often he can count on the aid of his equally concerned contemporaries and friendly counsel from more experienced teachers. Also, there is still much to be said for the system of assigning the basic lectures to the most experienced senior professors and the conduct of discussion groups—in sizes small enough to be manageable—to the graduate assistants. Nevertheless, when the system is abused, and undergraduate instruction is entrusted in large part to inexperienced and unsupervised subinstructors, particularly if they are themselves preoccupied with their own graduate study and teaching, the undergraduate student is sacrificed.

Another factor which is illuminated by the difficulty even a conscientious neophyte instructor has in learning the techniques of instruction is the strong tradition of amateurism in college teaching. As a group, college teachers have been loftily contemptuous of courses in education and absurdly vain about their innocence of any formal instruction in curriculum design, testing techniques, and formal classroom procedure. I venture that not one in fifty college professors has ever taken a course in the history of education or in learning theory. Moreover, in the process of learning by doing, when college teachers set out to teach with nothing before them but the remembered model of their own instructors, they are more often than not immune to any except self-criticism. Their undergraduate students, conscious of grades and unwilling to offend those with such power over them, incline not to protest directly if the teacher is dull, inchoate, or otherwise ineffectual. Professional taboos, together with their own heavy work loads, generally keep deans, chairmen, and even experienced colleagues out of the classroom of the neophyte instructor.

A closely related enemy of teaching excellence is the widespread misuse of examinations. What should be an invaluable teaching and learning device is too often regarded by the professor as a tedious chore and by the student as a threatening ordeal.

Another perennial champion in the lists against the development or maintenance of excellence is a blind conservatism, a characteristic inflexibility resisting the adopting and adapting of new techniques and technologies for instruction. How often have we heard in faculty meetings, "But are we yet ready to undertake this innovation?" Unhappily, for all their fancied radicalism, students are quite as conservative as faculty in their resistance to change. They hotly protest any proposed shift from the semester to the trimester or quarter system, from a long summer session to a short summer session, or vice versa, and evidence scant hospitality for televised instruction, automated laboratories, or other devices which properly used can actually improve instruction rather than constitute a shoddy ersatz operation. Perhaps this is only another aspect of the mystique of amateurism. However, it is distressingly apparent that in the main, college and university campuses which should be taking the lead in such matters are lagging far behind industry and the military. Efficiency need not, as some would have us believe, result inevitably in soulless stainless-steel robots. It ought properly to lead to better teaching with less effort for more people.

Faculties and faculty organizations such as the AAUP appear to be far more concerned with fringe benefits, tenure of appointment and other prerogatives, and political power within academic institutions than with policing the profession and either measuring or improving the quality of performance in instruction.

Indeed, a misapplication of the concept of academic freedom has been discouragingly successful in precluding the effective measurement and evaluation of teaching which is a necessary precondition to rewarding excellence and encouraging improvement. So long as professors hold the view that the classroom is the professor's inviolable castle, that student judgments are to be dismissed as feckless and irresponsible, and that although the dean and the chairmen are supposed to know about good teaching and bad teaching, they are not supposed to do anything to find out, the quality of teaching is in jeopardy.

A final item is the preoccupation of administrative officers with externals and with the urgent rather than the important. There is great pressure to focus attention upon buildings, public relations, and other matters of insuring that school keeps, rather than upon the instructional process itself.

Now that I have listed the pressures militating against quality in undergraduate instruction, let me essay briefly to indicate some things which may be done to counteract them. We must try in every way we can to balance teaching and research, rather than accepting the false dilemma of giving everything to one or the other. We must reassert through occasions like national meetings the importance of undergraduate instruction and insist on our several campuses that the most experienced and most gifted of professors participate in undergraduate as well as graduate instruction. We must abandon our cherished amateurism about the processes of teaching and learning and be as scientific, as intellectually curious, and as tough-minded about the processes by which we communicate the important knowledge in our special fields as we are about the ways in which we acquire that knowledge. This will mean significantly changing our attitudes and our practices in setting examinations (for example, making greater use of outside examiners, scientifically designed machine-graded quizzes, and much more thoughtfully prepared, read, and returned course examinations of all kinds). We shall have to learn to use effectively and relevantly the new technological tools for the purposes to which they can be adapted, rather than blindly resisting them as threatening what we prefer to call standards, but by which we frequently mean merely ingrained habits and prejudices. We will do well to refocus our attention upon the definition and resolution of significant problems in higher education, rather than upon jurisdictional disputes and unproductive power struggles. At the same time we are stoutly defending genuine academic freedom, we shall have to abandon its extension to immunity from evaluation or criticism. And we shall all—administration and faculty, with the thoughtful and reliable assistance the students are capable of providing if we will permit—need to refocus our attention upon the central and important matters of creating, maintaining, or restoring vitality and realistic standards of excellence throughout the process of undergraduate teaching.

XXIII

1965
Establishing
Priorities

Logan Wilson

❀❀❀❀❀❀❀❀❀❀❀❀❀❀❀❀❀❀❀❀❀❀❀❀❀❀❀❀❀❀

The era of the great society is also an era of great expectations for higher education. Most of us are doubtless pleased by this enhanced status for our institutions and ourselves, and why not? For many years we professional educators have urged the public at large to raise both the level of support and the level of expectation for educational enterprise. At long last, perhaps more as a result of changed circumstances than of our own persuasiveness, the American people are sold—and maybe oversold—on the values of higher education.

Within a single generation, we have witnessed a remarkable transition. The opportunity to go to college, traditionally regarded as a prerogative of the few, is now widely viewed as a right for all high school graduates, and indeed, as a duty for the majority. Those who teach them were once looked upon mainly as schoolmasters and schoolmarms for a privileged class of adolescents, but now professorial counsel is eagerly sought by business, industry, and government.

Even though some of us may look back nostalgically to the more halcyon years, from our vantage point in the mid-sixties it is clear that higher education confronts unprecedented opportunities and is being asked to assume unparalleled obligations. Not only are colleges and universities expected to transform youths in attendance, but also to play key roles in an effort to uplift the population at large. Whether it be eliminating poverty, reducing unemployment, improving morals, or getting a man on the moon, institutions of higher education are being drawn into a multitude of public concerns.

In a complex and growing society, this is understandable. Colleges and universities cannot stand still in purpose and scope; they have an inescapable obligation to provide better education for greater numbers, to enlarge and improve knowledge, and to serve society in unanticipated ways. They must be viable institutions, and they cannot ignore current problems and issues without losing their significance in a dynamic social order.

Even so, I would caution that neither our whole system of higher education nor any of its institutions should engage in the futile endeavor of trying to be all things to all men. If we saddle our institutions with responsibilities they cannot effectively discharge, or shift to them burdens which more logically belong to other agencies, we run the risk of damaging the integrity of academic endeavor and fragmenting its basic purposes. I hope we are beginning to realize that multiuniversities, like small colleges, can be overextended, too, and that it is essential for us to set priorities of effort among and within institutions of higher education.

In looking at this matter of priorities, let me begin by mentioning a few things which higher education cannot do. One of them is to transform native ability. In an ever more complicated social order where there are fewer and fewer jobs for individuals with limited intelligence and little education, it is unfortunate that an impediment of birth should remain a lifetime barrier; but in a cross section of a hundred persons there are about twenty whose intelligence quotients fall between 70 and 80, and several more of still lower mentality. Although the right kind and level of education can make most of them into more useful members of society, it needs to be emphasized that *higher* education is simply beyond their grasp. Between these individuals and the brighter members of our population, it is estimated that about forty-six persons, with IQ's ranging from 90 to 100, come within the range of "normal intelligence." Many four-year colleges would not admit youths with this apparent potential; most of them could enroll somewhere, however, and some of them would do quite well, both before and after graduation.

To be sure, there is no better mechanism than an open educational system for distributing the members of a society according to their aims and abilities; but we must bear in mind that the bright learn more readily than the dull and hence formal education on advanced levels does not necessarily foster egalitarianism. Those who mistakenly believe in higher education as an equalizer of individual differences must therefore find other grounds for upholding the notion that everybody ought to go to college.

No matter how much we may increase our support of formal schooling on all levels, it seems to me unreasonable, moreover, to expect classroom influences to substitute for families, neighborhoods, and churches; to bear the main burden of transmuting caste into class; and to reconstruct the whole society morally and aesthetically while leading it intellectually. We must recognize that the mass media, including advertising, and the values they implicitly or explicitly endorse, supply youth with many of its behavioral patterns. Other institutions must share importantly in the development of our human resources and in overcoming poverty, delinquency, and immorality.

Although it may be *infra dig* in academic circles to suggest that formal education can be overdone, I would suggest that it may be possible to have too much of a good thing even when the good thing is higher education. Human resources, like material resources, are subject to the law of diminishing returns; and at some point additional investment in education may make a lesser contribution to society than other forms of private or public expenditure. In many parts of the world overpopulation is a more serious immediate problem than undereducation. Even in a relatively affluent society the extension of the years of formal schooling on the one hand, and the earlier retirement and longer life of the older generation on the other, impose increasing costs on society; as more of these costs are borne by public agencies, some difficult choices will have to be made among alternative uses of resources.

Turning now from these disclaimers about education as the sure road to utopia, I want to emphasize my conviction that it is undoubtedly our most effective single way to improve the general welfare. Our colleges and universities do indeed have important roles as servants and shapers of the Great Society. The utterances of educators and others are replete with statements about the services of academic institutions. Various national committees and commissions in recent years have drawn up specifications of goals for all levels of education. President Lyndon Johnson, more than any other President in our time, has committed his leadership to a positive educational program for the entire nation.

American higher education assuredly does not lack objectives, but one of our major current problems is what to do about pressures and priorities. What do they mean to the 2,100 or so campuses throughout the nation? Pressures arise from such sources as local, state, and federal government; the growing and changing student population; demands for continuing education; increasing costs; industry, labor, business, and professional groups; the disadvantaged; women; the various academic disciplines; international needs—and a variety of other sectors.

Since even our so-called private institutions are really public service agencies, and all colleges and universities are supported by the larger society in one way or another, they can hardly ignore all of these pressures. Their real problem is how to serve contemporary society without becoming subservient to it. If they become mere knowledge factories geared solely to increasing human productivity and improving standards of material living, their time-honored commitment to the pursuit of truth, the advancement of higher learning, and the enrichment of our cultural heritage may fall into neglect.

Are they not obligated, as Harry D. Gideonse has suggested, to offset many of the influences exercised by the society itself in order to develop men and women fit for intellectual and moral responsibilities in an even better society?

When I referred to integrity of academic endeavor, I had in mind the historic fact that our leading institutions have been dedicated to high purposes, including transmission of the best that men have thought and said in the past. Colleges and universities serve by playing a contemplative and critical role, and if they become too enmeshed in daily affairs of the community at large, this function is bound to be eaten away. One evidence of what is already happening is the growing phenomenon of the faculty in absentia, and the fragmentation of intellectual effort and professional loyalties. Student loyalties also appear to be falling away in some places where centrifugal forces are not sufficiently countervailed by institutional cohesion and consistency of purpose.

As we confront the diverse and sometimes conflicting pressures surrounding us and try to set worthy priorities for endeavor, it would be well to remind ourselves that colleges and universities are the main trustees of civilization. Adherence to this trusteeship, I would insist, has undoubtedly been a prime factor in their enduring quality as human organizations.

In addition to consistency of purpose (without which there can be no integrity), institutions of higher learning also have leadership obligations. If they are to help create a greater society and a better world, they must be able to criticize as well as to comply, to shape as well as to serve. This in turn implies a reasonable freedom of choice with respect to the means and ends of higher education.

With these provisos ever in view, let us now focus attention on the broad problems of setting institutional priorities. Here I think we should reverse our usual approach and start with higher education as a whole rather than with individual institutions. Our past assumption has been that the separated aims and activities of existing colleges and universities would somehow add up to the best educational interests of the nation. In my judgment, this is no longer a valid assumption. Higher education has become too complicated, too costly, and too important in the national welfare for its basic decisions to be made haphazardly.

For a number of years I have had the growing conviction that one of higher education's most urgent needs is for coherent, unified planning. My conclusion is that we have entered an era when colleges and universities must cease to be a mere congeries and that they must somehow become a genuine system characterized by unity no less than diversity. In my opinion, there is no other way to expand and improve our institutions without an enormous waste of time, money, and effort. I set forth some of the particulars of this matter several years ago in a paper on "Basic Premises for a National Policy in Higher Education," and I have noted with interest that Mr. Conant's recent book, *Shaping Educational Policy,* deals with similar considerations.

Although I endorse Mr. Conant's proposal to use state governments as units to form an "Interstate Commission for Planning a Nationwide Educational Policy" for our public schools, the private sector's importance in higher education suggests to me that on upper levels it would be more feasible to work through a nonpolitical arrangement. An advantage of this approach is that it would build upon existing structures and utilize more fully the leadership of professional educators in setting and implementing priorities.

Whether enough educators are willing to subordinate their vested interests in particular departments, disciplines, projects, and institutions to place the common or national interest paramount remains to be seen. T. R. McConnell's view is that interinstitutional coordination is effective only when compulsory. And I agree that politically prompted schemes of mandatory coordination are pushing educators into thinking more realistically about the give-and-take of interinstitutional cooperation.

As was shown at the American Council on Education's 1964 annual meeting, traditional forms of institutional autonomy are being displaced by emerging patterns which emphasize interdependence rather than independence in the expansion and improvement of colleges and universities. Consortia, statewide and regional systems are evidences of a new era in the governance of higher education and reflect an inescapable need to think beyond the confines of a single campus in allocating priorities of educational effort.

The growth of federal aid to higher education in the fifty states has also led to the necessity for the establishment of central agencies, such as commissions, to determine institutional and program priorities. Although the academic community at large still uses divergent approaches to Congress, the American Council on Education is endeavoring to develop a more unified front, and each year it formulates and distributes widely a statement of program priorities. Neither the Council nor any other single agency can claim to be the one voice speaking for all of higher education, of course, but I am hopeful that we can reduce the babel of voices being heard in Washington and reach more agreement about how the pressures on higher education can be channeled constructively.

One of our current difficulties, it seems to me, is a reluctance in educational circles to face up to the need for a more logical division of labor among institutions to counteract indiscriminate local responses to pressures for proliferation. Despite our lip service to diversity and pluralism, it looks at times as if we were trying to homogenize higher education. One manifestation of this is the "university syndrome," which in effect means that a single institutional model is imitated so indiscriminately that many campuses begin to lose their unique character and purpose.

I would not argue that uniformization in higher education is invariably bad, but I do contend that variety of form and function is useful and should be maintained. Junior or community colleges, for example, can hardly serve their distinctive purposes if appreciable numbers of them yield to pressures to become higher-level institutions. Liberal arts colleges, technical institutes, and other distinctive kinds of higher-learning centers also have important functions which may be submerged if too many of them are transmogrified into so-called universities in response to local and popular pressures.

The pressure for funds also is tending to homogenize the support and control of our institutions as more and more public institutions seek to augment their budgets from private sources and more and more independent institutions rely increasingly on tax support. There are advantages to any institution in varied support, of course; but if forms of support and control become too mixed everywhere, then the duality of American higher education may be lost.

In short, a unified system of higher education should also be diversified, with each type of institution playing a distinctive role in the whole division of labor, and each having a unique character. All colleges and universities may share in varying degrees the collective functions of teaching, research, and public service; but every place needs its own priorities. Our common ends may be almost infinite, yet the local means to pursue them are always finite.

Even a Harvard or a California has to make decisions about the kind of clientele it wishes to serve, the caliber of faculty it wants to maintain, and the range of programs it will or will not carry forward. Where resources are more limited, operations should be within more restricted ambits, with no institution undertaking more than it can do well.

Since institutional mistakes in determining their priorities stem more commonly from overweening than from modest ambitions, it seems to me that many campuses would benefit from more insistence on adequacy and less rhetoric about excellence, more underpinning for basic programs and less dissipation of resources in a multitude of projects, more attention to strengthening the citadel of higher learning and fewer sorties in the countryside.

All of this may seem unduly conservative, but in my judgment the first order of business for administrators, faculty, and students alike is to foster the best possible campus environment for learning. Commenting on some current aspects of student behavior, Sidney Hook noted in *The New York Times Magazine* on January 3, 1965:

> *They cannot be encouraged too much to broaden their intellectual interests, and they certainly must not be discouraged from giving expression to their generous enthusiasms for civil rights, for human welfare, for peace with freedom. But good works off campus cannot be a substitute for good work on campus. Ultimately, the good causes our society always needs have a better chance of triumphing if their servitors equip themselves with the best education our colleges and universities can give them.*

Our primary obligation to students in residence implies a top priority for the teaching function. As I have said elsewhere, there is a danger in many places that the student, and particularly the undergraduate, may become the "forgotten man" as our institutions become increasingly involved in such off-campus concerns as aiding various levels of government with political problems, meeting miscellaneous demands for continuing education, lending staff personnel to the developing nations, and so on. These and many other endeavors have strong claims for academic attention, but in my opinion never to the extent that basic on-campus obligations come to be neglected. I would also add that because of our reluctance in academic circles ever to drop anything or anybody—from an unneeded course to an unwanted professor—some of our priority problems are self-made.

Research should have the next priority in many, but by no means all, institutions. In the foreseeable future I doubt that our nation needs or can fully support more than forty or fifty really distinguished, research-oriented universities. Such centers should be more numerous and more widely dispersed than at present, but it is not only wasteful but also futile to think that every locality should aspire to having one or more. Although research of the kind that contributes to the advancement of knowledge should be a major emphasis in perhaps two hundred of our institutions, I believe that on most campuses it is sufficient to expect the average faculty member to keep abreast of his field.

Since real creativity in research is a very scarce talent anyhow, I think that most faculty persons would benefit themselves and their institutions more by devoting greater effort to the improvement of teaching. Contrary to the "publish or perish" myth that is much talked about of late, in all except a few leading institutions less than 10 per cent of the faculty accounts for 90 per cent or more of all published research. My recommendation would be that we reduce the strain on the majority, trim the output of needless publication, and upgrade the quality of instruction by a more realistic adjustment of the talents available.

Insofar as research involves the production of new knowledge of theoretical or practical significance rather than keeping oneself well informed about a field, however, it does entail an institutional commitment of time and money as well as talent. It therefore follows that many kinds of research cannot be conducted by the faculty in their spare time with the same libraries and laboratories they use for undergraduate teaching.

For the institution with a heavy commitment to research, there are many kinds of policy questions to be answered. Who should make the decisions about the kinds of inquiry to be undertaken? What criteria should be used in selecting or rejecting proposals? Is the distinction between basic and applied research meaningless, and if not, does an academic institution abuse its societal role by engaging in development projects? Does the individual researcher owe his first loyalty to his college or university, to his discipline, or to the funding agency? To what extent should the availability of funds determine the directions of research? In answering these questions, it seems obvious that the institution with no priorities of its own will be the place where outside pipers will call its tune.

Although I would assign a third-rank priority to what is usually called "public service," it is true that teaching and research are themselves public services of indispensable importance to the larger society. Those miscellaneous other outside involvements that we have come to designate as public service are now considered to be legitimate claimants for faculty and staff attention. Beginning with the president, public service demands upon him are often so numerous and so pressing that he functions only residually as an educational leader on his own campus. Other staff persons and many faculty members are also likely to be drawn into a gamut of peripheral service activities having to do with everything from the local chamber of commerce to the most distant foreign country. Indeed, if all the outside demands were met—and few of them can be readily brushed aside as unworthy—nobody would be left on many campuses except students and custodial workers.

To my way of thinking, every institution needs therefore to engage continuously in a reassessment of its end and means. It must ask itself such questions as these: Is this service important or merely urgent? Would it strengthen or weaken activities with higher priorities? Can another agency do it just as well, or better? To be sure, a new project may be of special interest to the bursar's office or the public relations bureau, but we keep telling ourselves and others that capable academic personnel are in short supply. If this be true, then there ought to be devil's advocates in all institutions to deal with the proliferation of services.

I realize that at times I may have seemed to reflect the conscience of an educational conservative. If so, this has not been my intention, for I am a staunch believer in an enlarged and enhanced role for higher education as a prime mover toward the Great Society. As someone has aptly said, colleges and universities are the engines of modern civilization. I am confident that we can continue to step up their power and increase their load capacity. If we are to make them the main vehicles of social progress, however, I would urge their users to know where they want to go and to choose the main roads rather than the byways to get there.

XXIV

1966
New Roles
for Faculties

Talcott Parsons

❁❁❁❁❁❁❁❁❁❁❁❁❁❁❁❁❁❁❁❁❁❁❁❁❁❁❁❁❁❁

It is an old cliché to say that the core of a college or university consists of its faculty, but it remains as true as ever, and because of changes in the academic situation, perhaps it needs not only re-emphasizing, but reinterpretation.

The present unprecedented growth of the American system of higher education would not have been possible without a base created by a kind of structural revolution which is now about a century old; namely, the creation on this continent of a university system, a process which was well established by the beginning of the present century. Out of it has come a system which differs not only from what existed here in an earlier period, but also from the European systems, especially the German, from which we learned so much.

These processes have eventuated in a special type of system. It is both very extensive and very diverse—the latter feature going far back. A far higher proportion of the age cohort have recently had some higher education than has been the case for any other known society until very recently, and that proportion is rapidly increasing. The "full" university has become the central type, the leader in the system; but it is important to realize that there is an immense variety relative to it, especially of liberal arts colleges which have neither graduate nor professional schools, large urban and other institutions which are mainly devoted to general education, and a wide variety of institutions with primarily vocational emphasis, such as undergraduate engineering schools.

Three characteristics of the university which are distinct from but correlated with its size need emphasis here. First, it has become basically secularized, a process which occurred in the leading private institutions only after the Civil War, and has even begun to occur in the principal nonsecular subsystem, that sponsored by the Catholic church. (For example, a practicing Jew has been appointed dean of a professional school in a Jesuit-controlled Catholic university, namely Fordham.) Second, it has developed the graduate school of arts and sciences, a unique American contribution, devoted to the training of academic professionals over the whole range of intellectual disciplines, which, however, is combined with an undergraduate college largely devoted to liberal general education. Third, this faculty, which generally is responsible both for the graduate school and for the college, is a central faculty which is ringed by a set of professional faculties: law, medicine, education, business, and so on.

It is my contention that the principal features of the new academic professional, even in other than university-type institutions, are deeply dependent on the emergence of this university type. Just as the university professor has become the central type—as distinct from the one in a college—so within the university it is the member of the arts and sciences faculty, rather than of the professional faculty, who has become the central type.

Two further crucial developments were drastic innovations as compared to the pre-university American college. The first was the diversification of the curriculum which was a direct outcome of the differentiation of the body of knowledge into a universe of different disciplines, now generally classified as humanities, natural sciences, and social sciences, with each in turn subdivided into a number of principal and more or less prominent disciplines. The typical faculty of arts and sciences comprises, with some exceptions, the whole range of this system of disciplines; and any given member's colleagues are therefore to be found in all or most of them, whatever his own specialty may be. This development has very generally been seen as one of rapidly developing, if not galloping, specialization. That the whole range should continue to be included within the same faculty is a notable limitation on the tendency to organizational specialization. One might well ask, why not faculties of humanities only, or even of classical languages and literatures only? This limitation on organizational specialization is connected with two others which have already been mentioned: namely, the inclusion of professional faculties in the same university with the faculty of arts and sciences, and the tendency of the latter faculties to combine both graduate and undergraduate instruction.

The second innovation has been the professionalizing of the academic role. This has a number of facets. That it has been an occupational role is of course not new. In this respect, however, there has been development and crystallization. The teacher has become fully an appointee of an organization, paid a salary, relieved of the necessity for any financial dealings with his students, and in general bound to his appointment as a full-time job.

Connected with the development of graduate schools has been the increasing concern with standards of professional qualification. The basic concern has been with technical competence acquired through a process of formal training, with its major features becoming standardized. Nothing like governmental licensing has been advocated here, but the Ph.D. degree has in this country come increasingly to be the basic certificate of competence on the full academic level, though exceptions to its requirement even for the higher prestige institutions can still be found, and other bases may, of course, emerge.

Associated, then, with the extent and diversity of the system, there has been a process of extending the base of recruitment to the graduate schools in terms of social class, ethnic and regional origins, part of it strongly affected by talent searches on the part of the liberal arts colleges which in turn have fed the graduate schools. With the expansion of the whole system, the number of qualified graduate schools has substantially increased. In sum, there has developed an academic marketplace much wider than in other systems which has become progressively better integrated in terms of common standards.

In our history—as that of the Western world more generally —the focus of academic organization has been on the teaching functions. But this can scarcely be considered without raising the question of *what* is to be taught. The salient feature of the modern academic system in this respect is the development of the system of intellectual disciplines—predominantly secular now—and their incorporation as teaching subjects, in various combinations, in the whole system of higher education. Thus the diversification of the curriculum was a major aspect of the modernization process which led to the university in our sense—as distinct from the old religious-classical curriculum of American college tradition. Furthermore, this was the rationale of the emergent graduate schools, because it was these disciplines which defined the standards of competence for which training was required.

On the whole, however, the processes by which the disciplines came to develop, through scholarship and research, had not, in our tradition, been very closely integrated with those of the transmission of knowledge through teaching. Indeed, it was probably the most important contribution of the German model to the American system that a way had been found to integrate these, within the structure of university faculties. In our own earlier tradition, however, the relation had been informal with, on the one hand, a rather vague expectation that teachers on the higher levels would also be scholars, but with virtually no formalization of the expectation, and little acceptance by the university of responsibility to facilitate the process—it was a kind of noblesse oblige on the part of a cultural upper class. Thus the traditional scholar typically provided his own books. On the other hand, scholarship and research tended to be promoted by private associations of interested people, in Europe often with at least symbolic support from government, through academies and the like.

To simplify enormously, it can be said that, leaning on the German model, the leading American universities, through the establishment of graduate schools, brought research directly into the organization of their faculties in a new way. The justification for it, as often implicit as explicit, was along the line that the training of fully competent teachers in the newly developed stages of the academic disciplines required that their teachers in turn should be very especially competent. And what could be a more appropriate test of competence than that the teacher himself be a major contributor to the process of advancement of knowledge?

This bringing of the research function into the university faculty has proved to be a viable arrangement—it has stuck for a considerable time now. In so doing, it has, in an important sense, put the research function in a position of dominance in the system, the higher the level the more so. It is, broadly, the universities with prominent research contributors on their faculties which enjoy the highest prestige in the system generally. In recruitment of faculty members, the research standing of the departments and individual teachers in their training and, subsequent to that, their own research attainments, especially as evidenced through publication, have become the primary criteria which govern academic advancement.

Essentially, the obligation to contribute to the advancement of knowledge is not a matter only for individuals, but has become a corporate obligation of the academic system; and though by no means alone, this obligation has come to be centered here more than in any other sector of the social structure. By virtue of his participation in this corporate system, the individual assumes his share of the obligation.

The primacy of this obligation is clearly shown by an interesting controversy which, though nearly over, still reverberates. This is the controversy as to whether formal training in teaching methods should or should not be required of future college and university teachers, to match the formal training in the disciplinary subject matter itself. The general outcome of the controversy has been negative in well-known respects.

This does not, however, mean that the teaching function has been or is in danger of being abandoned or relegated to lower-level institutions. The conspicuous phenomenon is, rather, that the research and the teaching functions have come to be integrated in the same organizational units, coming to focus in the graduate parts of university faculties of arts and sciences, and that this integration has strong institutional support in the system as a whole, manifested especially in the valuational attitudes of their own members. Here a pilot study I have been involved with has found both overwhelming high valuation of research contribution and strong preference for a balance between research and teaching functions among academics, with little significant desire to specialize fully in one or the other direction. It is probably especially significant that the sentiments in favor of this balance extend to the highest prestige level of the academic system, among the people who clearly have the freest opportunity to become research specialists, unencumbered by teaching obligations.

These trends have brought about a professional structure which fuses the investigative function with that of the transmission of knowledge, both to the successors of the current generation of investigators and to a wider public of educated men. It is a structure which in a special way articulates the cultural and the social levels of human concern. The full institutionalization of the research function in the universities and beyond them has introduced an unprecedented dynamic factor making for change in our society. Some of its innovative contributions are readily assimilated, at least in early stages—most conspicuously those of physical technology. Others arouse intense resistance, as in many fields of social organization, but also, for example, of medicine in the case of Pasteur's discoveries. The preservation and development of roots in the structure of the society is a condition not only of the continuation of the scientific enterprise, but also of its whole beneficent impact on the society. The three main facets of the teaching function, that of academic professions centered in the graduate school, of applied professionals in the professional schools more generally, and of educated citizens through the undergraduate college, are the three main channels through which the substantive cultural content of the academic disciplines can be utilized in the going social world and, conversely, can be guided in its development by criteria of social value which at the same time are general enough not to restrict genuine technical creativity.

These considerations about the convergence of functions in the academic world raise important questions about the form of social organization which develops in response to these demands, but also in relation to a variety of other major developmental forces in modern society. Here a very clear-cut set of phenomena is involved. This centers on the distinctiveness of the organization of the academic profession, in particular the faculty as its primary unit. Perhaps the best available term to designate it is collegial structure. It is closer to the pattern of the voluntary association, and indeed in its own collective decision-making functions is one, than it is to the classical conception of bureaucracy with the implications of the primacy of line authority.

The term *collegial* means that, unlike most voluntary associations, membership involves an occupational commitment, to a job, as we say. This, however, is a job in which, at a certain organizational level, rights predominate over obligations, the most conspicuous cluster of such rights being what ordinarily is called those of academic freedom and tenure. The obligations, which are very real, are primarily cultural, rather than to the concrete social organization. Despite necessary differences in levels of distinction, the faculty and its most important subunit, the department, are basically companies of equals where major status differences are those of stages of career, especially the line between probationary and tenure status. This stands in sharp contrast to the pyramidal structure of bureaucratic hierarchies, with their steadily increasing concentration of all the components of status as one moves toward the top, which can often be occupied only by one individual at a time.

In a society where many say the process of bureaucratization is coming to dominate everything, it is notable that this type of organization has not only survived, but has actually been strengthened. This is partly through the general relative, as well as absolute, expansion and upgrading of the academic system, but also it is notable that it is strongest at the top of the academic pecking order in the high-prestige university faculties.

Concurrent with the strengthening of collegial structures, we have been seeing an immense growth in the complex we call university administration. This, of course, is a function of the sheer size and hence complexity of the institution. It also concerns the increasing importance of logistical support for the work of the faculties and students, buildings, libraries, laboratories with increasingly elaborate equipment, and the rest of the familiar story, which extends to the provision of parking facilities and the regulation of their use.

This development entails bringing into the academic institution increasing numbers of rather high-level personnel who are not themselves academics, but represent a whole range of professional and executive functions. This administrative bureaucracy could readily encroach seriously on the position of faculties as defined in the traditions of academic freedom and tenure, but the striking thing is how little this has taken place. For it not to occur, a set of delicate balancing mechanisms seems to be required; one of the most important is interpenetration of the two subsystems. Here I refer especially to the fact that department chairmen are almost always currently practicing academic men; deans very generally are, one may say, on temporary leave of absence; and even presidents have been, for the most part, recruited from the academic ranks, and belong to the fraternity. Thus the experiments of appointing people altogether from outside, as in the case of General Eisenhower at Columbia, have on the whole not worked out very happily.

The pilot study to which I referred above has found that the strongest sense of encroachment on their prerogatives on the part of faculties by their administrations is to be found in middle-grade institutions in which the administrations are committed to programs of expansion and upgrading. At the highest levels, however, this pressure is not strongly felt; both the individual faculty member and the department seem to be well satisfied with their level of autonomy.

It is our interpretation that this finding indicates an important new functional basis of the collegial structure of faculties. The older type, which was dominant before the development of the modern American-style university, essentially based its egalitarian structure on the status of faculty members as peers in the same upper class with each other and typically with the parents of their students —as scholars they were also gentlemen in the relevant sense. Now the collegial structure is increasingly grounded in the social recognition of the prestige of academic achievement—the Nobel Prize winner having become an important symbol. The new system has become sufficiently strongly institutionalized so that administrations have come, by and large, to define their functions as those of facilitating the central functions of the faculties, rather than treating them as employees whose activities are to be directed by their organizational superiors.

It is, in my opinion, fundamental that this delicate balance be maintained. The growth of administrative apparatus in the academic world is part of a much wider process in the society at large, of which the growth of government is a part. Durkheim was one of the first to see that such growth was a necessary aspect of the development of a pluralistic society through increase of what he called the division of labor. In my opinion, though subject to important conditions and some setbacks, academic freedom has not been threatened by the growth of university administration; rather, the latter has become an essential condition of the protection and extension of the former.

Finally, what of the student? He seems to be currently the most important focus of strain and of a certain amount of disturbance. Is he, as Paul Goodman seems to allege, a simple victim of an exploitative system?

First it should not be forgotten that there are, as a consequence of the differentiation of the academic system, many different kinds of students; and their problems are therefore by no means all alike. As manifested by protest, strain seems to focus on undergraduates in high-level large universities, the notable case so far being, of course, Berkeley.

A second relevant point is an application of what to all social scientists today is the familiar principle of relative deprivation. Certainly, in terms of American values, higher education is a good thing. Equally certainly, in recent years, more students have been receiving not only some higher education but better education—granting the complexity of the evaluative problem—than any preceding generation, particularly that of the parents of the great majority of them. Because the status of education has been rapidly improving, there is more, rather than less, discontent which focuses on higher levels of aspiration the possibility that, since things have progressed so far, they may—indeed, ought to—progress much farther, and that immediately. To take a fantastic example, five hundred Berkeley undergraduates may have the ambition to spend one hour a week discussing the profoundest problems of the philosophy of science with a Nobel Prize winner in physics from the faculty. This, however, is manifestly impossible, even if the faculty member in question did nothing else.

A third, not wholly unrelated, point may have some resonance among the more psychologically minded. This is the suggestion that the crisis of student morale may in part be a function of structural differentiation in ways which are parallel to a major change which underlies the modern era of society generally. In older societies, including most wholly or partially nonmodern ones today, the typical family household was at the same time the primary unit of societal function, especially through economic production—the peasant or family farm being a prototype. Here the father, as socializing agent, was (though engaged in adult responsibilities the child could share only with difficulty, when at all) continuously present; and his role was one into which his son could grow by gradual stages.

With the Industrial Revolution, more and more fathers worked outside the home in a factory or office, and did things their small children might have had increasing difficulty in understanding even if they could have spent long hours observing their performance. This differentiation of the occupational from the familial role and with it the alteration in the structure of parental roles, notably that of father, is crucial to the significance of the socialization problem as felt to be problematical in the Western world. I would go so far as to suggest that a Freud could not have emerged in a preindustrial society.

My suggestion is that, at the level of higher education, a new phase of this process has occurred and that it creates, this time not for Oedipal-stage children but for late adolescents, a parallel problem. The ideal old-style college was one where the faculty were wholly devoted to their jobs as teachers of undergraduates. Furthermore, they did this in a structural context in which, in the ideal case of the residential college, a clearly familistic relation was cultivated. That the teacher was symbolically in a father role scarcely needs emphasis.

Now, however, this father has become involved outside the ken of the undergraduate student, notably in his research. He has symbolically deserted the family of students for which, by becoming a college teacher, he took responsibility. Is it surprising that such a situation generates Oedipal resentment with typical ambivalence which goes with the fact that important and mysterious things go on in that laboratory where "father" is occupied, from which the "child" is unfairly excluded? Symbolically, then, the laboratory, or more generally the research role, is a kind of equivalent of the parental bedroom for the Oedipal child.

If this parallel has any relevance, student unrest may be part of the growing pains of a major system of the institutional structure of modern society. In my opinion, the development in this century of the academic system, seen in the broadest terms, is perhaps the most important sociocultural change which has occurred in the structure of society; and surprisingly to most, the United States has taken the definite lead in the development. The faculty has been and is the spearhead of this process. No aspect of our society is more urgently in need of being understood.

XXV

1966
Relevance of
Liberal Arts

David B. Truman

✿✿✿✿✿✿✿✿✿✿✿✿✿✿✿✿✿✿✿✿✿✿✿✿✿✿✿✿✿✿✿✿✿✿✿✿

When we speak of the liberal arts, we are in the first instance referring to certain subject matters or disciplines that collectively are presumed to have in distinctive degree the capacity to release a man's mind from those conditions that make him intellectually and morally servile. The classic liberal arts of the trivium and the quadrivium—grammar, rhetoric, logic, arithmetic, geometry, music, and astronomy—were regarded as those worthy of a free man because they sought to acquaint him with the modes of human thought and expression in their full range and with the grounds of human knowledge. Hence they were indispensable to his command of his own soul. Today we encounter difficulty in listing the liberal arts, and not merely because the quantity of knowledge is so great and its forms so numerous. The difficulty is at least as much that the liberal presumption concerning any set of subjects is so uncertain. One might assume, for example, a list composed of history, philosophy, literature, music, mathematics, physics, and biology and yet be forced to acknowledge that, as these subjects are often taught, none can be counted upon as being liberal.

Why? I submit that it is because we forget too readily that a liberal education is an experience that is philosophical, in the broadest sense, and that the particular subjects do not so much contain this quality as provide jointly a possible means of approaching it, as the trivium and quadrivium were intended to do. The liberal arts, then, include those subjects that can most readily be taught so as to produce an understanding of the modes of thought, the grounds of knowledge, and their interrelations—established and to be discovered. The range of these subjects is not unlimited, but if the process at which they aim is to succeed, none can stand alone. Their promise is collective. It is their bearing upon one another that lends them their liberal quality.

So regarded, the liberal arts have an objective relevance to contemporary needs that can scarcely be exaggerated. The grounds for this assertion are numerous, but I shall confine my argument to two: the implications of the contemporary crisis of values, and the problems inherent in the developing political role of science.

If we ask ourselves to whom the liberal arts are irrelevant, we cannot readily answer that it is today's undergraduates. Many of them, of course, will assert it; but we would be undiscerning if we did not look behind such assertions. It requires no extensive acquaintance with students to know that a larger proportion of the most intelligent among them are genuinely troubled, in floundering search for purpose, for meaning, for value—in themselves and in the world about them. Those who may reject the relevance of the liberal arts, as goal and not merely as present practice, are in fact, one suspects, declaring for closure, for the appearance of certainty that may go with an early and intentionally narrowing confinement to the boundaries of a particular specialty. In their often compulsive behavior they are, as much as their wandering peers, asking for the means of finding themselves, of achieving integrity, in a world of ambiguities.

The irrelevance can no more accurately be asserted of the society itself, for the malaise of the undergraduates in part reflects the world of their elders. These young people are, to be sure, the first generation from whose lives the ominous threat of nuclear warfare and the sometimes cloying consequences of what we euphemistically call general prosperity have never been absent. These, in combination with the love of absolutes that is normal in youth, undoubtedly have produced responses that are different in degree from those in older people. But if one considers the escapism and emptiness that are a part of the flight to suburbia, the cry for help that can be heard in the expansion of self-pity into the major preoccupation of a thriving cult, the fear and uncertainty that lead parents, however unconsciously, to seek security in simultaneously indulging and exploiting their children—if one considers these and similar symptoms, it is apparent that the call for meaning, for purpose, for value is not merely, or even primarily, a matter of a single generation.

Freedom of the intellect, and hence of the human spirit, from such anxiety and bewilderment is surely as central to the purposes of the liberal arts as ever in the past. Their relevance here lies precisely in their search for the relevant.

But the case for the relevance of the liberal arts can also be put in somewhat more concrete and more specifically societal terms, bearing on the place and the problems of natural science. One of the revealing divisions in much educational talk is the tendency to exclude the natural sciences from the liberal arts. The science major is one thing and the liberal arts student another. Why? Why this equating of the liberal arts with the humanities and the social sciences? The possible explanations are many, but they surely would include the somewhat different modes of thought in the two areas and, for those drawn toward the humanities, the often broader range of questions and the interpenetration of curiosities that may be encountered in those fields. The consequent truncation does violence not only to the historic conception of the liberal arts, but also to their essential objective—an understanding of the modes of thought over the whole range and an exploration of their interconnections.

In the student who is not going to become a scientist, the results of this division are serious. The ordinary citizen today, and tomorrow, has a stake in how the findings of science are geared to the purposes and values of society, for the character of that application will in considerable measure determine whether those purposes and values can be realistically entertained. But for the young physicist or biologist—given the easy arrogance that the contemporary prestige of the sciences nourishes—the consequences of a truncated education may be catastrophic. In him the society particularly needs the philosophical experience of the liberal arts in full sweep, not in some bobtailed version, if he is not to become an instrument for its destruction. As a relatively mature intellect, he needs to know other modes of human thought than the scientific.

This view is unacceptable to many scientists, but their usual counterassertion rests on a crudely empirical base that lacks much in the way of rationale. It is that if one is to do anything in science and hence if science is to progress, the budding scientist must start early, move fast, and look at nothing else. The view has some basis in experience, but what sort of scientist will it be likely to produce in a day when science does and should penetrate wider and wider areas of public policy?

To take a rather pedestrian example, the young scientist who notices a disproportion between the government resources allocated to moon landings and those assigned to the cause and cure of cancer may become curious about how such choices are made. If he has been educated and not merely trained, he is less likely to stop with the dangerously simple explanation of Szilard's dolphins, that such matters would be better dealt with if politicians thought as scientists. He might then be prepared to realize, and in good time, that the problems created when biologists learn to write the genetic code will not be completely amenable either to the scientific or to any other mode of thought in isolation. Can one ask for greater relevance?

The relevance I have discussed so far—to the confusions of the day and to the disturbances of science—is largely ascriptive, without subjective dimension. It provides no ready answer for the student who, having spent most of his Christmas holiday in the New York Public Library grinding out a paper on Milton, asked, as he looked out over the turbulent city, "What relevance does what I have been doing have to all of this?" A presumptuous question, perhaps, and yet one whose implications suggest the gap between our professions and our performance. Could the chairman of the English department have answered him? If he could, as he should, why need the question have been asked? The pertinence that can be established in principle too frequently is lost from sight. Why? In some cases, of course, it should be, since a superficial insistence on relevance is often a thinly disguised rebellion against discipline, an inability to accept the hard work without which one cannot enjoy learning for its own sake or find its relevance to experience. But that is not the whole story.

The heart of the problem, I am convinced, is in the structure, or nonstructure, of the curriculum. If the promise of the liberal arts is collective, then its realization assumes a structure, a system of priorities, collaboratively designed and, equally important, collaboratively operated. Such a structure, moreover, should ideally be based upon a defensible conception of the appropriate educational experience prior to college entrance, since priorities should be determined in part by what we can know of the psychological character of the college years and what can best be done at that stage.

What we label a curriculum too often can be called a structure only by courtesy. It is more likely to resemble a kaleidoscope whose position changes as it passes from one student hand to another. Whether a particular piece is seen at all is largely a matter of chance. Since a consistent design is absent from the whole, moreover, and its assembly is less the result of collaboration than of log-rolling, each segment is dealt with in comparative isolation. A partial coherence may be imposed by the departments or the disciplines, but these are only slightly larger fragments and provide no adequate means of achieving the collective goals of the liberal arts.

We should not wonder if students raise the question of relevance. Their intelligence should compel them to. We should also not wonder if in the sciences, where disciplinary coherence is strong enough to provide insulation from many doubts, students assume an attitude toward what they call the liberal arts that is somewhat like that of the late Charles Kettering when he described basic research as what you do when you do not know what you are doing. Nor should we be astonished if students without scientific aspirations criticize routine laboratories and rebel against required science courses that relate only to the next year of a sequence that they are not going to take. Finally, we should not be taken by surprise if students compulsively narrow the experience of their later college years in mute appeal to some graduate admissions officer. These responses may have other origins as well, but they follow naturally from a curriculum that lacks a structure designed and operated in conscious collaboration.

When I speak of structure I am not advocating rigidity and coverage; I am asking for coherence and for planned priorities. Nor am I, for example, raising the false issue of general versus special education, or opposing prescription to independent study. I am glad to associate myself with Mark Van Doren's view that "the ideal specialist is the fine end of education." The issue in specialization, then, is not whether, but when and how. Independent study, moreover, is a valuable pedagogical device, but that is all it is. It is not the equivalent of an educational design.

The potential relevance of the liberal arts as a collective enterprise has never been greater or more necessary than in today's society. The problem is to bring that potential to reality.

XXVI

1966
Fragmentation, Isolation, Conflict

Kenneth E. Boulding

❁❁❁❁❁❁❁❁❁❁❁❁❁❁❁❁❁❁❁❁❁❁❁❁❁❁❁

We are all aware that we are living in an extraordinary time, that in many ways the twentieth century is unique. There has never been anything like it before. There may never be anything like it again. It is a time which is both enormously hopeful and enormously dangerous. The hope and the danger both arise from the fact that we are in the middle of an extraordinary explosion in human knowledge, an acceleration which began perhaps three or four hundred years ago.

As one reads the record of evolution, it is clear that there are times when man's evolution goes into a higher gear and accelerates rapidly. The development of man himself was a great evolutionary transition. In man's own development, we can detect three great periods of transition. The first was the invention of agriculture and the movement from the paleolithic to the neolithic. The second was the development of cities and civilization. We are now in the middle of what I call the third great transition, perhaps even greater than the other two, in which civilization is passing away and something else is taking its place. I used to call this something else post-civilization; but I find that this term scares everybody, because, for some strange reason, civilization has an extraordinarily good press, especially among college types. Actually, civilization has been a rather disagreeable state of man. I suspect that man was happier in the neolithic, because civilization has been characterized by war, slavery, exploitation, and other disagreeable institutions.

Whatever civilization is, it is clear that it is passing away. The advanced countries even today are fantastically different from a hundred years ago, and are now moving toward what I call a developed society. This is still quite a long way off, for there are no signs that the process of this transition is slowing down. It will eventually slow down, I am sure, but not perhaps for a hundred, or even four hundred years; and in the meantime we are undergoing the most rapid social change of any human generation. One sees this especially in Japan, which has achieved the world's record for economic development—about 8 per cent per annum per capita increase in real income for the last twenty years. If they keep this up three or four generations, they will be very rich. Even at more modest rates of economic growth, the developed world at the end of two hundred years is very hard to visualize.

When I try to think about what the developed society might look like, the principal image that comes into my mind is that of earth as a spaceship, destination unknown; and the politics and the ethics of the spaceship are extraordinarily different from those of the past. Up to now, man has always lived on a great plane. He has never really believed the earth was round. I believed that the earth was round when I went around it and did not fall off, and certainly the astronauts believe it is round; but most of the societies of the past, even civilized societies, did not.

The economic life of a spaceship society is very different from that of the great plane. We shall have to lay a great deal more stress on conservation and the economizing of consumption. We have had, and still have, an economy in which we have extracted materials from the ground and eventually flushed them down the sewers, from which they go into pollutable reservoirs. Now we are beginning to run out of pollutable reservoirs. When I flew across the Great Lakes today, I wondered how long it would take to pollute them completely. As you know, we have already lost Lake Erie and will lose Lake Michigan very soon. It may take only twenty-five years before mankind faces a major crisis in the atmosphere, which is becoming polluted almost to the point where irreversible changes are taking place that are still imperfectly understood.

At any rate, it is obvious that our existing society is fundamentally suicidal; we cannot go on indefinitely, historically speaking, extracting things out of the earth and flushing them into the seas and lakes and atmosphere. Certainly, then, within five hundred years we shall have to develop an economy and society in which we recycle almost everything, with meticulous conservation of all materials, so that we get everything back from the sea and the atmosphere that we flush into it. We still do not have the technology for this, but that perhaps is just over the horizon. A society like this could still be affluent. But as someone has said, "Today we are not so much an affluent society as an effluent society."

Thus, the spaceship society will be a queer kind of mixture of affluence and extreme parsimony. It will have to be parsimonious not only with materials, but also in other things. Thus, there is no space in the spaceship for cowboys, even Texas cowboys. You cannot play cowboys and Indians in a spaceship; you cannot have horses or men on horseback in a spaceship. There is no room. You have to develop a much more modest society. Greatness is out, as far as I am concerned. It is corrupted inevitably into delusions of grandeur. Man is going to have to learn to live modestly, decently, politely, quietly; and the delusions of today we have to show up as delusions, and very dangerous delusions at that.

The spaceship earth may seem a long way off, but it may be closer than we think. We have to look at the present period as man's last chance to achieve this transition; that is, he will never again have a planet with fossil fuels and an unpolluted atmosphere, and in X years these resources will be gone. I sometimes think gloomily of economic development as the process which brings the evil day ever closer when everything will be gone. If we raise the standards of consumption of the rest of the world to American levels today, we will not have any fuels or ores left in one or two hundred years.

In a very real sense, this is man's only chance; we have a chance to convert our fossil fuels and oils into enough knowledge to enable us to do without them, and this is possible. I am a long-run optimist. I think we have a fair chance of making it. The present period is like the bridge of San Luis Rey; we are walking a very narrow tightrope over a very deep chasm, with some kind of promised land on the other side, and we could very easily fall off. That is why this is both a dangerous and a very exciting time.

The most obvious danger, certainly, over the next hundred years is a nuclear war or worse; and we must take this seriously, although no one does any more. But certainly it is still a possibility, and no matter what the probability is, it is too much for me. I think even if we suppose it to be only 1 per cent per annum (which I do not think is unreasonable in view of the nature of the international system), if we accumulate this over a hundred years, it looks very alarming. Certainly we have to regard the existing international system as fundamentally unstable and unviable. Stable deterrence, I think, is a delusion. The demonstration is very simple; deterrents would not deter if there were not a probability of the thing's going off. If there is a probability of its going off, accumulate this for long enough, and it goes off; there is no mathematical possibility of deterrence being really stable in the long run. We can only regard ourselves as pretty lucky that it has not gone off already, and we just have to take the chance that it is not going off and regard this as a period in which we can produce the changes in the international system that are necessary for true stability.

The present international system, I think, is not stable; if we add chemical and biological warfare, with their explosive possibilities, we have even a more frightening prospect than we have now. The longer we look into the future, with the existing system, the worse it gets. On the other hand, of course, there are changes going on in the international system. I am not sure it is always changing for the better; but there is, at any rate, a real possibility of developing an international system that does not have this positive probability of almost total disaster built into it.

There are other dangers besides nuclear. I suppose there is a real danger of enormous epidemics, especially with the development of biological knowledge and the conquest of space. I suppose this sounds like science fiction; but, as you know, you have to read science fiction nowadays to keep up with the news. There is real science fiction about this; remember, for instance, how measles killed the American Indian after 1600. That is why in 1620 the Pilgrims were able to establish a settlement on that implausible, rockbound coast. Just as it happened before, it could happen again. Something could get out of the labs. I think we are almost certainly on the edge of an enormous increase in biological knowledge. Even the last ten years in biology have been fantastic; today we stand in biology about where we did in nuclear science when I was born.

Now we know the code of life; we just do not know yet how to write it, but we shall probably be writing it soon. We may have artificial viruses and enormous changes within the genetic process. We may have coffee-flavored algae, artificial organisms; and perhaps in a hundred years artificial horses will replace these awful things that come out of Detroit. On the other hand, there is a great chance of these things going wrong; the earth is a terribly delicate system.

Another problem is, of course, our complete inability up to now to control the expansion of population. In fact, I am witness to this. I have five children myself, and this always makes my Malthusian speeches sound a little hollow. Still, we cannot go on expanding population exponentially at any rate whatsoever. This does not just mean planned parenthood; this means population control. How we are going to do this, I do not know. This does not mean just having a certain number of children; this means being prevented from having children. Nobody now is achieving this, not even the Japanese, who are closest to it. The population of Japan is increasing at 1 per cent per annum, which means doubling every seventy years. When you do this for a thousand years—which is not very much—Japan becomes awfully full.

Perhaps one of the most critical questions that we face in the next hundred years is what is the carrier capacity of the Spaceship Earth? How many can the Spaceship Earth carry, how big is the crew?

I do not know even the order of magnitude. I do not know whether this is a hundred million or a billion or ten billion or a hundred billion. If it is ten billion, we have a little time. If it is one billion, we are in trouble, because I do not know any way of reducing the human population except by disaster. If we have to reduce the population to even a billion, which is one-third of what we have now, and a fifth of what we are going to have in a few years, this is going to be tough. It means a hundred years or two of sheer agony for the human race ahead.

So I am not optimistic about this. I have my own scheme, which I call a green stamp plan for population control. Each person, on reaching adolescence, receives a hundred and ten green stamps, a hundred of which entitles the owner to have one legal child. Then we would set up a market so that the rich could buy them from the poor, and the philoprogenitive could buy them from the monks and nuns and people who do not want to have children. It is also a device for redistributing income, because the rich will have a lot of children and get poor, and the poor will have few children and get rich. I am afraid that no one takes this very seriously as yet.

Even more remote things worry me. We have examples in history of failure of nerve on the part of cultures, and this could happen to the whole human race, perhaps as a result of success. The thing that worries me more than anything else is success, because there is a very fundamental principle that nothing fails like success, because you do not learn anything from it. If then you have a success that is only partially understood, this can be very dangerous from the point of view of survival. To survive, you have to have a fair amount of failure and a good deal of inefficiency. As a matter of fact, that is one reason why universities are important; they constitute a kind of human liquid reserve for the society. Universities are a device for institutionalizing what the organization theory people call slack. We might, however, develop a culture which would paralyze the learning capacity of man; and all this tremendous knowledge explosion that we take for granted would come to an end, or even retreat. There have been societies which have lost knowledge.

Now we come to the cheerful part. As far as I can see, all the means of avoiding the dangers of this extraordinary transition period and bringing it to a succeessful conclusion revolve around a conscious development of what I call the integrative system. In my private ideology, there are really three great organizers of the great dynamic processes of society. One I call the threat system, where someone says, "You do something nice to me or I will do something nasty to you." Another is the exchange system, where someone says, "You do something nice to me, and I will do something nice for you." This is economics. This does not really cover the waterfront. There is something left over, which is sort of a ragbag, and I am not sure it is not a system. This is the whole can of worms that includes things like status, legitimacy, community, affection, trust, love, hate, and all these things that bind us together, whereby someone says, "Well, do something because of what you are and what I am and what we both are, because we are all in the same boat together, because we are all Americans, or all Michiganders, or all human beings." It is the sense of identity, of community.

The very identity of the individual depends on the integrative system that he is integrated into; for if an individual is not integrated into an integrative system, he does not have much identity. People lack identity because they do not have a community. We do not know much about the dynamics of the integrative system as an element in the total, all-around dynamics of society, and yet it is enormously important. I think this is the main key to social dynamics.

Suppose we look at just one aspect of this, which is legitimacy. If you lose legitimacy, you have lost everything. It then really does not matter how much threat capability or purchasing power you have. You can be rich and powerful and still be rejected; and even though threat capability and exchange capability both at times and places create legitimacy, at other times and places they also destroy it. There are some peculiar nonlinear relationships here. A very interesting example of this is what happens in a monarchy.

After all, the legitimacy of Queen Elizabeth depends on the fact that William the Conqueror was a bastard. Authority often begins by the exercise of the threat system, and then it becomes legitimized in some way. There came a period in history, however, when, if a monarchy was going to be retained, it had to give up power—threat capability—in order to retain legitimacy. Sometimes survival requires the abandonment of power.

We have had somewhat the same thing happen in the case of empire. In some way that we still do not understand, empire lost legitimacy and the old threat system could not put it together again. Similarly, the United States has enormous threat capability in southeast Asia, and yet we seem to be quite incapable of creating any legitimacy. As a result, we are helpless to do anything good. All we can do is evil, and this puts us in an unfortunate position. I do not really understand how communities, nations, or religions are created. These, however, are the most interesting phenomena of the integrative system. Who would have thought that an almost illiterate camel driver would establish the great civilization of Islam? Who would have thought that an old gentleman with a beard in the British Museum in the mid-nineteenth century would have caused so much trouble, and would have created an integrative system which now commands the allegiance of a rather large portion of the human race? For all I know, the most important events of this year may be happening in some obscure valley in Ethiopia, that nobody is going to hear from for fifty years. Some great prophet may be creating a great integrative system for the twenty-first century.

What it boils down to is that the basic dynamics of society depend on the human learning process. I do not know much about learning; I am just a teacher. And quite frankly, the more I teach, the less I know about it. I find it a baffling phenomenon. I am sure there are things like imprinting in the psyche. The psychologists say that if you catch the growing mind at the right moment with the right experience, you can imprint something into it which will profoundly affect its development. But we do not know much about the overall internal development of the image or knowledge structure, or how the teacher cooperates with this internal principle of growth of knowledge which can be called the inward teacher. The main business of the outward teacher is to create an environment which enables the inward teacher to produce knowledge. As yet, we understand this process very little.

The total dynamic process and the whole problem of the transition, as I see it, is how to write a scenario for mankind which can enable us to get across the gulf and to walk the tightrope—that is, how to develop and distribute knowledge and values that will produce the "noosphere," as Teilhard de Chardin calls it, which will permit human survival. We must work on this for a long time.

One of the crucial problems is the lack of any clear image of what we might call integrative development. There is such a concept, certainly; man can and does move towards wider and better communities, more realistic decision-making, and a smaller probability of making disastrous mistakes. It is hard to measure even the direction, however, of integrative development. We have nothing in the integrative system like the Gross National Product in economics. In economics we know when something is happening, whereas in the case of integrative development we are not sure. We do not have the information. In the integrative system it is hard to test the realism of our images or the consequences of our decisions.

I do not think the State Department or the people who run the international system, for instance, have any clear idea of integrative development. They tend to see the present international system as going on forever; they have no real sense of growth of the world integrative system, even though there is the beginning of a conscious effort toward this by cultural exchange and that kind of thing.

Partly, I think, this is a problem of historians. I have a great deal of prejudice against historians, because I cannot get them interested in history. Really, I suppose I want them to rewrite history in the light of integrative development. For example, in 1967 The University of Michigan celebrates its 150th anniversary, which is also the 150th anniversary of the Rush-Bagot Agreement which disarmed the Great Lakes. It is also the 100th anniversary of Canada. So it looks like a good opportunity to put on a pageant, or build a monument, or do something to celebrate the Rush-Bagot Agreement. I cannot get the history department interested in this. Yet the Rush-Bagot Agreement of 1817 was the beginning of 150 years of development of an integrative system, even though at first it was precarious. We almost went over the edge several times. We did not get "54-40," and we did not fight. Peace, however, eventually became a habit, and we developed a security community between Canada and the larger British complex and the United States. This did not have to happen; events might have located the first world war in Oregon.

There is an enormous bias among intellectuals in favor of what is. In fact, however, what is not is much more interesting than what is; and what is is only a very small example of what might be; in other words, existing systems are an imperfect and inadequate sample of the total possible range of systems. Integrative systems may be hard to perceive. Yet they do develop communities of various kinds, new legitimacies, loyalties and disloyalties; and these processes are not wholly random, even though all historical systems have strong random elements in them. Because of these random elements almost all actual images of society are tinged with superstition. Superstition is a perceived order in a random system. Even pigeons order random systems, as B. F. Skinner has demonstrated; and politicians and intellectuals do it all the time. They have this infernal rage for order when there is none, and find it extremely uncomfortable to live with randomness. Human history is a mixed system with great elements both of order and of randomness in it, but it is hard to perceive the order in the midst of so much randomness.

In the case of the integrative system, we do not really know what exactly are the values that we want to increase—the values of man for human survival. We can be pretty sure that things like love and benevolence are enormously good things and lead to the positive improvements, increasing returns, and external economies. If I am happy when you are happy, you are happy when I am happy. This is obviously a system with increasing returns which generates high levels of mutual well-being. These are important elements of the dynamics of the integrative system. Anything that extends the individual beyond himself and creates a satisfactory role and a personal identity, that gives him some sort of satisfactory relationship with other persons in a community, produces integrative development.

What we do not know is the role of consensus, dissensus, alienation, or of what we might call creative conflict; that is, of creative dissent or of different and competing subsystems in the development of integrative structures. What, for instance, is the value of variety and of the coexistence of different subcultures? What is the real role of coercion, of exchange processes, of legitimization?

I am deeply involved in conflict resolution. Nevertheless, I am not at all sure that all conflicts should be resolved. Some conflicts are too much fun to resolve. Some conflicts are very creative. I am not going to argue that conflict is necessarily a bad thing. The obvious position is that there is an optimum degree of conflict in any social situation. I became extremely aware of this when a student of mine produced a paper on conflict in the community in the school system in downtown Detroit. She was puzzled because she could not find any. There was none, because there was nothing. The picture of sheer apathy and nothingness in this transplanted Appalachian community was one of the most horrifying things I have read in a long time. Here is a subculture which has been losing content for ten generations. At the end of that time, you have an amount of nothing that can hardly be believed. Conflict would be a sign of something, some stirring of life.

In many situations, we have too little conflict. I suspect that until recently we had too little conflict in race relations, and the intensification of conflict is a sign of development. On the other hand, there is a profound tendency for conflict to get out of hand. The dynamics of conflict always tend to go into perverse dynamics; that is, the sort of dynamic process in which everybody makes everybody else worse off. We see this in the family very often, we certainly see it in international relations in things like arms races, and we see it in childhood problems. I often use my own children as an example of this. I have two little boys and two big boys, and the two little boys behave very much like an international system. They are always making each other worse off, always having verbal arms races, or worse, and they often have to be separated by the United Nations in the shape of parents. The two big boys, who used to be like the two little boys, now manage their conflicts better. They are nasty to each other in creative ways. I do not think they like each other any more, really, but as they have grown up they have learned how to live out their conflicts creatively.

We have the same problems at the university. One of the

problems of university administration is that university administrators want to minimize trouble rather than maximize its utility, and they often want to play down conflict when actually there is, often, too little conflict in the university situation. On the other hand, I know universities where there is too much, and the university is torn apart by factional strife.

One of the things to beware of is a certain oversimplification. We are all prone to oversimplify in things as complex as social dynamics and the social system. We find people who say, "All we need is that everyone love one another," or "All we need is world government," or "All we need is to hate the Communists," or something of this sort. None of this is satisfactory, simply because the world is a subtle and enormously complex dynamic process in which everything depends on everything else, and in which it is extraordinarily hard to tell even the direction in which you are going.

In this process of integrative development, whichever way it is going, the institutions of higher learning have a very important role. They represent the transmission element of the superculture. The superculture is the developing society. We see it most vividly in the airports, for all airports the world over are the same airport, except the Moscow airport, which has the Victorian charm so characteristic of the socialist countries. All superhighways are the same superhighway; all chemistry departments are the same chemistry department, almost; and in a very real sense, all universities are the same university. Any university person can go into a university anywhere in the world and be immediately at home, especially if he is in his own department. A chemist can go into a chemistry department in Tokyo, Peking, Moscow, Madrid, no matter where it is, no matter what the ideology is, and it is still chemistry. There is no such thing as Communist chemistry or Christian chemistry; there is just chemistry. Every discipline has a worldwide community. Insofar as the superculture is an integrative system, the universities are its church. Even though they have no pope, they have a solid ecumenical unity.

On the other hand, we all live in many local and national folk cultures which we rightfully cherish. One of the critical problems is how to reconcile the world superculture with the parochial, provincial, and special subcultures, the folk cultures in which we have all grown up and in which we find a great many things of value which we want, quite rightfully, to preserve. I do not want a world purely of universities and superhighways. I want a world of variety, and I want the Japanese to go on having the tea ceremony and the Kabuki, and I want us to go on having Lincoln's Birthday and the Fourth of July. The danger of a superculture is that it is fundamentally rather drab, and the things that give color and variety are precisely these elements of the folk culture with which it often comes into conflict. The management of the conflict between the innumerable folk cultures of the world and the developing world superculture is one of the most critical problems that we face today.

The universities have a peculiar responsibility because of the fact that they are, in a sense, at the interface between the superculture and the folk culture. I am all in favor of this. I do not want a denationalized, delocalized, devitalized, de-everything else university. The university must have a foot in both its own local culture and in the superculture, and it must live with this ambiguity. The university also needs to be self-conscious about this ambiguity; otherwise it gets itself into serious trouble—as indeed it does all the time. We all know the difficulties that universities have with their sponsors, their alumni, their students' parents, and even their students. University communities often tend to be at odds with their boards of governors, whether they are national, secular, or religious. This is not necessarily a bad thing. Actually, it is often a symptom of the creative tensions of the time. On the other hand, we have to learn how to manage this conflict; and I suggest that the great task of universities in the immediate future is how to become more self-conscious about their role in integrative development, and in the reconciliation of the development of the superculture with the preservation of folk cultures, human variety, and the different streams of human history.

The university will and must change along with the world around it. I am enormously struck, even as I look back on my own lifetime, with the contrast between my own University of Michigan and the Oxford of my student days. I can see a fantastic transition. As I look back on Oxford, it seems inconceivably parochial; it covered just the Western world. I suppose there was a professor of Oriental languages, but nobody knew who he was. Everybody was supposed to study Greek and Latin—the parochial tradition. By contrast, at the University of Michigan today I suppose as many people study Arabic, Sanskrit, Chinese, and Japanese as study Greek and Latin. The University of Michigan is a world university. It has 1,500 foreign students from all over the world, and nothing is alien to it. What has happened in my lifetime is the vanishing of the exotic.

This generation of students is going to produce enormous changes in our social, political, ethical, and religious life, both in and out of our universities. It is not going to be easy. In fact, I think we have some pretty rough years ahead; but if any organization is responsible for this transition—and it is a frightening one—it is the university. As a member of a university, I feel a little scared by my responsibility.

On the other hand, I am afraid it is no good to be frightened. We have to take our courage in both hands and go on; because there is no way back to Eden. The angel stands at its gate with the flaming sword, and once you have lost innocence, you have lost it. Once you wise up you can never wise down. There is no way to go but on to Zion, wherever and whatever it is.

That, I think, is the real task of the university.

XXVII

1967
Commitment
to Collaboration

Ernest L. Boyer

❀❀❀❀❀❀❀❀❀❀❀❀❀❀❀❀❀❀❀❀❀❀❀❀❀❀❀❀❀❀

The move to unite higher learning is an interesting turn of events, for what once was a vice has—with remarkable speed—become a virtue. Educators have long worshiped independence, autonomy, and—as the catalogues describe it—"the isolated college on the hill." Now higher educators are insisting they belong together. Indeed, the urge to unite has grown so intense that even Vassar looks longingly toward New Haven, and the president of Cornell tells his Princeton friends that all of us are now a part of one vast system. President Perkins, in his lectures on "The University in Transition," speaks approvingly of an interlocking educational network that runs "through the department, through the college, the university, the state, the regional compact, the national association, and the international body." Talk such as this should convince even the most reluctant joiner that, for better or worse, interinstitutional cooperation is here to stay.

The intensity of our commitment to collaboration is clear. However, our understanding of just what we mean by such commitment remains obscure. Clearly, enthusiasm for togetherness has outdistanced reason, and talk of cooperation has run far ahead of achievement. To illustrate: many of the voluntary associations have brought together clusters of private colleges which have joined forces because of proximity or common academic or fiscal concerns. Initially, when such alliances are formed, there is a burst of good will. Enthusiasm abounds, and one is convinced that the Amanist spirit has been reborn and that, just as in the communal colonies of old, all things will be held in common. But time passes, and so does the zeal. The partners remain confused, or intentionally fuzzy, about steps being taken to move them from dream to reality.

State systems, as well, are often elusive. A scattering of autonomous public institutions in a state are brought together to make certain that the use of resources makes fiscal and educational sense. And yet, long after such alliances are bureaucratically decreed, the coordinating councils, or what have you, that oversee the system often are hard-pressed to find ways to make the program work. For such boards it is often most difficult to develop a mosaic that is both acceptable to the colleges and satisfactory to the legislature.

This is the hard reality. As yet we are still very much in the dark about this thing called partnership in education. There is much confusion, and little interest, about the basic question of just how interinstitutional arrangement in higher education really can be made to work. We have a vague idea that, for educational reasons, we should work together and that, for political reasons, we must work together. And yet, how do we move from this vague commitment to a program that actually makes sense? How deep must the commitment be? What kinds of cooperative projects are most practical? Who should be involved in the planning of such projects? How are those who participate in cooperative activity to be rewarded? These perplexities bring me to suggest five ground rules that must be followed if any cooperative effort is to move from talk to action.

First, the commitment to cooperation must be deep. As I see it, all attempts at collaboration will fail unless those who enter the partnership understand just what is at stake. Cooperation is an investment and, like all social contracts, requires that some autonomy be surrendered to a greater good. You cannot talk about the exchange of faculty, about the transfer of credit, about the use of videotaped lectures, or about the building of a common library without facing the fact that all such schemes require shared planning. When several institutions are involved, decisions heretofore made locally now must be reached collaboratively.

Several years ago I directed a project that linked a large university with twenty-four surrounding elementary and secondary districts. The goals of the venture were nobly stated and enthusiastically endorsed. All partners agreed to work for greater continuity in the curriculum, new schemes in teacher improvement, and increased interschool use of faculty. After directing the project for three years, I can assure you that in a project of this type there is a great gap between drafting a plan and executing a program. Progress was made only after it became clear to all that curriculum improvement meant that curriculum planning had to be carried out *together,* that cooperatively developed in-service courses for teachers meant that the wishes of *many* districts must be considered, and that sharing faculty among districts called for an *interinstitutional* analysis of faculty loads. Vague commitments yielded to hard realities as the university and each district understood that programs historically developed in isolation now required interinstitutional consideration.

At the heart of this experience is a point worth noting. To enter an alliance does require that the partners give up something. It means that independent institutions surrender isolation for a greater good. It calls for a new way of thinking about how students learn, about where the resources of the colleges should be located, about the role of the professor, and above all about the independence of a single institution. Any college unwilling to reexamine these fundamental issues should never talk of joining with others.

Second, the structure sustaining intercollege cooperation must be appropriate. From my brief view of the scene I am convinced that very little is known about the organizational structure needed to support an interinstitutional program once the compact has been formed. If the system is created by legislative decree, very often a coordinating core is also formed to hold the alliance together. Almost inevitably, though, such legislation is subject to interpretation—indeed, it must be interpreted, inference must be drawn from it, and the permissiveness that should characterize it must be exercised if a workable organization is to emerge. The responsibilities of the new structure must be defined in detail, as must the authority upon which it can draw to help meet its obligations. What are the sources and the extent of its powers? How is it apportioned among the organization's components; and, most particularly, what is the management role of the central coordinating body?

These problems are even more acute and perplexing when voluntary associations are formed. Parenthetically, as a person who has become fairly familiar with the complexities of two mandated associations of educational institutions, I shock myself by asserting that a voluntary association faces even more acute and perplexing problems—and yet I believe it is essentially true.

What ingredients, fitted together in what ways, are needed to launch the new vessel and keep it afloat? Although each voluntary association must develop a structure to meet its own special needs, I submit several recommendations which in my view are universally valid. First, there must be a top-level board of governors whose powers, purposes, and composition are clearly defined. Campus leaders from each institution must participate actively in determining the shape and direction of the new enterprise. Second, task forces are needed for each specific project launched by the alliance. The personnel involved will vary from project to project, and those who eventually will be called upon to carry out a project must be involved in its planning. Third, there should be a coordinator or facilitator or secretary-general (please note that I deliberately avoid such terms as director and executive) who provides the organizational and supportive services. His is a most delicate and demanding role. He and his staff, no less than the governing board, will create the climate. The coordinator must manage the affairs of the consortium lest chaos result, but he will dictate cooperative efforts only at the risk of stultifying faculty interest and initiative. His is the pivotal position, yet his success can best be measured by how few pivotal actions he is forced to take.

All of this is to make clear that the good will of an alliance is not enough. It must follow a structure tailored to the special needs of the consortium to support the venture.

Third, the focus of interinstitutional cooperation must be specific and the moves decisive. Once collaboration is agreed to and a structure established, then the partners in the alliance must bring concreteness to the venture. They must take calculated risks, push for approval of pioneering projects, and see to it that the first few programs are properly launched.

Such ventures have a self-escalating quality. Action breeds action. Enterprise sparks enterprise, and even if early efforts are not howling successes, the byproducts cannot be ignored. Cross-fertilization, a breakdown of institutional isolation, and a reciprocity of respect are of immeasurable worth. Most importantly, quick action is called for to ensure that the whole idea is not overtaken by lethargy.

Keep in mind, however, that these decisive early moves must focus on projects that pose little threat to existing structures. They must start at points where the advantages are obvious and conflicts minimal. To illustrate: let us assume that consortium members decide that first they will design a common general education television course for all campuses. The problems are enormous. Local faculties must approve the professor and the content of the course. Displaced professors must be reassigned. The relationship of the piped-in course to the total general education program at each college must be examined. These complex organizational and human problems cannot be solved overnight, and to begin cooperation at this point alone is to court disaster.

On the other hand, consider the prospect of shared libraries or intercampus lectureships among colleges as early moves. These projects enrich each campus, and no basic overhaul of the system is needed. Quick, concrete action is possible. I do not wish to suggest that collaboration even at the outset should be bland. Rather, I propose that early cooperative steps among the colleges must relate to projects that are quickly achievable and clearly beneficial.

Fourth, participation in cooperative planning must be widespread. Any cooperative program, if it is to succeed, must involve in the planning those who will be called upon to carry on the work. As things now stand, consortia planning often brings together either top brass or technicians. These officials draft proposals in isolation, and yet these joint schemes ultimately call for a commitment from a host of other people all up and down the line. Key people frequently do not hear of the project until action is called for. Some time back I attended an intercampus session in which a group of presidents talked enthusiastically of working together. They committed their institutions in principle to a whole range of ventures related to curriculum, to teaching, and to library acquisitions. While this initial high-level commitment was noble and necessary, the presidents also agreed that they themselves would continue to serve as the planning board for the consortium. There was no hint that others would be brought into the planning or that help would be sought to tackle the myriad of details. More importantly, there was no talk of ways by which members of the faculty and staff would develop their own dedication to the scheme.

Soon thereafter I attended a second cooperation conference. Here the intercampus talk was carried on by technicians. The planning had to do with an intercollege information storage and retrieval system. Those attending the conference knew how to install cables and link computers, but, so far as I could tell, they had no power to decide what should be shared or what the relationship of the proposed network would be to educational programs back home. There was no evidence that the deans, or the professors, or the students, or even the librarians from the colleges had ever been asked what they would like to share or how such sharing could become a powerful part of the instruction on campus.

My fifth and final point is that the rewards for intercollege cooperation must be real. This brings me to the most delicate issue of all—the matter of money and honor. I submit that we cannot call upon faculty to give time to programs that extend beyond their own campus without rewarding them for the effort.

As things now stand, professors usually are rewarded for activities carried on in isolation, for projects and research that focus on the career rather than the institution. More often than not, professional payoff—in the form of salaries and tenure and promotion in rank—comes to those who give themselves single-mindedly to their own discipline, and surrender fully to their specialty. Anyone who looks at larger problems of the college, or works with colleagues from other colleges, does so at his own risk. Professors who take time to develop cooperative courses or plan joint seminars, or indexes for a new library system, or prepare to lecture often risk professional isolation. Such detours may prove fatal.

Members of the teaching faculty must be involved in inter-institutional cooperation. Indeed, many are eager to join in the effort. If clusters of colleges agree to work together, they also must agree that those who leave their routine commitments to make the cooperative project work will be rewarded. They must declare that such efforts will be given the highest priority and that those who participate will be fully honored when salaries are raised, promotions are made, and tenure is awarded.

XXVIII

1967
Learning Through Involvement

Martin Tarcher

✿✿✿✿✿✿✿✿✿✿✿✿✿✿✿✿✿✿✿✿✿✿✿✿✿✿✿✿✿✿✿✿✿✿

In 1930, that most misinterpreted and misapplied of all philosophers, John Dewey, wrote:

> *Our schooling largely evades serious consideration of the deeper issues of social life . . . the effective education, that which really leaves a stamp on character and thought, is obtained when graduates come to take their part in the activities of an adult society which puts exaggerated emphasis upon business and the results of*

business success. (*Individualism, Old and New.* New York: Minton and Balch.)

Dewey was criticizing a social philosophy which was geared to a world of scarcity. It was a world in which man's most urgent drive was to gratify basic material needs—to solve problems relating to the allocation of scarce material resources and to the production and distribution of material goods and resources. In such a social setting man learned to value productivity and the specialization that so increased productive efficiency. Unlimited wants and scarce means were accepted as the basic givens of economic principles and practice. Self-interest, in terms of gratifying material wants, became the major motivating force of human behavior. We adhered to "natural laws" and the laws of the "free" market, without which we believed there could be no freedom. Thus we came to see freedom as the absence or the minimum of government interference. And individualism, the exercise of freedom, became the desire and ability to compete. "Natural rights," particularly property rights, were viewed as more important than social responsibility and service to the community. Value we equated with price, and we learned to bestow higher rewards upon the manipulators of money than upon the teachers of our children. Power we recognized as superior to understanding. And the clash of vested interests in political and economic marketplaces we came to accept as the best means of determining social policy.

The 1930's were years of depression and want. Dewey was perhaps unrealistic or premature in depreciating the importance of productivity and the drive toward material goals. And perhaps it was necessary for the schools to produce graduates with the skills and attitudes required for survival and the struggle against scarcity. One might well argue that the materialistic values constituted major parts of a social philosophy which was very much in tune with the realities of the time.

But now the realities are changing. We are the first society in the history of mankind to reach the edge of abundance. With our unprecedented explosion in scientific and technological knowhow; with new frontiers of space and sea; with computers, still in the Model T stage, adding brainpower to the muscle capabilities of the machine and promising a cornucopia of goods and services; with the Keynesian tools of fiscal and monetary policy which, although imperfect, are a mighty advance towards economic growth and stability —we begin to realize that technologically, at least, we have the means for a massive and final assault against poverty and its culture, at home and abroad. We have the technology but we lack the social organization, the innovation of ideas. There are no limits on *how much* we can produce, but we appear unable to determine what is worth producing, and how to distribute equitably the fruits of our industry. Nor have we created the activities—call them work, leisure, or what you will—which develop creators rather than consumers, participants rather than spectators, doers whose doing is based on valid theory rather than thinkers who never do or doers who never think. Although they have been greatly modified, the values and assumptions of the world of scarcity are still very much accepted and applied by our political, economic, and social decision-makers. What is worse is that they are still accepted and perpetuated by most of the educators in most of our institutions of higher learning. The times call for new social goals, new values and assumptions, new institutional arrangements that will allow us to complete our unfinished war against scarcity and move beyond production to the development of human potentialities.

The intellectual leadership required for our social reconstruction will not come from the Pentagon, Capitol Hill, the business community, the labor movement, or from public, private, and voluntary agencies. These decision-makers are busily engaged in countless brush wars and minor skirmishes against the symptoms of social problems. They are activists, unconcerned with theory. And they fail to realize that they are applying the tired theories of defunct economists and philosophers to problems that will have to be explained by new theories, attacked through new social institutions. The leadership will come when our colleges and universities—which are or should be concerned with theory—turn their unique resources and innovative capabilities to the tasks of social reconstruction. Unfortunately, we in education are caught up in the very web of values and assumptions that it is our responsibility to review, in the social arrangements that it is our responsibility to change. Our reconstruction, then, must begin in the schools themselves. And the time has come to ask what changes are required in the structure and organization of our colleges and universities. Clearly this is a question that has no simple, single answer. It must be approached through the thoughts, experiments, and actions of all educators concerned with the future of man.

I would like to suggest one idea that I hope will prove worthy of consideration and experimentation. It is based upon three assumptions. The first is that higher education is largely irrelevant unless it performs its function as society's instrument for continuous, constructive self-criticism and social change. The second is that higher education should help students to gain a theoretical framework of values and ideas, and scientific habits of thought and action —so that as future entrepreneurs, legislators, scientists, and educators they may better understand, control, and improve their natural-social environments. The third is that schools will perform neither of these functions until they become integrative rather than fragmenting; until we eliminate the narrow, restrictive, disciplinary boundaries.

I recently attended the annual meeting of the American Economics Association. In the informal hallway sessions, the names of economist critics of economic theory cropped up constantly. "Galbraith, Theobald, Boulding? They're not economists, they're social philosophers," was the frequent comment, always spoken with opprobrium. And of course, the speakers, the specialists in monetary or fiscal policy, shipping procedures, econometrics, and GNP accounting, were correct. For the subjects of their remarks are indeed social philosophers. But what kind of social scientist is an economist, political scientist, sociologist, or psychologist who is not also a social philosopher? He is bound to be a narrowly overspecialized technician, a mechanic who, to use an old cliché, knows more and more about less and less. This is not a plea for the end of specialization, but for the end of narrow specialization. We need specialists who are broad-gauged, who see the data and theory of their discipline within the broader context of our natural-social realities; who know how to relate verifiable evidence from other disciplines to their own areas of competency; and who, because of this extension into related subjects, constantly improve their own comprehension and capabilities.

There is no knowledge without understanding of relationships. And the relationships we wish to understand are those between man and nature, man and man in his natural and social settings. No meaningful relationships or problems, however, are so obliging as to fall graciously within the limits or boundaries of any single discipline. As long as we ignore the comprehensiveness of all things, as long as we continue to divide our institutions into clearly defined and delimited departments and cram each department with sharply defined and delimited specialties within specialties, we shall continue to graduate men and women who accept rather than question old values and assumptions—who are alienated from the realities of their time. It is an unusual student who can, without direction from his teachers, tie fragments of knowledge into a meaningful whole—into a framework for understanding his community, his nation, his world. Perhaps we can eliminate such fragmentation by building areas of our curricula, especially at the undergraduate level, not around disciplines but around questions and problems. "What is the nature of our natural and social environment? How have we organized ourselves to meet specific social needs, and what values, beliefs, and attitudes underlie these institutional arrangements? What are the forces presently at work—the trends and developments effecting change? What are the problems, the opportunities and challenges created by these developments? What alternatives for action are open to us, and what are the likely consequences of each alternative?"

I hope and expect that the institution of the future will have learned that both the best teaching and the best learning occur in the course of research involvement. By research, however, I do not mean opinion surveys, participant observation, or any other technique which limits itself to the accumulation and classification of data—the description of what is. I am referring to scientific method, to laboratory experimentation in which scientists ask questions; select a problem; obtain, analyze, and evaluate data; predict the consequences of data changes; choose a course of action; and use symbolic tools to simulate actual conditions and test the selection made. This is a method not of description, but of change. In this laboratory environment, small groups of students with similar educational aims and backgrounds could be apprenticed to small groups of faculty with related but varied specialties. Together, students and faculty would attempt to solve the real problems of real environments, both natural and social—wherever possible linking the two. The students, working as scientists with scientists, would have a voice in the selection of a project. Let us take an illustration.

Consider a research problem for budding social scientists. A group could assume the role of legislators in an actual American city. The task would be to legislate social improvement, overcoming whatever opposition and obstacles might appear. To begin, the group would necessarily apply itself to the first question around which our curriculum is based. "What is our environment, our community, like?" The students would find that a study of this community requires not a detailed knowledge of any one discipline, but an understanding of social institutions. How, for example, is this community organized to allocate its resources and produce and distribute goods and services? How does it maintain law and order and effect change? What arrangements does this community make for educating its young? Where have these and other social institutions been effective and where are they breaking down? From here the group moves to our next curriculum question. "Why are the social arrangements as they are? What are the historical circumstances behind their formation? Under what values and assumptions were the people operating who were responsible for the creation of such institutions? Are the assumptions still valid?" And so to the third curriculum question. "What are the forces presently at work—the trends and developments affecting change?" Here the group is confronted with the effects upon the community of cybernation and automation, of decisions made by the Common Market in Europe, of national economic policies, of the gain or loss of a defense contract, of a movement to the city of poor farmers or southern Negroes in search of a better life.

Once they recognize and understand the forces operating to change our city, the group can move on the fourth curriculum question. "What are the problems, the opportunities, and the challenges created by these developments?" In attempting to answer this last question, the group cannot long remain aloof from the human condition. For they are no longer dealing with egos, ids, and superegos, but with human beings whose usefulness is seemingly destroyed by new machines, with people caught up by forces they can neither understand nor control. Finally they can consider such questions as "What alternatives of action are open to us as legislators? What bills should we try to pass? What would be the likely consequences if our bills became law? What new potential problems can we antici- pate and what additional legislation could prevent these problems or modify their effects? What legislation, in other words, will allow us to make maximum use of our technology and our resources, and help us to design institutions which will improve the quality of our lives?"

The method need not be limited to the social sciences. Why, for example, cannot a group of students and scientists in the health and medical field take as a research problem the improvement of medical and health facilities in an actual village in India, or in a ghetto of an urban center in the United States? Following the same procedures as we have outlined, they could learn much about the relationship between the physical sciences and the social environ- ment. And much data and theory could be made available by our institutions of higher learning to decision-makers, to those responsi- ble for health and medicine in the villages and ghettos of the world.

This educational approach would not allow the students to go off in all directions. Faculty still has the major responsibility of introducing or directing the students, at the appropriate times, to the essential data and theory from each of the disciplines involved. A theoretical framework must be developed, a framework which ex- pands as new data and theory are introduced. The students work with the theory, use it, link it to what they already know, and apply it to the problems of their community. They relate theory to prac- tice, concentrate on connections, and develop that most important habit of the learning process—the ability to place objects and events in new relationships. In the course of studying and analyzing the community, the student also becomes familiar with such tools for obtaining data as statistical skills. But in learning statistical theory, for example, he will not be dealing with the subject in the abstract. He will apply the theory immediately and directly to obtaining and evaluating data referring specifically to the community under study. Similarly, opinion research techniques might be taught through the designing of an actual survey to be taken in the community.

In attacking problems through this research method, stu- dents get new data; make, discover, learn from, and correct mistakes; bring to light new problems; and disclose gaps in present knowledge. When they achieve their end—draw their conclusions or solve their problem—all this new knowledge becomes part of the means to new ends. In analyzing the meaning of their accomplishment, in going over all they have learned, the students and faculty will think in terms of the next step. "Where do we go from here? What is the next problem we should attempt to solve? How can our new knowledge be of value in defining and attacking our new problem?" Thus, the group moves from problem to problem, bringing in faculty from other disciplines as needed. The theoretical framework is systematically expanded. And without such a framework, all the facts in the universe will not help the student to understand that universe.

Learning through research involvement of this type is certainly more exciting than the passive absorption of facts and ideas as disseminated, in lectures or discussion, by teachers anxious to get back to their research. This is not intended to imply that every subject or area of study can or should be taught in this manner. Nor does it mean that the research participants will not attend lectures, take part in discussions, use learning machines, or read books. It does mean that the year's reading, writing, listening, and discussing will be purposive. It will be directed towards the solution of specific problems. It will be preparation for research activity—means to the data and ideas pertinent to the student's project. Finally, such projects are the beginning, not the end of learning. They provide the breadth and scope necessary for the student to become broad-gauged before he becomes a specialist. And when the time arrives for him to select his area of specialization, he will be able to draw upon an experience which involved him in the material and meaning of many disciplines.

When this method is applied in the schools, the nature of the projects—the disciplines included and the ease or difficulty of the problems to be solved—would depend upon the goals and upon the prior education and experience of the students. Undoubtedly, problems of a more technical nature would be the basis for programing in the two-year community colleges. This does not mean vocational training as we know it. In our changing society the only skills that will not quickly become obsolete are the skills of learning themselves.

The subject matter will differ in community colleges, colleges, and universities. But the projects will have things in common. They will provide a framework for understanding the nature of man and his environment. They will emphasize the communication skills necessary for research. And they will attempt to develop a scientific approach to experience, scientific habits of thought and action.

There are, I believe, many advantages to be gained through this approach. First, it cuts down the artificial and destructive barrier we have built between teaching and research. Faculty will view students not as killers of their more important and more profitable research time, but as apprentices who can contribute significantly to research. Students will learn not through absorption and regurgitation, but in the way scientists have always learned—in the process, the act of discovery itself. And students will have no cause for complaints about not getting to see, know, or work with faculty. It is probable, too, that students, who are still young enough to avoid complacency, will keep faculty close to the problems, the realities, the relevancies of the real world.

The second advantage is that faculty will be forced to broaden its scope. No longer will it be possible for specialists to limit their reading and talking solely to their own alter egos, and to repeat continuously the same errors. It is easy for a narrow specialist to maintain his myth of value neutrality when his only serious intellectual contacts share his discipline, his values, and his myth. But when the same specialist must work with faculty from other disciplines, it is not likely that he will long go unchallenged. The unlimited wants, the material self-interest, and the narrow concept of freedom of our economist, for example, will not easily slip by the anthropologist or psychologist who might see man not as an accumulator, but as a being whose self-interest lies in a struggle for identity, in an attempt to learn and to fulfill his creative potentialities.

The third advantage of our method is that it develops a sense of community. Administrators, faculty, and students become participating members rather than managers, employees, and products of the bureaucratic organization. No matter how large the school, the method narrows it down to small, manageable groups of individuals, working cooperatively and sharing common goals. Gone is the impersonality of the multiversity. The participants all share a role in the determination of purpose, content, and method. The students help to select the problems to be solved. And they share the responsibility for the tasks that lie ahead. Their community, however, is not the community of a monastic order. The school takes its problems and its data from the broader community. In turn, it gives the community that which only higher education can give—valid theory to direct the course of social action. In other words, the school becomes relevant. It stops fiddling while society writhes. It becomes the source of our needed social reconstruction.

One can correctly point out that educators are very much involved in the community today—that as consultants to government, business, and labor and through their research efforts, they make major contributions to social action. True, but they are not their own masters. It is their employers or grantors who ask the questions and decide what problems are to be solved. Generally, these employers seek competitive advantage rather than criticism. Whether the purpose of the assignment is to produce a better missile, test a better pill, make workers happy so that they will produce more, outsell Product X, or design an improved pension plan, it is to do better that which is already being done. Thus, our consultants are in the service of the existing institutional arrangements, of the status quo. They are not our specialists in constructive criticism and social change.

We arrive at the fourth and last advantage. The method helps the student to develop commitment to society and to social goals. It is therefore an attack upon that malignancy which plagues modern man—the boredom and cynicism which we call alienation. The theories of alienation are legion and pervade the pages of social criticism; nor has the theme been missed by the humanities. Wherever there is literature, art, or the mass media, there can be found the lonely, pathetic, apathetic, alienated man—be he dropout, hippie, alcoholic, addict, Hell's Angel, or clean-shaven businessman or college professor who wonders why, with all his success, he is bugged by guilt, dissatisfaction, a feeling that he is somehow without feeling. Certainly when one is at a loss to understand his environment—when he is the object, not the subject, of change—when he is buffeted by events he can neither comprehend nor control—he will be alienated. The method, by getting the student to doubt, question, and test; by introducing him to risk and experimentation; by giving him authority as well as responsibility; by providing the opportunity for sharing purposes and efforts with others; and by posing for his consideration not a jungle of isolated courses and facts and unrelated texts, but the real problems of real people in real communities helps him to develop the values and theory for understanding his environment and becoming a self-directing citizen.

The approach I have attempted to describe has been tried, with, I believe, some success—admittedly on a very modest scale. It is clear that I have left many questions unanswered and many details to be worked out. There is room for much improvement, improvement that I hope many educators will make. Perhaps the most important criticism that can be leveled against the method has already been made by E. M. Hutchinson, who, in reviewing the book *Leadership and the Power of Ideas,* in which I expounded the approach, stated, "One doubts whether even the most affluent society could generalize such a training method in a foreseeable future, and to that extent it was an abstraction from reality."

In response to this criticism, I must first reiterate that the approach is not proposed as a panacea, but rather as one method to be tested and improved along with many others. More important, I believe that what appears idealistic today may well prove to be very realistic in the near future. Our danger lies not in being idealistic, but in underestimating the fantastic potentialities of our science and technology. There is no future for timidity or negativism in education. We can no longer afford either the mentality or the institutions of the age of scarcity. Industry has already begun to recognize that the future lies in education and the development of brainpower. The corporation invests in research and development; moves into the mass media; purchases or merges with publishing and textbook companies; and obtains substantial contracts for operating Job Corps centers, poverty programs, and training programs and for trying to solve social problems we in education too frequently ignore. The business community anticipates the day when total or partial disarmament will call for vast expenditures to be invested in education —and it makes its plans.

If educators are to control the purposes, the content, and the methods of that education, we must be bold, imaginative, and experimental. We must prepare now for the time when education is recognized as America's greatest growth industry in the best sense of the term; when we will support it as we have conquered scarcity, and can move on to our next task—the development of humanhood; when the thing becomes secondary and the end is man.

XXIX

1968
Twelve Hypotheses of Student Unrest

S. L. Halleck

❀❀❀❀❀❀❀❀❀❀❀❀❀❀❀❀❀❀❀❀❀❀❀❀❀❀❀❀❀❀❀

Students can no longer be taken for granted. It does not matter that a great majority of students remain largely content, conservative, and apathetic. A determined minority of restless college students have forced us to examine and sometimes change institutions, rules, and values that were once considered inviolate. The most significant aspects of student unrest can be described as follows:

(1) Some students reject the political and economic status

quo and are making vigorous attempts to change the structure of our society. These are the student activists. (2) Some students reject the values of their society as well as the values of their own past and are developing a style of life that is contradictory to the Western ethics of hard work, self-denial, success, and responsibility. These students sometimes participate in efforts to change the society, but for the most part they are withdrawn and passive. They can be described as alienated. (3) Both activist and alienated students tend to come from affluent middle- or upper-class homes. They are sensitive and perceptive individuals. They are also highly intelligent. (4) Both activist and alienated students have difficulty in relating to the adult generation. They are articulate, irreverent, humorless, and relentless in their contempt for what they view as adult hypocrisy. Such youth are highly peer-oriented. They turn to one another rather than to their parents when shaping their belief systems or when seeking emotional support. (5) Alienated students and, to a less extent, activist students, find it difficult to sustain goal-directed activity. Their capacity to organize for any kind of action is limited. They often fail at work or school. Even their political efforts seem highly disorganized. (6) Alienated students live at the edge of despair. Although they seem at times to be enjoying life, there is always a sense of foreboding about them. Often they become depressed and suicidal. Activist students are more emotionally stable but are also prone to deep feelings of helplessness and self-pity.

There is no dearth of explanations of the above phenomena. Some explanations seem to be based on opinions that support the prejudices of differing political viewpoints. Others are more scientific and are presented with analytic objectivity. No hypothesis thus far advanced can be considered a sufficient explanation of student unrest. At best, each is only a partial explanation.

Certain propositions often made about students are not hypotheses but value judgments. The unsupported statement that the behavior of our restless youth represents a healthy and sensible response to the corruptions of our world is exhortative rather than explanatory. Such a position is embraced by those who are discontent with the status quo, and wish to emphasize and exploit student restlessness as a phenomenon that justifies their own grievances. Similarly exhortative are unsupported statements that students are more emotionally disturbed than they used to be. Implying that students act as they do because they are mentally ill serves to demean their behavior by casting doubts upon the validity of the messages that behavior is designed to communicate.

A more interesting proposition concerning student unrest is that it is neither new nor exceptional. Precedents can be cited in our history when students were even more restless than they are now. Periods of unrest do seem to run in cycles, and it is conceivable that we happen to be in an active phase of a predictable cycle. This proposition is reassuring to those who look forward to a quiet future. Its weakness, however, is that it assumes that those forces that make for cyclical behavior will remain relatively constant. My own opinion is that the world is changing so rapidly that using historical precedents to predict future behavior is a risky business. We can deplore student unrest or we can welcome it, but we cannot ignore it or simply wait for it to go away.

Those who are critical of student activism and alienation are most likely to seek its causes in factors that they believe have created a moral weakness in our youth. They believe students are restless because they lack discipline, values, or purpose. These deficiencies are believed to originate within the disturbed family, particularly that family which has been influenced by affluence, liberal thinking, and modern psychological notions of child rearing. While these hypotheses may also appeal to those who are sympathetic toward students, they are primarily critical in the sense that they imply that something is wrong with those students who protest or withdraw.

Perhaps the commonest explanation of student unrest is that it is the result of too much permissiveness in rearing children. The proponents of this view argue that some parents have, through painstaking efforts to avoid creating neuroses in their children, abdicated their responsibility to teach and discipline their children. In doing so they have reared a generation of spoiled, greedy youth who are unable to tolerate the slightest frustration without showing an angry or infantile response.

Although the permissiveness hypothesis has been used in the crudest manner to berate and deplore the behavior of youth, it cannot be lightly dismissed. There is considerable evidence that activist and alienated students are members of well-educated families, deeply

committed to liberal doctrines. In such homes children are given unusual freedom to criticize, debate, and question. Restless students
also have frequently attended primary and secondary schools dedicated to the ideal of progressive education, schools that, in their
efforts to maximize freedom and creativity, seek to minimize discipline and frustration.

It can, of course, be argued that children raised in permissive
homes will be better citizens than those raised in stricter homes. Restless students do seem to be more open to ideas, more involved with
social issues, and more flexible than their peers. The critics, however,
can point to other characteristics of restless students that seem to be
related to their permissive upbringing, and that are not so salutary.
The response of such students to discipline, for example, is, in no
useful sense, adaptive. Arbitrary regulations enrage them. Even
rational forms of discipline, such as the need to master basic concepts before moving on to more abstract ideas, bother them. Restless students also react inappropriately when their demands are not
immediately accepted. They are prone at such moments to protest
violently, to give up and withdraw, or to wrap themselves in a cloak
of despair. Much of their abrasiveness and much of their ineffectiveness can be explained by their uncompromising demands for immediate gratification. This inability to tolerate frustration or delay
must be considered a weakness or defect.

A second hypothesis focuses on the concept of responsibility.
Many who are concerned about the dangers of permissiveness also
believe that our culture has been "psychologized" to the extent that
youth become unwilling to assume responsibility for their own behavior. The expansion of the social and psychological sciences has
confronted the public with elaborate deterministic explanations of
behavior. When a behavior is totally explained, there is a tendency
for people to act as though they are no longer responsible for that
behavior. They confuse the theoretical issue of scientific determinism
with the society's practical needs to have its citizens remain accountable for their own actions.

When the sociologist documents the impact of poverty and
discrimination upon Negro youth, he is conducting a logical and
scientific exercise. The subjects of his research, however, are tempted
to utilize his findings to support an individual and collective feeling

of responsibility. The Negro adolescent who participates in a riot, for example, might sincerely believe he could not do otherwise, being moved by forces over which he has no control. Psychological explanations are also utilized to avoid accountability. It is becoming more common to hear criminals say, "I should not be held responsible for what I have done because I am mentally ill."

Psychiatry, particularly Freudian psychiatry, has been maligned as a critical agent in producing a climate of nonresponsibility. While there is nothing in the theoretical doctrines of psychoanalysis that favors abdicating personal responsibility, it does seem that the psychiatrist's ability to expand and legitimize the mental illness role has had an impact on the manner in which people view the question of responsibility. Behavior once considered bad is now considered sick. Sickness implies that one cannot help himself or that one is not responsible for his actions. The proponents of the nonresponsibility hypothesis would argue that by expanding the sick role to include forms of behavior that were once considered in terms of good or bad, the healing professions have helped create a social climate in which more people manage to avoid accountability for their actions. Youth growing up in such a society are tempted to behave in a pleasure-seeking, antisocial, and irresponsible manner. Many feel that this is exactly what restless students are doing.

The evidence that activist and alienated youth are deeply influenced by a climate of irresponsibility is inconclusive. Some activist students are often impressively willing to hold themselves accountable for their actions. On the other hand, most alienated students are not. They tend to seek medical or psychiatric excuses from their obligations at the first sign of stress. They also have a discouraging tendency to break laws and to insist that their own personal needs and problems are such that they should not be held accountable for these actions.

The situation with regard to use of marijuana is a case in point. Thousands of students use this drug illegally, yet it is practically impossible to organize students to do anything to legalize the sale of marijuana. When students are occasionally arrested for smoking marijuana, they almost always avoid punishment by becoming informants and thus not only avoid legal accountability but seem unable to adhere to their perceived obligations toward their deviant subcultures. It is almost as if they say, "Because the world is so bad and because it has treated me so badly, I cannot be blamed for my actions. There is no point in holding me accountable for things I cannot help doing anyway."

A third hypothesis that appeals to critics of student unrest is based on the alleged hazards of growing up in an affluent society. It is sometimes argued that affluence that is unearned, and that is unaccompanied by a tradition of service and commitment, creates a sense of restlessness, boredom, and meaninglessness in our youth. The child raised in an affluent society has difficulty finding useful goals. He does not learn to use work or creativity as a means of mastering some aspect of the world. He therefore, according to this argument, is trapped in a never-ending search for new diversions and new freedoms, which sooner or later begin to feel sterile and un-gratifying.

Man seems less likely to be troubled if he is distracted by some monumental task that dominates his life goals. In a relatively poor society, the very need for survival creates a structured and seemingly purposeful life. In an affluent society, man has the time and freedom to contemplate the meaning of his existence. Many restless students do come from affluent homes, and many have decided that their lives are devoid of meaning. Sometimes it seems that their provocative behavior is designed primarily to invent new struggles and even imaginary hardships that will free them from their lethargy and help them atone for their guilt over having it so good.

The affluence hypothesis has certain undertones of criticism directed toward the parents of restless students. Affluence, after all, does not always produce protest or indolence. Traditionally, many of our most useful public servants have been products of wealthy homes. The critics of student unrest would reserve their harshest barbs for those newly affluent parents who have themselves become so caught up in materialistic pleasure-seeking life that they have failed to meet their responsibility of teaching children the kinds of values that would lend meaning to a young person's existence.

A number of explanations of student unrest focus upon the disturbed family. According to this hypothesis, activist and alienated students behave as they do because they are responding to an unresolved conflict within the family unit. It is usually suggested that the restless student has been subjected to too much pressure by his parents or is acting out a need of his parents. A more general approach to the problem focuses on a family structure in which the father is a weak or shadowy figure. This approach emphasizes the breakdown in authority of the paternal figure, the confusion of sexual roles in our society, and the break with tradition that such confusion produces.

The evidence for the existence of a high degree of pathology in the families of restless students is inconclusive. Sociological studies of students and their families do not support any family pathology hypothesis. In fact, such studies suggest that activist students, at least, come from rather stable families. Psychiatrists, on the other hand, find some evidence of serious familial conflict in most of the families of restless students they treat. It must be emphasized, however, that the psychiatrist deals with only a small proportion of such students.

If family disorganization is an important cause of student unrest, the manner in which it exerts its influence must be complex and subtle. Sociological techniques are simply too superficial to get at the complexities of the problem. The findings of psychiatrists are based on depth explorations, which may be valid for some families but which cannot be generalized. Neither sociologists nor psychiatrists can provide valid answers. The most we can say is that some aspects of student restlessness may be directly related to family pathology. Certainly, it is conceivable that in today's highly charged social climate, even minimal family disturbance may be translated into highly provocative behavior.

The next group of hypotheses places the student in a favorable light. These hypotheses view him as a victim of man-made circumstances and maintain that student unrest is a legitimate and rational effort to change these circumstances. The student is viewed as either a helpless victim of a world he never created, or as a hero seeking to cleanse the world of the evils of previous generations. To be useful, these hypotheses must not simply define what is wrong with the world, but must suggest how various factors have made students more capable of perceiving and acting upon the injustices and irrationalities of our world.

The first of these "favorable" hypotheses focuses on the cold war. This generation of students has grown in an age when the world has been divided into two large camps that have been competing with each other ideologically and politically; and since the Russians launched their first satellite, the competition has also been educational. Students today are trained in a school system that emphasizes the competitive acquisition of knowledge as a source of power and stability. By the time they leave high school, they are better educated than any previous generation of students; but they are also more overworked.

All of this emphasis on education and competition is not easily sustained after the student arrives at the university. By this time he is at least partially burned out. The personal benefits of intensive studying and searching for a profitable career begin to appear less attractive in an affluent world and particularly in a world that seems to be making it increasingly difficult for a young person to become an integral part of the economic system. As the student comes to view the implications of our competitiveness with Communism as a never-ending phenomenon, he also begins to question the social value of his efforts. Even if he maintains his enthusiasm for academic work through the undergraduate years, by the time the student reaches graduate school, he increasingly asks himself whether the competitive search for knowledge is worth it. At this point he begins to view our competition with the Communist world (and sometimes competitiveness itself) as a form of mass paranoia, and he views the university as an agent of the government that contributes to the perpetuation of the paranoid system. He reacts by protest or withdrawal.

The second "favorable" hypothesis focuses on the war in Vietnam. Although student unrest began long before the war in Vietnam ever escalated to massive proportions, there can be little doubt that in the past few years this conflict has been the major factor influencing the behavior of students. The war is particularly unpopular on our campuses. A large proportion of students, perhaps the majority, see it as a misguided effort. A significant minority see it as wholly immoral. Much of the restless behavior of students can be directly related to their efforts to do something to stop the war or to their sense of total frustration when they feel powerless to stop it.

The draft and the inequities engendered by the II-S defer-
ment also contribute to unrest. The major issue here is fear. The
average male student is plagued with fears that he will fail in school,
will be drafted, and will run the risks of being killed in a conflict
he may not consider vital to our interests. A second issue is guilt.
The university student knows that he is spared from military service
only because he is richer or smarter than someone else. While he
may believe that the war is immoral, he also knows that his privileged status is immoral. When he accepts the II-S status he suffers
guilt. Much of the activism on our campuses is a means of atoning
for that guilt. Much of the alienation on our campuses is a means of
denying the relevance of the society that created such guilt.

Students also feel some shame in not participating in those
aspects of military service that might make them feel more masculine. It is rare for anyone even in peacetime to embrace military
service eagerly, and a normal late adolescent has justifiable concern
with interrupting his career to face the harshness of life in the service. The unpopularity of this war gives the student a cogent reason
for avoiding military service; but it does not resolve his nagging fears
that he is somehow or other being cowardly or less masculine by
being treated specially.

It is also true that the antiwar climate on our campuses
makes the student progressively more disinclined to serve in this war
the longer he remains on campus. Education breeds a dislike of
violence. Furthermore, whatever romantic thoughts a young man
may have about the war at the age of eighteen are somewhat atten-
uated with a year or two of maturation. Students spend many hours
arguing about the war, the draft, and means of avoiding the draft.
This preoccupation creates a highly tense situation in which the
student feels supported only by his peer group. He begins to relate
to subcultures that become progressively more separated from the
rest of the nation and particularly from the adult generation.

A third hypothesis favorable to students is offered by those
who believe that student unrest is an appropriate response to the
deterioration of the quality of life in America. Overpopulation,
which results in crowds, traffic jams, and mass-production businesses,

has taken much of the joy out of life in our towns and cities. Personal care or service is hard to find in any shop, restaurant, or hotel. People begin to feel faceless and insignificant.

Students, it can be argued, are among the first to sense the painful anonymity associated with bigness. This is a particularly serious problem on overcrowded campuses where students are painfully isolated from their teachers and other adults. A sense of student-faculty intimacy and a sense of scholarly community are sorely lacking on any of our large campuses. Students find it difficult to develop a sense of identification or loyalty toward a monolithic and impersonal university. In their complaints that they are treated like numbers or IBM cards, they strike a poignant note for all of us.

Overcrowding is only relative and would not be so destructive were it not for the manner in which we have incredibly neglected the planning and development of town and country. Our cities grow with no respect for the land. Beauty and wilderness are easy prey for the builder and contractor. Clean air and clear streams are almost a thing of the past. An adolescent who grows up in a world in which he must sit back and watch beauty fade while pollution advances comes to despair of the future. One way of looking at student unrest is as a massive reaction to the destruction of that kind of world and way of life that their forebears enjoyed but that will be denied to them. It is not uncommon to hear a student say to an adult, "In your world life had some hope and meaning, but in the world you have left for me, these qualities are gone."

A fourth hypothesis comes out of political hopelessness. Many individuals see our mass society as immune to change. It has been argued that our society is so complex, our systems of checks and balances so intricate, and our interplay of pressure groups so self-equalizing that really effective change is no longer possible. Our business-oriented economy has so indoctrinated us into the role of credit-bound consumers that we are all beholden to a way of life that may not be in our best interests. An increasing number of radical students are convinced that the forces of government, industry, and education are totally interdependent and allied to one another for the purpose of warding off any reasonable attempts to change the society. They believe that our country has developed a system of life that simply absorbs legal efforts to change

our society, even protest, in a manner that ultimately preserves
the status quo. In this regard it is somewhat distressing to note
the manner in which hippies and protesters have not only been
institutionalized as part of our folklore and humor but have been
exploited by the advertising industry, an institution they initially
intended to destroy.

Guided by the philosophy of Herbert Marcuse, many students are convinced that constructive change within our society is
not possible by working through the system. They do not have any
sort of vision as to what will replace the old order, but they are
convinced that our society is fundamentally irrational and must be
destroyed. They do not reject illegal acts or even violence as agents
of destruction.

A fifth hypothesis favorable to students centers on civil
rights. The civil rights movement not only increased youth's awareness of a historical injustice that made it difficult for them to be
proud of this country, but also served as a training ground for
future radicals. The new campus protest began at Berkeley when students demanded the right to work freely on their own campuses
on behalf of oppressed Negroes. Many campus radicals shaped their
images of the Establishment and of unreasonable authority on the
basis of their early work in the civil rights movement. Students
throughout the country have developed an amazing empathy and
identification with Negroes. Their commitment to the Negro cause
has taught them the psychological meaning of oppression and has
encouraged them to seek out and attack sources of oppression in
their own lives.

I should like now to present three hypotheses—or, perhaps,
groups of hypotheses would be more accurate—which are neither
favorable nor unfavorable to students. Some explanations of student unrest focus upon impersonal processes. The causes of unrest,
according to these hypotheses, are not to be found in the actions
or philosophies of other men, but are believed to reside in changes
in our highly complex society, which seem to create the need for
new modes of psychological adaptation.

The first of the "neutral" hypotheses focuses on modern
technology. Man has always lived with hope, particularly with the
hope that his efforts in the present will be rewarded with gratifica-

tion in the future. A certain degree of predictability in the future enables one to make commitments to goals and to other people. To the extent that we live in a society in which past, present, and future lose their interrelatedness, the power of hope to shape man's behavior is diminished. New means of adapting to the world must then be found and the manner in which people relate to one another must be profoundly altered.

Postwar America has been characterized by a massive and continuous growth of technology. Our society is one in which the conditions of everyday life are constantly changing. Moreover, the rate at which technology changes our lives is itself increasing. No one can predict what life will be like in twenty years, ten years, or even five years. Today's knowledge, today's work skills, and today's values may be totally irrelevant to tomorrow's world. Kenneth Keniston has described the manner in which some youth, when exposed to an ever-increasing rate of technological growth, come to perceive that the values of the past will be totally inappropriate for the world in which they will be adults. Moreover, they feel powerless to anticipate or direct the future. In this environment, hope no longer sustains. It is adaptive to be cool, to learn to live in the present.

What are the advantages and disadvantages of living in the present? The advantages are more or less obvious. One is more flexible and, superficially at least, more comfortable. It is not necessary to delay gratification nor need one allow himself to be tortured by the mistakes of the past nor to be deluded by unrealistic hopes for the future. The disadvantages of life in the present are more subtle, yet more powerful. To live in the present one must narrow his commitments. He must travel lightly and be ready for anything. More intimate relationships are unlikely since they cannot be sustained by reference to past experience nor by promises of a better future. Passion and romantic longing must be avoided because they may breed pain or impair one's flexibility. In short, if carried to extremes, life in the present is a selfish life incompatible with the growth of that intimacy and passion that man has always found essential to a fulfilled life.

Distrust of the future and a determination to live in the present seem to be characteristic of both activist and alienated students. The student activist seeks immediate change and has difficulty in developing the patience or optimism for long-term planning. The alienated student adopts the philosophy of the hippie. Believing that the only certainty in life is change, or uncertainty itself, he adapts by "doing his own thing" and behaves as though he is responsible only to himself.

A second group of hypotheses in our "neutral" category attempt to relate the growth of new media, particularly television, to the troubling behavior of students. It can be argued, for example, that simply by being available to publicize the activities of protestors and hippies the media exaggerate the importance of these groups. The television camera forces all of us to take seriously forms of behavior that might have been dismissed lightly in earlier decades. Conceivably, the media may be creating a climate of expectation in which youth are subtly seduced into dissenting roles that may not represent their actual interests.

It is also true that many television commercials, radio ads, and most modern music are directed toward the youth market. The self-consciousness of youth is thereby heightened. They are made more aware of their potentialities and sometimes develop an exaggerated sense of their own power.

Another attempt to relate changing media to student unrest has been implied in the writings of Marshall McLuhan. McLuhan believes that electronic media are bringing us all closer together in a more truly communal and shared society than ever existed. Our youth, who have grown up with the new media, are ready for such a society. Elders, who are committed to sustain the institutions of the past, are not. Much youthful rebellion can then be visualized as an effort to make older people see that the world has changed and that many of the values of the past are now irrelevant.

Although McLuhan's hypothesis has some attractiveness, it does not seem as plausible as those that focus upon the psychological impact of the content of media. Frederic Wertham believes that the massive degree of violence that young people see on television makes them more violent and less responsible. Vance Packard, for example, has argued that chronic exposure to the values implied in TV commercials could create a generation of unrealistic, demanding, and present-oriented youth. I would like to propose my own hypothesis of student unrest based on the manner in which the media influence the character structure of youth by prematurely confronting them with the harsh truths and realities of life.

As an animal whose growth and development requires him to be dependent on others for a long period of time, man learns to rely on others for an optimal amount of structure and order in his life. It is obvious that authority is not always benevolent, not just; and yet it is true that no man can be at ease if he does not commit a part of himself to some authority, whether it be his church, his family, his government, or an ideology. Nor can one come to develop a firm sense of who he is without making such commitments. It is at least partly through experiencing limitations that are imposed by others, by respecting others, and by emulating those who are respected that one finds his own identity. The process by which one comes to terms with authority is not always deliberate nor rational. Sometimes even benevolent authority relies on faith, mystique, or untruth to retain its control.

This is especially relevant to the situation of young people. The most well-meaning parents must on occasion deceive their children because they know that children would find many of the hard and cynical facts of life unbearable. Until recently it was possible for young people to begin to experience the world as adults know it only after they had reached adolescence. Most of the time the adolescent absorbed this new knowledge gradually and painlessly. Even when he did feel that his parents had been hypocritical or had deceived him, his awareness of their dishonesty came so gradually that his resentment and rebelliousness were restrained. Today it is different. One of the significant developments in postwar America has been the influence of mass communication media, particularly television, which are capable of disseminating information to all age groups immediately.

Even before adolescence, television acquaints youth with the cynical facts of life at a time when such truths may be indigestible. Other media communicate knowledge so quickly now that there is little opportunity for anyone to live comfortably with myth or self-delusion. Beliefs that were once casually accepted are vigorously scrutinized. The belief that there is equality for all Americans can hardly be sustained when one has a front row seat from which he can observe the Negro's unsuccessful struggle to maintain a decent life in this country. Blind faith in the veracity of leaders of nations is quickly lost when one can watch the proceedings of an organization such as the United Nations in his own living room. I have no doubt that diplomats have always lied to one another, but what is new about this world is that children can now watch them lie in living color.

The hypocrisies of older generations have always been with us. What is new today is that it is ridiculously easy to expose them. The effect on our youth of premature emergence of truth has been to create a deep skepticism as to validity of authority. Neither the family, the church, the law, nor any institution demands the automatic respect it once did. There may be other factors contributing to this decline in respect for authority, but in my opinion it is best understood in terms of the psychological impact of our new media.

A third "neutral" hypothesis has to do with the reliance on scientism. Today's restless youth have grown up in a world that has sought answers to the questions of life not in religious faith but in science. Many of us believe that science can provide all the answers. We ask that the speculations and opinions of the social sciences contain the same hard truths as more rigorous findings in the physical and biological sciences. In my work with students, I am often impressed to find how easily they believe or once believed in the perfectibility of man. Hostility is seen not as an innate quality of man but as a response to frustration. The teachings of the social psychologist that aggression is a learned phenomenon have gained prominence over Freud's more ominous warnings that aggression is innate.

This generation of students seems to have grown up with the belief that original sin, in the religious sense, or Thanatos, in the psychoanalytic sense, does not exist. Much of this belief has been reinforced by the mode of their existence. Many are affluent and have grown up in suburban communities where, except for what they see on television, they are shielded from the tragedies of life. The realities of their own lives convince them that whatever calamities are imposed upon others are not inevitable. Statements such as "life is a vale of tears" or "the mass of men lead lives of quiet desperation" seem absurd to them. In their adherence to scientific rationality, they also cannot accept guilt. They are convinced that in a perfectible world man should be joyful and guiltless.

When a person raised with such beliefs encounters the harsh realities of life, he has little to fall back upon. If he perceives his own aggressive tendencies, he is frightened by them and attempts to deny them. He may project his anger upon those who he feels are frustrating him, or he may simply deny that such anger exists. When he perceives the evil of others, he is mortified. In his conviction that there are rational solutions to any problem, he cannot help but be intolerant of the irrationalities of those who prevent progress. In his belief that life and especially the sexual aspects of life can be enjoyed without guilt, he becomes highly disturbed when he discovers that he cannot escape his past and that a certain amount of guilt is inevitable. He even becomes plagued with additional guilt over the realization that he is guilty.

The restless student is one who has taken literally the message of science, rationality, and perfection. He is more open to action and change than were earlier generations of students. At the same time, however, he is not equipped to understand or deal with the depth of that irrationality in man that resists change and leads man to seek his own destruction. Too often such a student finds it necessary to construct devil theories of history, in which the existence of evil is attributed to only a few who block the progress of the many. He has sacrificed the comfort and patience that come with the idea of accepting original sin. Sometimes the student becomes totally overwhelmed with the irrational aspects of the world and reacts by totally abandoning his earlier beliefs. In their disillusionment, some alienated students seem to be turning away from the promises of scientism and searching for solace in the most dubious forms of mysticism, magic, and astrology.

Hopefully this review of twelve hypotheses—or, rather, groups of hypotheses—has been more than an exercise in cataloging. By emphasizing the diversity of explanations of student unrest, I have attempted to demonstrate the intellectual futility of searching for simple explanations of highly complex phenomena. As citizens, we may wish either to support or to attack the causes that the restless students have dramatized. But as scholars concerned with educating and understanding and helping students, we need a more objective approach. We must recognize that there is some truth to the most critical as well as the most sympathetic hypotheses.

Some of the hypotheses suggest guidelines for action. The critical hypotheses remind us that youth are not always as wise or powerful as we might suspect. Like adults, their actions are determined as much by personal weaknesses and selfishness as by sensitivity or idealism. While youth certainly do not need more paternalism and coddling, they still need our understanding and guidance. They can still learn much from adults who are committed to the pursuit of ideals in a climate of tolerance, compassion, and responsibility. The critical hypotheses need not be used only to berate students. If their validity is appreciated, they can be helpful in freeing adults from that unreasonable guilt that impairs an honest confrontation with the issues the students have raised.

The sympathetic hypotheses emphasize the unusual degree of stress this generation of students has experienced. Those hypotheses that invoke the war, overpopulation, and pollution as sources of stress forcefully remind us that student unrest is often an appropriate response to what sometimes seems to be a hopelessly troubled world. Other hypotheses raise many questions for those entrusted with the management of our universities. Does the emphasis on education as a means rather than an end have any meaning in an affluent society? Should youth be encouraged to remain in a passive role as students throughout the first third of their lives? Are there means of bringing young people into important roles in the power structure of our universities and our social system before they reach the age of twenty-five or thirty? Is the II-S classification anything more than a bribe that weakens the moral position of dissenting students and creates havoc on our campuses? Should it be abolished? To what extent can we continue to depersonalize and enlarge our campuses without creating a generation of alienated youth who feel no sense of identity, no sense that they have a voice in what is done to them, and no sense of commitment to anything but their own interests?

It is my belief that the neutral hypotheses are the most intriguing and the most powerful valid explanations of student unrest. At the same time they are the most difficult to live with optimistically. If progress itself, in the form of technology, science, or new media is the most severe stress in the lives of our young people, then we are faced with a seemingly impossible task, namely how to control progress and change rather than allowing these forces to control us.

Students have demonstrated to anyone who is willing to read their message that a complacent drifting into the future, an unchecked growth of technology, science, and media cannot take place without profoundly altering the nature of human existence and the character of man. Some of the behaviors of youth, including many forms of student activism, are efforts to warn us of overwhelming danger. They are adaptive insofar as they seek to ward off social calamity. Other behaviors of our youth, such as profound alienation, are by-products or symbols of a process of social decay that may well be irreversible. They are efforts to live with a calamity that already exists.

Faced with the grim realities of the postwar world, how will man continue to survive with dignity? Most of our counselors, scientists, and theologians have faith in man's infinite capacity to adjust. They seem convinced that man can mold his personality, can adopt new values, and can learn to live in a flexible and uncommitted manner. Some find cause for optimism in the possibility that man might learn new methods of child rearing so that he may overcome the psychological lag between his needs and the demands of the new world. I wish I could share this optimism, but I cannot. It is not likely that child-rearing methods can be changed quickly enough to keep up with the rate of technological change. It is also possible that some of man's psychological needs are immutable. I doubt that man can live without intimacy, without compassion, without ideology, without faith, without autonomy, without privacy, and without beauty, and still be man.

The only effective solution would require a drastic revision of many of the traditions and structures of our society. Our first need is to study and to plan, to determine what kinds of technological progress are consistent with making man a better human being and what kinds are not. The latter must ultimately be rejected. We must find a way to communicate those values that are essential to man's survival to our children in an open and questioning but noncynical manner. We must reexamine our time-honored reverence for affluence, power, and bigness, and face the possibility that affluence bores, that power corrupts, and that big institutions diminish the stature of man. In a nation struggling with an unpalatable war and an excruciating racial problem, these problems may seem premature, vague, and almost grandiose. Where can one begin?

If we do nothing else, we must at least begin to study the impact of technological progress upon man's personality. Only a handful of scientists and philosophers are seriously concerned with the study of man's psychological future. No university or government agency has ever created a department or institute to study this problem. This need is immediate and critical. Only man's intellect and reason can protect him from himself. If we deny the existence of the problem, if we equivocate, or if we merely drift, man's tenure on earth will have been truly absurd and meaningless.

And Now the Future

Lewis B. Mayhew

❀❀❀❀❀❀❀❀❀❀❀❀❀❀❀❀❀❀❀❀❀❀❀❀❀❀

The future of American higher education is emerging in a climate of disillusionment and criticism expressed both outside and inside the academy. Although some disenchantment is likely to be ephemeral and some criticism superficial, all will have effect as colleges and universities change or do not change in response. Further, these shadows are deepened by a national mood of despair over an uncertain end to an unpopular war, the possibility of major economic depression, distrust of government, destruction of natural resources, and evidence of loss of standards or criteria of morality in public and in private life.

Outside higher education, the political backlash is perhaps the most immediately dangerous element, although in the long term it may be less devastating than the disillusionment of the Negro community. Whereas only thirty repressive bills regarding student protest were passed during the summer of 1969, over 130 were proposed. In Congress, tax reform, which is bound to be destructive to private universities, is discussed with no attention paid to claims that the legislation would eliminate a national resource. In states such as California and Minnesota, officials were elected and given power in support of plans and promises to end university independence and to restore law and order on the campus. And the federal administration, heedful chiefly to one economic theory, imposed budget and spending restraints which fell most hurtfully on colleges and universities, and the students who attend them and the research that they do. Local communities which once consistently approved bond issues and tax overrides to support their junior and state colleges have changed, and during 1968 and 1969 rejected pleas for increased money even when the overcrowding of institutions visibly validated statistical claims. This political backlash is well revealed in the threats, veiled yet real, which both responsible and vindictive public officials made. A Southern governor said, "Campus chaos has made the entire question of university governance and operation a matter of great public moment, and those public officials directly involved in the planning, financing, and control of higher education need to take a more active interest in campus planning."[1] And Edith Green, long-time friend of higher education, remarked that "the hostility of our Congress to student violence will be reflected in cutbacks of money on every level of education," and went on to say that much needed support for private education simply could not be provided because the climate of opinion in Congress was so adverse to higher education.[2] In California, its governor wanted to violate the law, as interpreted by the Supreme Court, and fire an assistant professor because of political affiliation.

Then there is disillusionment within the Negro community over the fact that the promise of the Supreme Court decision of 1969 and subsequent legislation were not redeemed by a higher edu-

[1] Mills E. Godwin, Jr., *The College Campus in 1969,* Atlanta: S.R.E.B., 1969, p. 1.

[2] Edith Green, "Congress and College Violence," *Compact,* 1969, *3* (4), 21.

cation serving chiefly a white clientele with an idiom and rhetoric irrelevant to black experience in America. Negro leadership slipped from the hands of those who searched for assimilation into the larger society to those who felt separatism was the only solution. These leaders demanded special consideration for Negroes in colleges, separate programs of black studies, and black control of all parts of higher education which involved Negroes. This shift is well revealed by the fact that Negro leadership in Harlem had originally supported the idea of a Columbia-University-built gymnasium as a contribution to the black community but changed and claimed the building, if constructed, would be one more symbol of the unregenerated racism which characterized the American university. The depth of feeling is expressed in a demand for black mathematics unsaturated with middle class referents such as stocks and bonds. "Rather the teacher might ask in order to whet the ghetto child's appetite for math, 'If you loot one store and burn two, how many do you have left?' "[3] Negroes are saying they can no longer trust the leadership of white American higher education and that their only hope is to proceed alone but demanding unconditional help on their own terms from the white Establishment.

Especially sinister is the broadened base of questioning of the rights of college professors to the protection of academic freedom and to tenure. These were acquired on the argument that professors, since they must deal with sensitive and controversial matters in the presence of the young at an impressionable age, should be accorded special freedom from a society whose values might be questioned. But average Americans and the political leaders who sought to attract their vote began to see tenure as nothing more than undeserved job security, and academic freedom as a cloak for subversive and quite likely perversive thoughts and activities. In California, legislation was prepared to terminate tenure and in Florida a state representative urged that tenure not be extended to such fields as education in order to keep professors alert and growing intellectually. He would be willing to accept the concept of tenure only if the achievement of higher education would be exposed to evaluation by the

[3] Nathan Hare, "The Case for Separatism: Black Perspective," in James McEvoy and Abraham Miller, *Black Power and Student Rebellion*, Belmont: Wadsworth, 1969, p. 234.

political arm and if higher education would consider seriously how to increase competitive pressures to improve professional performance. Questioning the rights of academic freedom increasingly comes from various segments of society and not just from the right. Negroes and some white liberals demanded that Arthur Jensen's appointment be terminated when he as a scholar summarized studies on intelligence and generalized that race and intelligence were related.

An important post-World War II index of public favor for higher education is the amount of support provided for university research. During the late 1950's and early 1960's, universities and the federal agencies which supplied them research funds assumed a constantly expanding research budget. The leaders of the National Institutes of Health, for example, assumed that spending for health-related research would continue from approximately $1.4 billion in 1963 to $3 billion in 1970. To this end they confidently emphasized training programs to produce the thousands of scientists who would be needed during the decade of the seventies. Then began the era of disenchantment. Costly undertakings such as Operation Mohole, the attempt to probe below the earth's crust, proved a scientific fiasco. Congress began to scrutinize research contracts, and the elitism of science which favored relatively few institutions was forced to give way as restricted research funds were spread to more institutions and different parts of the country. And the scientific community got the message. Ivan L. Bennett of Johns Hopkins University, for example, claimed that "Science . . . can no longer hope to exist, among all human enterprises, through some mystique, without constraints or scrutiny in terms of national goals, and isolated from the competition for allocation of resources which are finite. . . . Unless we biomedical scientists are prepared to examine our endeavors, our objectives, and our priorities, and to state our case, openly and clearly, the future will be difficult indeed."[4] By 1969 the honeymoon was over, and higher education was told that substantial cuts in research budgets were to be expected (20 per cent for the National Institutes of Health). Nor could a change be anticipated when the war in Viet Nam finally ended. Colleges and universities

[4] Daniel S. Greenberg, *The Politics of Pure Science,* New York: New American Library, 1967, pp. 287–288.

were told that university leaders were in for a protracted struggle in coming years. An adviser to President Nixon warned, "I think they have to realize that there are going to be a lot of claims on postwar funds and that the case for higher education is going to have to be pretty strong. . . ."[5]

Even those old friends to higher education, the foundations, reflected the critical mood. Indexes of foundation giving revealed a substantial drop in the proportion of funds going to higher education after 1965. Spokesmen for major foundations mounted studies of university activities and became critical of practices once studies were completed. For example, the Ford Foundation claimed that university investment policies were inadequate and that they would have to change if they were to expect future foundation support.

Above all, students personified most clearly the mood of public disillusion about higher education. Protest which began in 1964 over matters of free speech gradually increased in range and intensity so that by 1969 some of the more militant students could believe that higher education was so bad that it should be destroyed, while more moderate students insisted that the size, curriculum, system of governance and priorities were wrong and should be changed quickly while there was yet time. They gradually sensed the growing syndicalism within the American professoriate and sought to reduce it through direct student participation in governance. The mood of despair was exemplified by students who preferred to jeopardize institutional financial stability rather than have the university conduct research of which they disapproved, or by those who viewed the university as just one repulsive element of the military-industrial-education complex, designed to use people and natural resources only to perpetuate a moribund capitalism.

Criticism from within higher education may be even more devastating and in the long run more telling, if only because those who express concern know intimately of what they speak. Some have finally become concerned about the unplanned, almost mindless, growth explosion which could very well destroy institutions because much of what is being done as part of this growth is a sham.[6] Others have at last recognized that the headlong rush on the part

[5] *Chronicle of Higher Education,* September 15, 1969.

[6] Edward H. Levi, reported in *Los Angeles Times,* July 6, 1967.

of institutions into graduate programs will, unless checked, result in serious oversupply of Ph.D.'s by the mid-1970's, yet can find no way to slow down this overproduction. Several institutions finally recognized that they had overexpanded during the 1960's and had overanticipated increased federal support, and began retrenchment. The Graduate School of Arts and Sciences at Harvard, for example, plans a 20 per cent cutback in graduate enrollment by 1972, and Stanford has begun systematic review of programs to find those which could or should be curtailed. And a few candid scientists finally have seen that universities had asked for and expected more research money than they could wisely use and that this fact alone could bring about a drying up of research funds.

The growth within institutions of higher education of interest in trade unionism and collective bargaining reveals a deep distrust of traditional styles of governance based on shared respect and responsibility. In effect those who would place their trust only in the negotiated contract are saying that individuals can no longer trust boards of trustees and central administration. This feeling is sufficiently widespread that professional organizations such as AAUP have had to accept the strike as legitimate if they are to retain membership.

Then some of the most respected practices of colleges and universities have come in for thoughtful and research-based criticism. College admissions based on prior academic records and measures of academic aptitude have finally been shown to be predictive of little more than college grades which are not particularly related to subsequent adult performance. College grades have finally been shown to be capricious, arbitrary, unreliable, and quite frequently unfair, and institutions have been forced to consider other means of assessment of which the pass-fail is but one widely used example. Critics within higher education have shown that colleges fail because neither their curricula nor style of teaching had much effect on the lives of students. Studies of college graduates have also revealed that graduates felt about their colleges as people felt about Willy Loman. They liked them, but not too much.

As indexes of this mood, all colleges and universities have begun to experience financial limitations; private institutions, drops in enrollment; public institutions, legislative scrutiny; and all of them, the constant threat of campus violence. So sharp are these evidences of dissatisfaction, that higher education has begun to respond. By examining these responses, something of the shape of the future of higher education, at least into the decade of the eighties, can be seen.

First, collegiate institutions have begun to experiment with long-range planning. For generations this was not done, and institutions had no financial plan beyond the next year's budget, no academic plan other than the yearly increments to the curriculum, and no physical plant plan other than the dusty panoramic view lodged in the president's office. Finally, stimulated by such external requirements as foundation or federal government demands, mandates of statewide coordinating agencies, or a sudden awareness of a financial crisis, institutions have begun, often quite awkwardly, to plan for the future. These efforts have taken many forms: faculty task forces, outside consultants, presidential planning, creation of planning offices, or some combination of these. And the efforts have met with varying success, from accurately projecting a decade ahead to complete rejection by faculties on which responsibility for implementation finally rested. By 1969, however, the idea of planning had become firmly rooted in the folklore of higher education, and some institutions had begun to experiment with more refined computer-based approaches to planning.

A second response—in part a reaction to even earlier and happier conditions—has been the surge of four-year institutions to begin graduate and advanced professional work, and to emphasize research regardless of whether or not the institution had library or laboratory or faculty resources of a quality needed to support graduate work. The model being followed was the prestige university whose graduate faculties attracted contract research and whose faculties gained light teaching loads and national prominence. The ready rationalization was that the society needed so many professional and technical workers that all institutions must create or expand capacity to train these needed people. Even in the face of a changed and less-favorable climate, institutions still persist in this quest and seem likely to continue to do so unless forced to slow down by outside forces such as a coordinating agency or legislature, or unless persuaded to do so by mounting evidence of the real drain on institutional resources which graduate education makes or of the fact that an oversupply of graduate-degree holders is in sight.

A third response, particularly among private institutions, has been a search for innovations in education, through which high-cost private education can be competitive with lower-cost but more inflexible public institutions. In a sense this has become a marketing solution to problems of finance and has resulted in such things as overseas experiences, different patterns of academic scheduling, greater independent and tutorial study programs, newer courses designed to appeal to the young in the late twentieth century, search for some unique academic symbol such as a center for the performing arts which might attract students, improving the amenities of residence hall life, or radically different time requirements for different sorts of courses. Thus, Antioch College has created a highly flexible freshman year for all students; Beloit has a degree program embracing overseas experience, off-campus experience, and an extended period for independent study; and Stanford is trying to provide freshman seminars for all entering students. Presumably these innovations are educationally valid, and a desire to improve education partly motivates experimentation, but in essence they represent a response to a competition which because of political or fiscal limitations cannot innovate quite so rapidly, or an effort to placate dissenting students questing for relevance in the curriculum.

Belated is the flurry of activity to create programs of black studies to symbolize concern for the struggle of Negro students for a unique and valued identity and to respond to the demands placed by militant members of Black Student Unions and similar organizations. These attempts have ranged from quite serious symposium planning and then adoption of black studies into the departments of institutions wealthy enough to recruit an able faculty, to the almost frenzied approval of new courses over one summer, to be taught by Negro ministers, members of Urban Leagues, or self-styled spokesmen for the black community. While most programs are still too new to be evaluated, early evidence suggests that some in a proper institutional climate have prospered and are generally well regarded by the entire academic community, as is true at Stanford or Antioch; others, such as the black studies program at San Francisco State, have been so militant and destructive of academic values as to attract political reprisals. A body of literature and opinion about black studies is developing, as also literature and artifacts to be used stressing black experience and black creativity and some graduate programs to prepare professors. Whether or not these developments will proceed fast enough to provide a firm foundation for sustained black studies programs in many institutions is as yet unclear, but such developments do suggest a generally serious effort for higher education to be responsive to a long-neglected need.

Although the dogma of American higher education has, at least since the turn of the century, proclaimed that the faculty was the university, in general it was central administration which set goals, allocated resources, and made the critical decisions. This was true whether an institution was a junior college ruled by a former school superintendent, a state university possessed of a large unwieldy academic senate, or a prestige private institution such as Stanford or Columbia, which allowed professors great personal freedom but which concentrated power to make decisions in the hands of a president and a few administrative associates. As campus unrest expanded, as criticism of how institutions were governed increased, and as the growth of trade unionism threatened, colleges and universities began to experiment with various forms of shared-responsibility system of campus governance. Faculty senates or associations were authorized and given considerable power over not only the traditional matter of the curriculum, but even over finances. Joint faculty-student judicial bodies were created to handle disciplinary matters and to advise and consent to administrative actions to preserve order on the campus, and boards of trustees reorganized themselves to include faculty points of view, whether the new members were from that institution or another. In spite of the well-recognized principle that faculty groups tended to be conservative and that governance by consensus tends to be inflationary with respect to cost, institutions felt compelled not only to rectify previous imbalance of power which favored presidents, but even to create new imbalances favoring faculties. This swing toward faculty involvement went so far in some institutions that central administration found itself without the power necessary to maintain institutional financial security or the means to deploy resources to meet new and unexpected challenges.

As private higher education began to experience serious financial difficulties and faced competition from well-supported, organized state systems of higher education pledged to create institutions within commuting distance of every student in the state, they began to form new organizations and structures that might enable them to remain competitive. To effect some economies to scale and to provide for greater curricular richness, a number of regional consortia of private colleges were formed, such as the Great Lakes College Association or the Associated Colleges of the Mid-West. Some institutions located within reasonable distance from each other merged, as did Case and Western Reserve; others engaged in close cooperation, as did St. Catherine's and St. Thomas' in Minnesota. Several pairs of institutions adopted such radical devices as that of a smaller institution actually moving onto the campus of a larger, but still preserving the identity of each institution. And a few private institutions sought some organic relationship with a neighboring public university while still maintaining their private character. It is true that many cooperative ventures have not accomplished the critical task of effecting economies; but they generally have been able to contribute additional services such as joint overseas experiences for students, in-service training programs for faculty, or strengthened library holdings in specialized fields. And as conditions worsen for private institutions during the seventies, the number and variety of cooperative attempts seem likely to increase.

As an additional response to financial pressures, both private and public institutions began to explore sources of funding that had previously been the almost exclusive domain of the other. Private institutions argued that public support from the state was in the long term good public policy, for if private institutions were forced to close, the states would have to build new facilities. They urged that states create large scholarship programs which students could use in either public or private institutions, and some form of direct subsidy such as the payment of an amount for every degree produced. Presidents of private institutions who in the sixties had ignored state coordinating groups began to accept appointments so they could influence state policy in ways favorable to their institutions. On the other side, public institutions enlarged development capacity and began to mount fund-raising drives equal in magnitude to those of the private sector.

Institutions and the various regional and national organizations which served them finally became convinced that if the case for higher education were to be made effectively and if its needs were to be met, higher education should speak with a unified voice from a consistent generally accepted policy base. To accomplish this, first, the major associations such as the American Council on Education and the American Association for Higher Education began to coordinate efforts to influence federal policy. Then several attempts were made to create policy-making agencies which could first assemble needed research and then make policy pronouncements. The Carnegie Corporation created the Carnegie Commission on Higher Education to help chart the future. Several of the large foundations agreed in principle to support a self-perpetuating policy commission, and the larger Washington-based associations retrieved long-dormant plans for commissions on broad educational policy. Some of the individual membership organizations also began to investigate ways of cooperation so that the voices of individuals concerned with higher education might become more influential. Even individuals in the federal administration, especially the United States Office of Education, began to see that both their interests and those of colleges and universities generally could be served through some more consistent policy formulation. One result has been the financing of a congress for higher education intended to advise the federal government on overall policy. Intended as one kind of an elite group concerned with overall policy is the Academy of Education, which, with foundation support, hopes to become as influential as the National Academy of Science.

Under threat of state legislatures and Congress to impose regulations unless institutions could curb student dissent and campus violence, colleges and universities finally began to correct some of the abuses which in part had given rise to campus protest and to develop plans for containment of violence should it erupt. Students were given larger voice in controlling their private lives. Procedures were developed so that students could be insured of something similar to due process, and students were placed on faculty and administrative committees and even on a few boards of trustees. At the same time, plans were developed as to how and when to use legal aid such as the police or court injunctions, and how to insure punishment after campus outbursts without precipitating still more unrest. All of this was quite foreign to the traditions of higher education, and for the first several years after 1964 when the students at the University of California at Berkeley initiated the Age of Protest, institutions moved slowly. Indeed, by 1967 students at Berkeley had been granted no more freedoms than they had had before the free speech movement. But with the occupation of buildings at Columbia and later at Cornell, and with the increased militancy of such student groups as the Students for a Democratic Society and Black Student Unions, institutions began to change rapidly. Probably the years of 1969 and 1970 will have seen more fundamental changes in the relationship of students to higher education than have happened since the founding of Harvard.

Last among the major responses, although many other reactions could be described, was the determination on the part of colleges and universities to find out more about themselves. For most of its history higher education had remained immune to scholarly study of the sort focused on other social institutions such as the family. Professors studied everything except their own professional practice and institutions, conducting business without recording essential data upon which wise decisions should be based. Stimulated by growing public skepticism as to institutional honesty and by real concerns as to how effective higher education really was, colleges and universities attempted a variety of activities to gain greater understanding of themselves. Offices of institutional research were created to audit internal educational efforts. Departments of higher education were created to study higher education and to prepare better-qualified administrators. Centers for research in higher education were strengthened and released a flood of information about students, governance, and even faculties. Generally such activities implied the hope that through more precise knowledge could come better decisions and greater public understanding and an overall improvement of college education. Perhaps, if the next step can be taken, that is, enticing people to read what is known, such an idea can be realized.

It is from such responses and the conditions which provoked

them that the future of higher education will be fashioned. First, and most obviously, the organization of higher education, especially public higher education, will be complex and at least statewide. During the 1960's, states created state coordinating councils; or gave power of control to state boards of education; or expanded the province of a university board of regents to include all institutions; or created two- or three-part state systems, a university system, state college system, and a junior college system. Although by 1969 the achievement of such agencies was not as great as had been hoped, they had become significant enough so the tendency toward centralization is not likely to be reversed. Higher education has come to be such a major part of state budgets that individual institutions will not be allowed to continue unsupervised. However, the precise form which will generally prevail is in some doubt. Some feel that coordination is not sufficient and that some suprainstitutional board with power to control is necessary. Others believe that, especially in the larger states, a state is too large a territory for a single board to control and that a regional board, responsible for all types of public higher education in the region of a state, would be preferable. This might take the form of the board of trustees for the senior institution in the region, which would absorb nearby state and junior colleges. Also debatable is the responsibility for private higher education. It seems obvious that if the states do provide public money for the support of private higher education, some form of control will follow. This control may simply be accreditation of new programs, or it might involve actual veto power over professional programs whether new or old. In 1969 there is just not enough evidence on the basis of which to anticipate the future.

The last half of the decade of the sixties brought the condition of Negroes and other minority groups starkly to the attention of higher education. Predominantly Negro colleges were examined, were frequently found wanting, and efforts were made to strengthen them. Predominantly white institutions revised admission policies and actively recruited Negro students. Negro students in turn demanded such special attention as black studies, black residence units, and black administrative officers sensitive to their unique needs and condition. The number of Negro youth entering higher education increased at a faster rate than did the number of white youth. All of this is history. For the future, for at least another generation it seems likely that predominantly Negro colleges will continue to exist. The actions of several Southern states to create or maintain two institutions in the same town is illustrative. When black colleges have been closed in favor of integrated ones, the proportion of Negro high school graduates attending colleges dropped. Predominantly white institutions in the South have not expanded capacity for Negro youth rapidly enough to absorb those who would attend had the Negro colleges closed. But throughout the nation, if present rates of change continue, each year larger and larger numbers of Negro youth are attending colleges, and it seems reasonable that by the year 2000 or 2011 Negroes will be represented in colleges and universities proportionate to their representation in the total population. Some plead that this change be accelerated. However, unless special efforts are made to finance in full Negro attendance, including allowance for forgone income, the present economic condition of the Negro community and the present tendencies of costs to students of higher education, when combined, will not allow faster increases.

Black studies also face an unknown future. By 1969 institutions had begun to create programs and departments of black studies, usually with full black faculty; but they experienced the serious problems of lack of qualified professors, lack of sufficient volume of scholarly materials, and frequently such militant conduct of professors and students in the departments as to alienate the rest of the campus. On the positive side, however, graduate schools began programs to prepare specialists in African history, Negro music, and Negro history; and publishers started to produce needed monographs, texts, and the results of several centuries of Negro scholarly and literary contributions. Eventually these activities will provide a secure base for some institutions to maintain black studies equal in every respect to other sorts of disciplinary effort, but in the large majority of institutions it appears likely that black studies will prove to have been a fad, just as Far Eastern Studies and Special Programs for the Gifted proved to be fads earlier. Unless there are enough trained professors, adequate library holdings, and a generally accepted conventional wisdom, as is true for courses in Western Civilization, interdisciplinary programs do not last.

American higher education, even in the strongest institutions, has been administrator-centered, with great powers concentrated in the hands of and exercised by presidents. However, during the sixties, first faculty and then students sought a greater voice in governance. Faculty senates were created, students were included on faculty committees and even on boards of trustees, and, in some institutions, an era of governance by consensus was established. In others, particularly junior and state colleges, faculties embraced the ideas of trade unionism and labor negotiations and moved toward an adversary style of governance with central administration and boards of trustees forced into the conventional role of management. These developments reduced the power of central administration and its flexibility to deal with sudden new demands. In some institutions presidents lost so much prerogative either upward to state systems or downward to faculties and students that when confronted with such demands as immediate establishment of programs of black studies, they were powerless to respond. Prestige private universities discovered that governance by consensus tends to be inflationary with respect to cost, at a time when costs had to be curtailed. Then, too, in the late 1960's legislators and other supporters of higher education came to believe that faculties and students had been given too much, as evidenced, for instance, by the questioning of faculty tenure. In view of the fact that faculty advantage, caused by the low supply and great demand for professors during the 1960's, will probably disappear before the end of the decade of the 1970's (there will be an oversupply of Ph.D.'s in most fields), and that the realization that large organizations cannot function without effective executive power, some restoration of power to presidents and central administration seems likely. This does not mean a return to authoritarianism. Faculty and students each have much to contribute; and faculty especially need control over the curriculum and conditions of student entry and exit into college. It does mean, however, that presidents and central administration will be able to control the budget, make needed administrative appointments, and veto faculty recommendations for promotion and tenure. Syndicalism is still foreign to the American style of conduct of affairs and the tradition of strong executive power, great.

One recent development, however, which will last and become even more significant than it presently is, will be constitutionalism in higher education. During most of the history of American higher education, student behavior was governed through loose principles describing ideal conduct and interpreted variously by administrative officers. Similarly, faculties did business without specific handbooks, grants of power, or faculty constitutions. For the most part, faculty meetings were rather pro-forma discussions without specific allocation of responsibility to the faculty, on the assumption that things would work out and that on any critical matter the board of trustees would finally decide. However, the time for such informal devices has ended, and students and faculty each demand and expect specific listing of powers, duties, rights, responsibilities, and sanctions when they are appropriate. Thus, the offenses over which an institution has jurisdiction are listed, the penalties which may be imposed enumerated, and judicial procedures described in detail. Faculty by-laws and constitutions are drawn with care, for the wording can be subjected to judicial review. In institutions whose faculties have elected an adversary position about governance, the ways in which elections for bargaining agents are conducted are similarly specified, as are the terms of working contracts.

Some believe that such trends have made colleges and universities much more bureaucratic than they need be; but there appears no significant force to cause a reversal of the tendency. Institutions will become larger, and their members more heterogeneous with respect to values, background, and interests. The older, more informal ways presupposed a generally held system of values, and that condition will no longer obtain. Future campus governance will be more complex and more bureaucratic.

These trends seem well established. However, there are significant matters concerning which the future is quite uncertain. First among these is the role that the arts and humanities shall play in campus life. There are some who believe that campuses must become the chief impresarios for the arts, especially the experimental arts—the avant-garde. There are those who believe that man's salvation depends on the arts becoming central, for it is through the arts that man best expresses his humanity. There are those who believe that use of leisure is the most perplexing problem facing modern man in an advanced technology and that the arts and humanities represent the best way of dealing with leisure. And there are those who believe that there has been a real cultural revolution in the United States and that the arts each year will become increasingly essential. But there is contrary evidence. College students do not attend artistic events in large numbers. College course work in the arts is historical and critical rather than aesthetic and emotional. Young people talented in the arts are not encouraged to attend college and may actually be penalized because of their artistic interests. Which of these countertendencies will succeed cannot be anticipated, except that some resolution will come.

Although the need to solve the problems of an urban society is recognized and the potential role of higher education is accepted —based on the earlier success of land grant colleges in solving agricultural problems—whether higher education will take that role is uncertain. There is much talk of urban institutions, urban grant institutions, centers for urban studies, and service to the urban condition. But it is still talk. No way yet has been found to finance continued studies of urban problems. Especially social science research on such things as educating ghetto children has been generally unproductive. Faculty members in urban institutions have tended to see these professional futures more closely allied to conventional research than to service to the city, hence have been unwilling to engage in extension work or other similar activities. So once again clouds surround the future, although probably urban problems will become so acute as to force solution—if not by higher education, then by some other social institution.

The last imponderable is the most crucial: How central in the life of the nation will higher education be in the future? James Perkins expressed the dream of the 1960's with his remark that the American university had become the pivotal institution, and others, the hope that the university had become the modern church and cathedral. Certainly it has become central in the production of workers and in the conduct of some research; but examined in the light of political power, social criticism, formation of national values, setting of standards of taste, or even affecting seriously the lives of its graduates, this desired centrality seems still remote. Only as higher education repairs its damaged credibility is it likely to become the true cathedral of a secular and sensate society.

Index